HOLY WEEK CHANTS

HOLY WEEK CHANTS

PALM SUNDAY THROUGH EASTER SUNDAY

FROM THE 1962 ROMAN MISSAL

IN GREGORIAN CHANT

LATIN AND ENGLISH TEXT

JUSTITIAS BOOKS

This book contains excerpts of the approved texts, melodies, and rubrics found in the following editions:

Graduale Romanum (ed. Vaticana, 1908)
Graduale Romanum (ed. Desclée, 1961)
Liber Usualis (ed. Desclée, 1962)
Missale Romanum, editio typica (ed. Vaticana, 1962)
Ordo Hebdomadæ Sanctæ Instauratus (ed. Desclée, 1961)

The revised prayer *Pro conversione Iudæis,* as published in *L'Osservatore Romano,* Feb. 6, 2008, *"Nota della Segreteria di Stato"*

Biblical texts based on Douay-Rheims (Challoner) translation of Sacred Scripture. The translation of the Order of Mass originates in a 19th century prayerbook, as collected in *The Saint John Fisher Missale*:

http://musicasacra.com/sjfm/

(ad usum privatum)

ORDINARY OF THE MASS

MASS OF THE CATECHUMENS

When the Priest goes towards the altar, the choir begins the Introit antiphon.

Prayers at the Foot of the Altar

The Priest: In nómine Patris, et Fílii, et Spíritus Sancti. Amen.

Ant. Introíbo ad altáre Dei.

The Ministers (or Servers): Ad Deum, qui lætíficat iuventútem meam.

The Priest: In the name of the Father, and of the Son, and of the Holy Spirit. Amen.

Ant. I will go in to the altar of God.

The Ministers (or Servers): To God who giveth joy to my youth.

¶ *The psalm is omitted through Holy Week, and resumed on Easter Sunday.*

Psalm 42: 1-5

P. Iúdica me, Deus, et discérne causam meam de gente non sancta: ab hómine iníquo et dolóso érue me.

M. Quia tu es, Deus, fortitúdo mea: quare me repulísti, et quare tristis incédo, dum afflígit me inimícus?

P. Emítte lucem tuam et veritátem tuam: ipsa me deduxérunt, et adduxérunt in montem sanctum tuum et in tabernácula tua.

M. Et introíbo ad altáre Dei: ad Deum, qui lætíficat iuventútem meam.

P. Confitébor tibi in cíthara, Deus, Deus meus: quare tristis es, ánima mea, et quare contúrbas me?

M. Spera in Deo, quóniam adhuc con-

P. Judge me, O God, and distinguish my cause from the nation that is not holy: deliver me from the unjust and deceitful man.

M. For thou, O God, art my strength: why hast thou cast me off? And why do I go sorrowful whilst the enemy afflicteth me?

P. Send forth thy light and thy truth: they have conducted me and brought me unto thy holy hill, and into thy tabernacles

M. And I will go in to the altar of God: to God who giveth joy to my youth.

P. I will praise thee on the harp, O God, my God: why art thou sorrowful, O my soul? and why dost thou disquiet me?

M. Hope in God, for I will still give praise

fitébor illi: salutáre vultus mei, et Deus meus.

P. Glória Patri, et Fílio, et Spirítui Sancto.

M. Sicut erat in princípio, et nunc, et semper: et in sǽcula sæculórum. Amen.

℣. Introíbo ad altáre Dei.

℟. Ad Deum, qui lætíficat iuventútem meam.

℣. Adiutórium nostrum in nómine Dómini.

℟. Qui fecit cælum et terram.

Confiteor

Confíteor Deo omnipoténti, etc.

M. Misereátur tui omnípotens Deus, et, dimíssis peccátis tuis, perdúcat te ad vitam ætérnam.

P. Amen.

M. Confíteor Deo omnipoténti, beátæ Maríæ semper Vírgini, beáto Michaéli Archángelo, beáto Ioánni Baptístæ, sanctis Apóstolis Petro et Paulo, ómnibus Sanctis, et tibi, pater: quia peccávi nimis cogitatióne, verbo et ópere: mea culpa, mea culpa, mea máxima culpa. Ideo precor beátam Maríam semper Vírginem, beátum Michaélem Archángelum, beátum Ioánnem Baptístam, sanctos Apóstolos Petrum et Paulum, omnes Sanctos, et te, pater, oráre pro me ad Dóminum, Deum nostrum.

P. Misereátur vestri omnípotens Deus, et, dimíssis peccátis vestris, perdúcat vos ad vitam ætérnam.

M. Amen.

---

to him: the salvation of my countenance and my God.

P. Glory be to the Father, and the Son, and to the Holy Spirit.

M. As it was in the beginning, is now, and ever shall be: world without end. Amen.

℣. I will go in to the altar of God

℟. To God, who giveth joy to my youth.

℣. Our help is in the name of the Lord.

℟. Who hath made heaven and earth

I confess to almighty God...

M. May the almighty God have mercy upon thee, forgive thee thy sins, and bring thee to life everlasting.

P. Amen.

M. I confess to almighty God, to blessed Mary ever Virgin, to blessed Michael the Archangel, to blessed John the Baptist, to the holy Apostles Peter and Paul, to all the saints, and to thee, father, that I have sinned exceedingly in thought, word and deed: through my fault, through my fault, through my most grievous fault. Therefore I beseech blessed Mary, ever Virgin, blessed Michael the Archangel, blessed John the Baptist, the holy Apostles Peter and Paul, all the saints, and thee, father, to pray for me to the Lord our God.

P. May the almighty God have mercy upon you, forgive you your sins, and bring you to life everlasting.

M. Amen.

P. Indulgéntiam, absolutiónem et remissiónem peccatórum nostrórum tríbuat nobis omnípotens et miséricors Dóminus.

M. Amen.

P. Deus, tu convérsus vivificábis nos.

M. Et plebs tua lætábitur in te.

P. Osténde nobis, Dómine, misericórdiam tuam.

M. Et salutáre tuum da nobis.

P. Dómine, exáudi oratiónem meam.

M. Et clamor meus ad te véniat.

P. Dóminus vobíscum.

M. Et cum spíritu tuo.

Orémus.

A ufer a nobis, quǽsumus, Dómine, iniquitátes nostras: ut ad Sancta sanctórum puris mereámur méntibus introíre. Per Christum Dóminum nostrum. Amen.

Orámus te, Dómine, per mérita Sanctórum tuórum, quorum relíquiæ hic sunt, et ómnium Sanctórum: ut indulgére dignéris ómnia peccáta mea. Amen.

P. May the almighty and merciful Lord grant us pardon, absolution, and remission of our sins.

M. Amen.

P. Thou wilt turn again, O God, and quicken us.

M. And thy people shall rejoice in thee.

P. Show us, O Lord, thy mercy

M. And grant us thy salvation.

P. O Lord, hear my prayer.

M. And let my cry come unto thee.

P. The Lord be with you.

M. And with thy spirit.

Let us pray.

Take away from us our iniquities, we beseech thee, O Lord, that we may be worthy to enter with pure minds into the Holy of Holies. Through Christ our Lord. Amen.

We beseech thee, O Lord, by the merits of thy saints, whose relics are here, and of all the saints, that thou wouldst vouchsafe to forgive me all my sins. Amen.

¶ *At Solemn Mass, incense is blessed:*

Ab illo benedicáris, in cuius honóre cremáberis. Amen.

Be blessed by him, in whose honor thou art burnt. Amen.

Kyrie

The Priest now reads the Introit antiphon and then the Kyrie, said alternating with the ministers. Meanwhile, the choir continues with the Kyrie when the Introit antiphon is completed.

K ýrie, eléison. Kýrie, eléison. Kýrie, eléison.

Christe, eléison. Christe, eléison. Christe, eléison.

Lord, have mercy. Lord, have mercy. Lord, have mercy.

Christ, have mercy. Christ, have mercy. Christ, have mercy.

Kýrie, eléison. Kýrie, eléison. Kýrie, eléison.

Lord, have mercy. Lord, have mercy. Lord, have mercy.

Gloria

If it is to be said, when the Kyrie is finished, the Priest intones the Gloria in excelsis, which is continued by the choir as he says it in a low voice.

Glória in excélsis Deo. Et in terra pax homínibus bonæ voluntátis. Laudámus te. Benedícimus te. Adorámus te. Glorificámus te. Grátias ágimus tibi propter magnam glóriam tuam. Dómine Deus, Rex cæléstis, Deus Pater omnípotens. Dómine Fili unigénite, Iesu Christe. Dómine Deus, Agnus Dei, Fílius Patris. Qui tollis peccáta mundi, miserére nobis. Qui tollis peccáta mundi, súscipe deprecatiónem nostram. Qui sedes ad déxteram Patris, miserére nobis. Quóniam tu solus Sanctus. Tu solus Dóminus. Tu solus Altíssimus, Iesu Christe. Cum Sancto Spíritu in glória Dei Patris. Amen.

Glory be to God on high. And on earth peace to men of good will. We praise thee. We bless thee. We adore thee. We glorify thee. We give thee thanks for thy great glory. O Lord God, heavenly King, God the Father almighty. O Lord Jesus Christ, the only-begotten Son. Lord God, Lamb of God, Son of the Father. Who takest away the sins of the world, have mercy on us. Who takest away the sins of the world, receive our prayers. Who sittest at the right hand of the Father, have mercy on us. For thou only art holy. Thou only art the Lord. Thou only art most high, O Jesus Christ. Together with the Holy Spirit, in the glory of God the Father. Amen.

Collect

℣. Dóminus vobíscum.
℞. Et cum spíritu tuo.
Orémus.

The Lord be with you.
And with thy spirit.
Let us pray.

The Priest sings the above and the Collect prayer in one of the following tones:

Ferial or Festal Tone

℣. Dóminus vo-bíscum. ℞. Et cum spí-ri-tu tu-o.

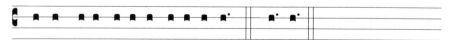

...per ómni- a sǽcu-la sæcu-ló-rum. ℞. Amen.

Ancient Solemn Tone

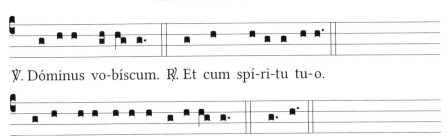

℣. Dóminus vo-bíscum. ℟. Et cum spí-ri-tu tu-o.

...per ómni- a sǽcu-la sæcu-ló-rum. ℟. Amen.

Ancient Simple Tone

For the prayers at the Asperges, Blessings, and Litanies

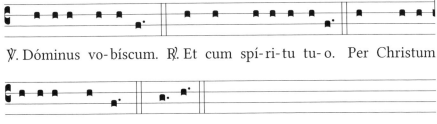

℣. Dóminus vo-bíscum. ℟. Et cum spí-ri-tu tu-o. Per Christum

Dóminum nostrum. ℟. Amen.

Epistle and Gradual

The ministers or servers respond Deo Grátias *at the conclusion of the Epistle.*

The Gradual is sung, and if there is a Tract, it follows. On Wednesday in Holy Week, the Gradual is sung after the Lesson and the Tract after the Epistle. On Easter Sunday, the Alleluia chant and Sequence follow the Gradual.

Gospel

At Solemn Mass, the Deacon:[1]

D. Munda cor meum ac lábia mea, omnípotens Deus, qui lábia Isaíæ Prophétæ cálculo mundásti igníto: ita me tua grata miseratióne dignáre mundáre, ut sanctum Evan-

Cleanse my heart and my lips, O almighty God, who didst cleanse the lips of the prophet Isaias with a burning coal: and vouchsafe, through thy gracious mercy, so to purify me that I

---

[1]*Or, if there is no Deacon, the Priest:* Munda cor meum ac lábia mea, omnípotens Deus, qui lábia Isaíæ Prophétæ cálculo mundásti igníto: ita me tua grata miseratióne dignáre mundáre, ut sanctum Evangélium tuum digne váleam nuntiáre. Per Christum Dóminum nostrum. Amen.—Iube, Dómine, benedícere.—Dóminus sit in corde meo et in lábiis meis: ut digne et competénter annúnties Evangélium suum. Amen.

gélium tuum digne váleam nuntiá-re. Per Christum Dóminum nostrum. Amen.

Iube, domne, benedícere.

P. Dóminus sit in corde tuo et in lábiis tuis: ut digne et competénter annúnties Evangélium suum: In nó-mine Patris, et Fílii, et Spíritus Sancti. Amen.

may worthily proclaim thy holy Gospel. Through Christ our Lord. Amen.

Pray, Sir, a blessing.

The Lord be in thy heart and on thy lips, that thou mayest worthily, and in a becoming manner, announce his holy Gospel: In the name of the Father, and the Son, and the Holy Spirit. Amen.

Then, in one of the tones below, he sings the Gospel:

℣. Dóminus vobíscum.

℟. Et cum spíritu tuo.

℣. Sequéntia (*or* Inítium) ✛ sancti Evangélii secúndum *N.*

℟. Gloria tibi, Domine!

The Lord be with you.

And with thy spirit.

The continuation (*or* beginning) of the holy Gospel according to *N.*

Glory be to thee, O Lord!

Gospel Tone

℣. Dóminus vo-bíscum. ℟. Et cum spí-ri-tu tu-o.

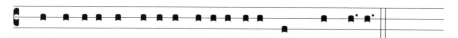

✛ Sequénti- a sancti Evangé-li- i secúndum Matthǽ-um.

℟. Gló-ri- a ti-bi, Dómi-ne.

Gospel Tone, ad libitum

℣. Dóminus vo-bíscum. ℟. Et cum spí-ri-tu tu-o.

✛ Sequénti- a sancti Evangé-li- i   secúndum Matthǽ-um.

℟. Gló-ri- a ti-bi, Dómi-ne.

Ancient Gospel Tone

℣. Dóminus vo-bíscum. ℟. Et cum spí-ri-tu tu-o.

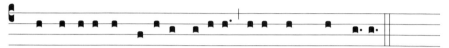

✠ Sequénti- a sancti Evangé-li- i secúndum Matthǽ-um.

℟. Gló-ri- a ti-bi, Dómi-ne.

(In a Low Mass, the server responds Laus tibi, Christe *at the conclusion of the Gospel.)*

The Priest then kisses the Gospel book, saying:

Per Evangélica dicta, deleántur nostra delícta.

By the words of the Gospel may our sins be blotted out.

MASS OF THE FAITHFUL

Credo

If it is to be said, the Credo follows the Gospel (or sermon). The Priest intones the Credo from the altar, and it is continued by the choir and congregation, p. 58 or p. 225.

Credo in unum Deum, Patrem omnipoténtem, factórem cæli et terræ, visibílium ómnium et in visibílium. Et in unum Dóminum Iesum Christum, Fílium Dei unigénitum. Et ex Patre natum ante ómnia sǽcula. Deum de Deo, lumen de lúmine, Deum verum de Deo vero. Génitum, non factum, consubstan-

I believe in one God, the Father almighty, maker of heaven and earth, and of all things visible and invisible. And in one Lord Jesus Christ, the only-begotten Son of God. Born of the Father before all ages. God of God, light of light, true God of true God, begotten, not made, consubstantial with the Father: by whom all things were made.

tiálem Patri: per quem ómnia facta sunt. Qui propter nos hómines et propter nostram salútem descéndit de cælis. * Et incarnátus est de Spíritu Sancto ex María Vírgine: et homo factus est. Crucifíxus étiam pro nobis: sub Póntio Piláto passus, et sepúltus est. Et resurréxit tértia die, secúndum Scriptúras. Et ascéndit in cælum: sedet ad déxteram Patris. Et íterum ventúrus est cum glória iudicáre vivos et mórtuos: cuius regni non erit finis. Et in Spíritum Sanctum, Dóminum et vivificántem: qui ex Patre Filióque procédit. Qui cum Patre et Fílio simul adorátur et conglorificátur: qui locútus est per Prophétas. Et unam sanctam cathólicam et apostólicam Ecclésiam. Confíteor unum baptísma in remissiónem peccatórum. Et exspécto resurrectiónem mortuórum. Et vitam ventúri sǽculi. Amen.

Who for us men and for our salvation came down from heaven. And was incarnate by the Holy Spirit of the Virgin Mary: and was made man. He was crucified also for us: suffered under Pontius Pilate, and was buried. The third day he rose again, according to the Scriptures. He ascended into heaven: and sitteth at the right hand of the Father. And he shall come again in glory to judge both the living and the dead: and of his kingdom there shall be no end. And I believe in the Holy Spirit, the Lord and lifegiver: who proceedeth from the Father and the Son. Who together with the Father and the Son is adored and glorified: who spake by the prophets. And I believe in one holy Catholic and Apostolic Church. I confess one baptism for the remission of sins. And I await the resurrection of the dead. And the life of the world to come. Amen.

Offertory

℣. Dóminus vobíscum.
℟. Et cum spíritu tuo.
     Orémus.

The Lord be with you.
And with thy spirit.
     Let us pray.

And the choir immediately begins the Offertory antiphon, which the Priest also reads aloud.

Offering of the bread

Súscipe, sancte Pater, omnípotens ætérne Deus, hanc immaculátam hóstiam, quam ego indígnus fámulus tuus óffero tibi Deo meo vivo et vero, pro innumerabílibus peccátis, et offensiónibus, et neglegéntiis meis, et pro ómnibus circumstántibus, sed et pro ómnibus fidélibus chri-

Accept, O holy Father, almighty and eternal God, this immaculate victim, which I, thy unworthy servant, offer to thee, my living and true God, for my innumerable sins, offenses, and negligences, and for all here present, as also for all faithful Christians, both living and dead: that it may be profitable for sal-

stiánis vivis atque defúnctis: ut mihi, et illis profíciat ad salútem in vitam ætérnam. Amen.

Deus, qui humánæ substántiæ dignitátem mirabíliter condidísti, et mirabílius reformásti: da nobis per huius aquæ et vini mystérium, eius divinitátis esse consórtes, qui humanitátis nostræ fíeri dignátus est párticeps, Iesus Christus, Fílius tuus, Dóminus noster: Qui tecum vivit et regnat in unitáte Spíritus Sancti, Deus, per ómnia sǽcula sæculórum.

vation both to me and to them unto life eternal. Amen.

O God, who, in creating human nature, didst wonderfully dignify it, and hast still more wonderfully restored it, grant that, by the mystery of this water and wine, we may become partakers of his divinity, who vouchsafed to become partaker of our humanity, even Jesus Christ our Lord, thy Son: Who lives and reigns with thee in the unity of the Holy Spirit, one God, forever and ever.

Offering of the wine

Offérimus tibi, Dómine, cálicem salutáris, tuam deprecántes cleméntiam: ut in conspéctu divínæ maiestátis tuæ, pro nostra et totíus mundi salúte, cum odóre suavitátis ascéndat. Amen.

In spíritu humilitátis et in ánimo contríto suscipiámur a te, Dómine: et sic fiat sacrifícium nostrum in conspéctu tuo hódie, ut pláceat tibi, Dómine Deus.

Veni, sanctificátor omnípotens ætérne Deus: et béne✝dic hoc sacrifícium, tuo sancto nómini præparátum.

We offer unto thee, O Lord, the chalice of salvation, beseeching thy clemency: that in the sight of thy divine majesty it may ascend with the odor of sweetness for our salvation, and for that of the whole world. Amen.

In the spirit of humility and with a contrite heart, let us be received by thee, O Lord: and grant that the sacrifice we offer in thy sight this day may be pleasing to thee, O Lord God.

Come, O sanctifier, almighty, everlasting God: and bless this sacrifice, made ready for thy holy name.

¶ *At Solemn Mass, and whenever incense is used:*

Per intercessiónem beáti Michaélis Archángeli, stantis a dextris altáris incénsi, et ómnium electórum suórum, incénsum istud dignétur Dóminus bene✝dícere, et in odórem suavitátis accípere. Per Christum Dóminum nostrum. Amen.

May the Lord, by the intercession of blessed Michael the Archangel, standing at the right hand of the altar of incense, and of all his elect, vouchsafe to bless this incense, and receive it as an odor of sweetness. Through Christ our Lord. Amen

Incénsum istud a te benedíctum ascéndat ad te, Dómine: et descéndat super nos misericórdia tua. Amen.

May this incense, blessed by thee, ascend to thee, O Lord. And may thy mercy descend on us. Amen.

Incensation — Psalm 140: 2-4

Dirigátur, Dómine, orátio mea, sicut incénsum, in conspéctu tuo: elevátio mánuum meárum sacrifícium vespertínum.

Let my prayer, O Lord, ascend like incense in thy sight: and the lifting up of my hands be as an evening sacrifice.

Pone, Dómine, custódiam ori meo, et óstium circumstántiæ lábiis meis:

Set a watch, O Lord, before my mouth: and a door round about my lips,

Ut non declínet cor meum in verba malítiæ, ad excusándas excusatiónes in peccátis.

That my heart may not incline to evil words: to make excuses to sin.

Accéndat in nobis Dóminus ignem sui amóris, et flammam ætérnæ caritátis. Amen.

May the Lord enkindle in us the fire of his love, and the flame of everlasting charity. Amen.

Lavabo — Psalm 25: 6-12

Lavábo inter innocéntes manus meas: et circúmdabo altáre tuum.

I will wash my hands among the innocent: and will encompass thy altar, O Lord

Dómine: Ut áudiam vocem laudis, et enárrem univérsa mirabília tua.

That I may hear the voice of praise, and tell of all thy marvellous works.

Dómine, diléxi decórem domus tuæ et locum habitatiónis glóriæ tuæ.

I have loved, O Lord, the beauty of thy house: and the place where thy glory dwelleth.

Ne perdas cum ímpiis, Deus, ánimam meam, et cum viris sánguinum vitam meam:

Take not away my soul, O God, with the wicked: nor my life with bloody men.

In quorum mánibus iniquitátes sunt: déxtera eórum repléta est munéribus.

In whose hands are iniquities: their right hand is filled with gifts.

Ego autem in innocéntia mea ingréssus sum: rédime me et miserére mei.

As for me, I have walked in my innocence: redeem me, and have mercy upon me.

Pes meus stetit in dirécto: in ecclésiis benedícam te, Dómine.

My foot hath stood in the right path: in the churches I will bless thee, O Lord.

Glória Patri, et Fílio, et Spirítui Sancto.

Glory be to the Father, and to the Son, and to the Holy Spirit.

Sicut erat in princípio, et nunc, et semper, et in sǽcula sǽculórum. Amen

As it was in the beginning, is now, and ever shall be, world without end. Amen.

¶ *The* Glória Patri *is omitted during Holy Week and resumed on Easter Sunday.*

Súscipe, sancta Trínitas, hanc oblatiónem, quam tibi offérimus ob memóriam passiónis, resurrectiónis, et ascensiónis Iesu Christi, Dómini nostri: et in honórem beátæ Maríæ semper Vírginis, et beáti Ioannis Baptistæ, et sanctórum Apostolórum Petri et Pauli, et istórum et ómnium Sanctórum: ut illis profíciat ad honórem, nobis autem ad salútem: et illi pro nobis intercédere dignéntur in cælis, quorum memóriam ágimus in terris. Per eúndem Christum Dóminum nostrum. Amen.

Receive, O holy Trinity, this oblation which we make to thee, in memory of the passion, resurrection and ascension of our Lord Jesus Christ, and in honor of Blessed Mary, ever Virgin, of blessed John the Baptist, the holy Apostles Peter and Paul, and of these and of all the saints, that it may be available unto their honor and our salvation, and may they vouchsafe to intercede for us in heaven, whose memory we celebrate on earth. Through the same Christ our Lord. Amen.

P. Oráte, fratres: ut meum ac vestrum sacrifícium acceptábile fiat apud Deum Patrem omnipoténtem.

P. Pray, brethren: that my sacrifice and yours may be acceptable to God the Father almighty.

M. Suscípiat Dóminus sacrifícium de mánibus tuis ad laudem et glóriam nóminis sui, ad utilitátem quoque nostram, totiúsque Ecclésiæ suæ sanctæ.

M. May the Lord accept the sacrifice at thy hands, for the praise and glory of his name, for our good and the good of all his holy Church.

The Priest replies in a low voice: Amen.

Secret

In a low voice, the Priest prays the Secret prayer, which is proper for each Mass.

The conclusion is sung aloud, as in the tone for the Preface, below.

Preface

The Priest continues aloud, and the choir responds.

Per ómnia sæcula sæculórum.	...forever and ever.
℟. Amen.	Amen.
℣. Dóminus vobíscum.	The Lord be with you.
℟. Et cum spíritu tuo.	And with thy spirit.
℣. Sursum corda.	Lift up your hearts.
℟. Habémus ad Dóminum.	We have lifted them up to the Lord.
℣. Grátias agámus Dómino, Deo nostro.	Let us give thanks to the Lord our God.
℟. Dignum et iustum est.	It is right and just.

Solemn Tone

PER ómni- a sǽcu-la sæcu-ló-rum. ℟. Amen. ℣. Dóminus vo-bíscum. ℟. Et cum spí-ri-tu tu- o. ℣. Sursum corda. ℟. Habémus ad Dóminum. ℣. Grá-ti- as agámus Dómi-no De- o nostro.

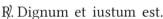

℟. Dignum et iustum est.

Ferial Tone

PER ómni- a sǽcu-la sæcu-ló-rum. ℟. Amen. ℣. Dóminus vo-bíscum. ℟. Et cum spí-ri-tu tu-o. ℣. Sursum corda. ℟. Habé-

mus ad Dóminum. ℣. Grá-ti- as agámus Dómino De-o nostro.

℟. Dignum et iustum est.

More Solemn Tone

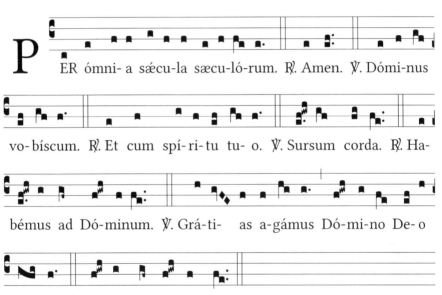

ER ómni- a sǽcu-la sǽcu-ló-rum. ℟. Amen. ℣. Dómi-nus

vo-bíscum. ℟. Et cum spí-ri-tu tu- o. ℣. Sursum corda. ℟. Ha-

bémus ad Dó-minum. ℣. Grá-ti- as a-gámus Dó-mi-no De-o

nos-tro. ℟. Dignum et ius-tum est.

Preface of the Holy Cross

Masses of the Season from Passion Sunday through Holy Thursday inclusive

Vere dignum et iustum est, æquum et salutáre, nos tibi semper et ubíque grátias ágere: Dómine sancte, Pater omnípotens, ætérne Deus: Qui salútem humáni géneris in ligno Crucis constituísti: ut, unde mors oriebátur, inde vita resúrgeret: et, qui in ligno vincébat, in ligno quoque vincerétur: per Christum, Dóminum nostrum. Per quem maie-

It is truly meet and just, right and salutary, that we should always, and in all places, give thanks to thee: O holy Lord, Father almighty, eternal God: who didst set the salvation of mankind upon the tree of the cross, so that whence came death, thence also life might rise again: and he that overcame by the tree, on the tree also might be overcome. Through Christ our Lord: through

státem tuam laudant Angeli, adó-rant Dominatiónes, tremunt Pote-státes. Cæli cælorúmque Virtútes ac beáta Séraphim sócia exsultatió-ne concélebrant. Cum quibus et no-stras voces ut admítti iúbeas, depre-cámur, súpplici confessióne dicéntes: Sanctus...

whom the Angels praise thy majesty, the Dominions adore, the Powers trem-ble. The Heavens, and the Virtues of the heavens, and the blessed Seraphim, do celebrate with united joy. In union with whom, we beseech thee, that thou wouldst command our voices also to be admitted, with suppliant confession, say-ing:

Preface of Easter

Masses of the Season from Easter through the Ascension exclusive

¶ *At the Easter Vigil:* in hac potíssimum nocte; *through the Easter Octave:* in hac potíssimum die; *otherwise:* in hoc potíssimum.

Vere dignum et iustum est, æquum et salutáre: Te quidem, Dómi-ne, omni témpore, sed in hac potís-simum die (in hoc potíssimum) glo-riósius prædicáre, cum Pascha no-strum immolátus est Christus. Ip-se enim verus est Agnus, qui ábstu-lit peccáta mundi. Qui mortem no-stram moriéndo destrúxit et vitam resurgéndo reparávit. Et ídeo cum Angelis et Archángelis, cum Thronis et Dominatiónibus cumque omni mi-lítia cæléstis exércitus hymnum gló-riæ tuæ cánimus, sine fine dicéntes: Sanctus...

It is truly meet and just, right and salutary: that we should always, but more especially on this day (at this time), extol thy glory, when Christ our Pasch was sacrificed. For he is the true Lamb that hath taken away the sins of the world; who by dying hath overcome our death, and by rising again hath restored our life. And therefore with the Angels and Archangels, with the Thrones and Dominions, and with all the hosts of the heavenly army, we sing a hymn to thy glory, evermore saying:

Sanctus

After the Preface, the choir immediately begins the Sanctus, *which is said also by the Priest and Ministers in a low voice.*

Sanctus, Sanctus, Sanctus Dómi-nus, Deus Sábaoth. Pleni sunt cæli et terra glória tua. Hosánna in excélsis.

Holy, holy, holy, Lord God of hosts. Heaven and earth are full of thy glory. Hosanna in the highest.

Benedíctus qui venit in nómine Dómini. Hosánna in excélsis.

Blessed is he that cometh in the name of the Lord. Hosanna in the highest.

CANON OF THE MASS

Te ígitur, clementíssime Pater, per Iesum Christum, Fílium tuum, Dóminum nostrum, súpplices rogámus, ac pétimus, uti accépta hábeas et benedícas, hæc ✚ dona, hæc ✚ múnera, hæc ✚ sancta sacrifícia illibáta, in primis, quæ tibi offérimus pro Ecclésia tua sancta cathólica: quam pacificáre, custodíre, adunáre et régere dignéris toto orbe terrárum: una cum fámulo tuo Papa nostro *N.* et Antístite nostro *N.* et ómnibus orthodóxis, atque cathólicæ et apostólicæ fídei cultóribus.

We therefore, humbly pray and beseech thee, most merciful Father through Jesus Christ, thy Son, our Lord, that thou wouldst vouchsafe to accept and bless these gifts, these presents, these holy unspotted sacrifices, which in the first place we offer thee for thy holy Catholic Church: to which vouchsafe to grant peace, as also to protect, unite and govern her throughout the world, together with thy servant *N.*, our Pope, and *N.*, our Bishop, and as also all orthodox believers and professors of the Catholic and Apostolic Faith.

Commemoration of the living

Meménto, Dómine, famulórum famularúmque tuárum *N.* et *N.* et ómnium circumstántium, quorum tibi fides cógnita est et nota devótio, pro quibus tibi offérimus: vel qui tibi ófferunt hoc sacrifícium laudis, pro se suísque ómnibus: pro redemptióne animárum suárum, pro spe salútis et incolumitátis suæ: tibíque reddunt vota sua ætérno Deo, vivo et vero.

Be mindful, O Lord, of thy servants and handmaids, *N.* and *N.*, and of all here present, whose faith and devotion are known unto thee, for whom we offer: or who offer up to thee, this sacrifice of praise for themselves and all their families and friends: for the redemption of their souls, for the hope of their safety and salvation: and who pay their vows to thee, the eternal, living and true God.

¶ *On some occasions, the beginnings of the following two prayers are proper.*

Communicántes, et memóriam venerántes, in primis gloriósæ semper Vírginis Maríæ, Genetrícis Dei et Dómini nostri Iesu Christi: † sed et beáti Ioseph, eiúsdem Vírginis Sponsi, et beatórum Apostolórum ac Mártyrum tuórum, Petri et Pauli, Andréæ, Iacóbi, Ioánnis, Tho-

In communion with, and honoring in the first place the memory of the glorious ever Virgin Mary, Mother of our Lord and God Jesus Christ; † as also of the blessed Joseph, her spouse, and thy blessed Apostles and Martyrs Peter and Paul, Andrew, James, John, Thomas, James, Philip, Bartholomew,

mæ, Iacóbi, Philíppi, Bartholomǽi, Matthǽi, Simónis et Thaddǽi: Lini, Cleti, Cleméntis, Xysti, Cornélii, Cypriáni, Lauréntii, Chrysógoni, Ioánnis et Pauli, Cosmæ et Damiáni: et ómnium Sanctórum tuórum; quorum méritis precibúsque concédas, ut in ómnibus protectiónis tuæ muniámur auxílio. Per eúndem Christum Dóminum nostrum. Amen.

Matthew, Simon, and Thaddeus: Linus, Cletus, Clement, Sixtus, Cornelius, Cyprian, Lawrence, Chrysogonus, John and Paul, Cosmas and Damian, and of all thy saints, through whose merits and prayers, grant that we may in all things be defended by thy protecting help. Through the same Christ our Lord. Amen.

H anc ígitur oblatiónem servitútis nostræ, sed et cunctæ famíliæ tuæ, quǽsumus, Dómine, ut placátus accípias: ¶ diésque nostros in tua pace dispónas, atque ab ætérna damnatióne nos éripi, et in electórum tuórum iúbeas grege numerári. Per Christum Dóminum nostrum. Amen.

We therefore, beseech thee, O Lord, to be appeased and accept this oblation of our service, as also of thy whole family: ¶ dispose our days in thy peace, command us to be delivered from eternal damnation, and to be numbered in the flock of thy elect. Through Christ our Lord. Amen.

Q uam oblatiónem tu, Deus, in ómnibus, quǽsumus, bene✚díctam, adscríp✚tam, ra✚tam, rationábilem, acceptabilémque fácere dignéris: ut nobis Cor✚pus, et San✚guis fiat dilectíssimi Fílii tui, Dómini nostri Iesu Christi.

Which oblation do thou, O God, vouchsafe in all respects, to make blessed, approved, ratified, reasonable and acceptable: that it may become for us the Body and Blood of thy most beloved Son, Jesus Christ our Lord.

Consecration of the bread

Q ui prídie quam paterétur, accépit panem in sanctas ac venerábiles manus suas, et elevátis óculis in cælum ad te Deum, Patrem suum omnipoténtem, tibi grátias agens, bene✚díxit, fregit, dedítque discípulis suis, dicens: Accípite, et manducáte ex hoc omnes.

Who, the day before he suffered, took bread into his holy and venerable hands, and with his eyes lifted up towards heaven, unto thee, God, his almighty Father, giving thanks to thee, did bless, break and give to his disciples, saying: Take and eat ye all of this.

Hoc est enim Corpus meum.

For this is my Body.

Consecration of the wine

Símili modo postquam cenátum est, accípiens et hunc præclárum Cálicem in sanctas ac venerábiles manus suas: item tibi grátias agens, bene✝díxit, dedítque discípulis suis, dicens: Accípite, et bíbite ex eo omnes.

In like manner, after he had supped, taking also this excellent chalice into his holy and venerable hands: again giving thee thanks, he blessed, and gave to his disciples, saying: Take, and drink ye all of this.

Hic est enim Calix Sánguinis mei, novi et ætérni testaménti: mystérium fídei: qui pro vobis et pro multis effundétur in remissiónem peccatórum. Hæc quotiescúmque fecéritis, in mei memóriam faciétis.

For this is the Chalice of my Blood, of the new and eternal testament: the mystery of faith: which shall be shed for you and for many unto the remission of sins. As often as ye do these things, ye shall do them in remembrance of me.

Prayers after the Consecration

Unde et mémores, Dómine, nos servi tui, sed et plebs tua sancta, eiúsdem Christi Fílii tui, Dómini nostri, tam beátæ passiónis, nec non et ab ínferis resurrectiónis, sed et in cælos gloriósæ ascensiónis: offérimus præcláræ maiestáti tuæ de tuis donis ac datis, hóstiam ✝ puram, hóstiam ✝ sanctam, hóstiam ✝ immaculátam, Panem ✝ sanctum vitæ ætérnæ, et Cálicem ✝ salútis perpétuæ.

Wherefore, O Lord, we thy servants, as also thy holy people, calling to mind the blessed passion of the same Christ thy Son our Lord, his resurrection from the dead, and glorious ascension into heaven: offer to thy most excellent majesty of thy gifts and grants, a pure victim, a holy victim, an immaculate victim, the holy Bread of eternal life, and the Chalice of everlasting salvation.

Supra quæ propítio ac seréno vultu respícere dignéris: et accépta habére, sicúti accépta habére dignátus es múnera púeri tui iusti Abel, et sacrifícium Patriárchæ nostri Abrahæ: et quod tibi óbtulit summus sacérdos tuus Melchísedech, sanctum sacrifícium, immaculátam hóstiam.

Upon which vouchsafe to look with a propitious and serene countenance: and to accept them, as thou wert graciously pleased to accept the gifts of thy just servant Abel, and the sacrifice of our patriarch Abraham: and that which thy high priest Melchisedech offered to thee, a holy sacrifice, an immaculate victim.

Súpplices te rogámus, omnípotens Deus: iube hæc perférri per manus sancti Angeli tui in sublíme al-

We most humbly beseech thee, almighty God: command these things to be carried by the hands of thy holy An-

táre tuum, in conspéctu divínæ majestátis tuæ: ut, quotquot ex hac altáris participatióne sacrosánctum Fílii tui Cor✠pus, et Sán✠guinem sumpsérimus, omni benedictióne cælésti et grátia repleámur. Per eúndem Christum Dóminum nostrum. Amen.

gel to thine altar on high, in the sight of thy divine majesty: that as many of us as, by participation at this altar, shall receive the most sacred Body and Blood of thy Son, may be filled with every heavenly benediction and grace. Through the same Christ our Lord. Amen.

Commemoration of the dead

Meménto étiam, Dómine, famulórum famularúmque tuárum N. et N., qui nos præcessérunt cum signo fídei, et dórmiunt in somno pacis.

Be mindful, O Lord, of thy servants and handmaids N. and N., who are gone before us with the sign of faith, and slumber in the sleep of peace.

Ipsis, Dómine, et ómnibus in Christo quiescéntibus locum refrigérii, lucis et pacis, ut indúlgeas, deprecámur. Per eúndem Christum Dóminum nostrum. Amen.

To these, O Lord, and to all that rest in Christ, grant, we beseech thee, a place of refreshing coolness, light and peace. Through the same Christ our Lord. Amen.

Nobis quoque peccatóribus fámulis tuis, de multitúdine miseratiónum tuárum sperántibus, partem áliquam et societátem donáre dignéris, cum tuis sanctis Apóstolis et Martýribus: cum Ioánne, Stéphano, Matthía, Bárnaba, Ignátio, Alexándro, Marcellíno, Petro, Felicitáte, Perpétua, Agatha, Lúcia, Agnéte, Cæcília, Anastásia, et ómnibus Sanctis tuis: intra quorum nos consórtium, non æstimátor mériti, sed véniæ, quǽsumus, largítor admítte. Per Christum Dóminum nostrum.

And to us sinners, thy servants, hoping in the multitude of thy mercies, vouchsafe to grant some part and fellowship with thy holy Apostles and Martyrs: with John, Stephen, Matthias, Barnabas, Ignatius, Alexander, Marcellinus, Peter, Felicity, Perpetua, Agatha, Lucy, Agnes, Cecilia, Anastasia, and with all thy saints: into whose company we beseech thee to admit us, not weighing our merits, but pardoning our offenses. Through Christ our Lord.

Conclusion

Per quem hæc ómnia, Dómine, semper bona creas, sanctí✠ficas, viví✠ficas, bene✠dícis et præstas nobis.

By whom, O Lord, thou dost always create, sanctify, quicken, bless, and give us all these good things.

Per ip✠sum, et cum ip✠so, et in ip✠so, est tibi Deo Patri ✠ omnipoténti, in unitáte Spíritus ✠ Sancti, omnis honor, et glória.

Through him, and with him, and in him, is to thee, God the Father almighty, in the unity of the Holy Spirit, all honor and glory. Forever and ever. Amen.

He sings the last of the conclusion aloud:

...Per ómni- a sæcu-la sæcu-ló-rum. ℟. Amen.

Pater noster

Orémus.

Let us pray.

Præcéptis salutáribus móniti, et divína institutióne formáti audémus dícere:

Instructed by thy saving precepts, and following thy divine institution, we presume to say:

Pater noster, qui es in cælis: Sanctificétur nomen tuum: Advéniat regnum tuum: Fiat volúntas tua, sicut in cælo, et in terra. Panem nostrum cotidiánum da nobis hódie: Et dimítte nobis débita nostra, sicut et nos dimíttimus debitóribus nostris. Et ne nos indúcas in tentatiónem.

Our Father, who art in heaven. Hallowed be thy name. Thy kingdom come. Thy will be done on earth as it is in heaven. Give us this day our daily bread. And forgive us our trespasses, as we forgive them that trespass against us. And lead us not into temptation. ℟. But deliver us from evil.

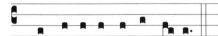

℟. Sed lí-be-ra nos a ma-lo.

The Priest answers Amen *in a low voice, and continues:*

Líbera nos, quǽsumus, Dómine, ab ómnibus malis, prætéritis, præséntibus et futúris: et intercedénte beáta et gloriósa semper Vírgine Dei Genetríce María, cum beátis Apóstolis tuis Petro et Paulo, atque Andréa, et ómnibus Sanctis, da propítius pacem in diébus nostris: ut, ope misericórdiæ tuæ adiúti, et a peccáto simus semper líberi et ab omni perturbatió-

Deliver us, we beseech thee, O Lord, from all evils, past, present, and to come: and by the intercession of the blessed and glorious Mary, ever Virgin, Mother of God, together with thy holy Apostles, Peter and Paul, and Andrew and of all the saints, mercifully grant peace in our days, that through the assistance of thy mercy we may be always free from sin, and secure from all disturbance.

ne secúri. Per eúndem Dóminum nostrum Iesum Christum, Fílium tuum: Qui tecum vivit et regnat in unitáte Spíritus Sancti Deus.

Through the same our Lord Jesus Christ, thy Son: Who lives and reigns with thee in the unity of the Holy Spirit, one God, forever and ever.

He breaks the host at the conclusion, and sings the end aloud:

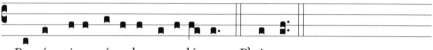

...Per ómni- a sǽcu-la sæcu-ló-rum. ℟. Amen.

℣. Pax Dómi-ni   sit semper vo-bíscum. ℟. Et cum spí-ri-tu tu-o.
May the peace of the Lord be always with you.

Hæc commíxtio, et consecrátio Córporis et Sánguinis Dómini nostri Iesu Christi, fiat accipiéntibus nobis in vitam ætérnam. Amen.

May this mixture, and consecration of the Body and Blood of our Lord Jesus Christ, be to us that receive it effectual to eternal life. Amen.

Agnus Dei

The choir begins the Agnus Dei, *while the Priest says it alternately with the ministers (or servers) in a low voice.*

Agnus Dei, qui tollis peccáta mundi: miserére nobis.

Lamb of God, who takest away the sins of the world, have mercy on us.

Agnus Dei, qui tollis peccáta mundi: miserére nobis.

Lamb of God, who takest away the sins of the world, have mercy on us.

Agnus Dei, qui tollis peccáta mundi: dona nobis pacem.

Lamb of God, who takest away the sins of the world, grant us peace.

Preparation for Communion

Dómine Iesu Christe, qui dixísti Apóstolis tuis: Pacem relínquo vobis, pacem meam do vobis: ne respícias peccáta mea, sed fidem Ecclésiæ tuæ; eámque secúndum voluntátem tuam pacificáre et coadunáre dignéris: Qui vivis et regnas Deus per ómnia sǽcula sæculórum. Amen.

O Lord Jesus Christ, who saidst to thine Apostles: Peace I leave with you, my peace I give unto you: look not upon my sins but the faith of thy Church; and vouchsafe to it that peace and unity which is agreeable to thy will: Who live and reign, one God, forever and ever. Amen.

In a Solemn Mass, the Priest kisses the altar, and then embraces the Deacon for the kiss of peace.

℣. Pax tecum.

Peace be with thee.

℟. Et cum spíritu tuo.

And with thy spirit.

Dómine Iesu Christe, Fili Dei vivi, qui ex voluntáte Patris, cooperánte Spíritu Sancto, per mortem tuam mundum vivificásti: líbera me per hoc sacrosánctum Corpus et Sánguinem tuum ab ómnibus iniquitátibus meis, et univérsis malis: et fac me tuis semper inhærére mandátis, et a te numquam separári permíttas: Qui cum eódem Deo Patre et Spíritu Sancto vivis et regnas Deus in sǽcula sæculórum. Amen.

Lord Jesus Christ, Son of the living God, who, according to the will of the Father through the cooperation of the Holy Spirit, hast by thy death given life to the world: deliver me by this thy most sacred Body and Blood from all my iniquities and from all evils: and make me always adhere to thy commandments, and never suffer me to be separated from thee: Who with the same God the Father and Holy Spirit live and reign, one God, forever and ever. Amen.

Percéptio Córporis tui, Dómine Iesu Christe, quod ego indígnus súmere præsúmo, non mihi provéniat in iudícium et condemnatiónem: sed pro tua pietáte prosit mihi ad tutaméntum mentis et córporis, et ad medélam percipiéndam: Qui vivis et regnas cum Deo Patre in unitáte Spíritus Sancti Deus, per ómnia sǽcula sæculórum. Amen.

Let not the partaking of thy Body, O Lord Jesus Christ, which I, all unworthy, presume to receive, turn to my judgment and condemnation: but through thy goodness, may it be to me a safeguard and remedy, both of soul and body: Who live and reign with God the Father, in the unity of the Holy Spirit, one God, forever and ever. Amen.

Holy Communion

Communion of the Priest

Panem cæléstem accípiam, et nomen Dómini invocábo.

I will take the bread of heaven, and call upon the name of the Lord.

Dómine, non sum dignus, ut intres sub tectum meum: sed tantum dic verbo, et sanábitur ánima mea.

Lord, I am not worthy that thou shouldst enter under my roof: say but the word, and my soul shall be healed.

Corpus Dómini nostri Iesu Christi custódiat ánimam meam in vitam ætérnam. Amen.

The Body of our Lord Jesus Christ preserve my soul unto life everlasting. Amen.

¶ *If there are no other communicants present, the choir begins the Communion antiphon as the Priest communicates.*

Quid retríbuam Dómino pro ómnibus, quæ retríbuit mihi? Cálicem salutáris accípiam, et nomen Dómini invocábo. Laudans invocábo Dóminum, et ab inimícis meis salvus ero.

What shall I render to the Lord for all he hath rendered unto me? I will take the Chalice of salvation, and call upon the name of the Lord. Praising, I will call upon the Lord, and I shall be saved from my enemies.

Sanguis Dómini nostri Iesu Christi custódiat ánimam meam in vitam ætérnam. Amen.

The Blood of our Lord Jesus Christ preserve my soul unto life everlasting. Amen.

Communion of the Faithful[2]

The Priest turns towards the people and holds up the Host, saying:

Ecce Agnus Dei, ecce qui tollit peccáta mundi.

Behold, the Lamb of God, behold him who taketh away the sins of the world.

He then repeats three times:

Dómine, non sum dignus, ut intres sub tectum meum: sed tantum dic verbo, et sanábitur ánima mea.

Lord, I am not worthy that thou shouldst enter under my roof: say but the word, and my soul shall be healed.

The Priest then distributes Holy Communion to the faithful, as the choir begins the Communion antiphon. If there are many communicants, the antiphon may be sung with its psalm, and repeated.

To each communicant, the Priest says:

Corpus ✝ Dómini nostri Iesu Christi custódiat ánimam tuam in vitam ætérnam. Amen.

The Body of our Lord Jesus Christ preserve thy soul unto life everlasting. Amen.

Purifications and Ablutions

Quod ore súmpsimus, Dómine, pura mente capiámus: et de múnere temporáli fiat nobis remédium sempitérnum.

Grant, Lord, that what we have taken with our mouth we may receive with a pure mind: and of a temporal gift may it become to us an eternal remedy.

Corpus tuum, Dómine, quod sumpsi, et Sanguis, quem potávi, adhǽreat viscéribus meis: et præsta; ut in me non remáneat scélerum má-

May thy Body, O Lord, which I have received, and thy Blood which I have drunk, cleave to my bowels: and grant that no stain of sin may remain in me,

cula, quem pura et sancta refecérunt sacraménta: Qui vivis et regnas in sǽcula sæculórum. Amen.

who have been refreshed with pure and holy sacraments: Who live and reign forever and ever. Amen.

Postcommunion

After the Priest reads the Communion antiphon, he turns towards the people, saying:

℣. Dóminus vobíscum.

The Lord be with you.

℟. Et cum spíritu tuo.

And with thy spirit.

Orémus.

Let us pray.

The Priest sings this and the Postcommunion prayer in the same tone as the Collect, p. 4.

¶ *On the Monday, Tuesday, and Wednesday of Holy Week, the Prayer over the People is said after the Postcommunion. These are prefaced by an invitation by the Deacon (or the Priest):*

Humiliáte cápita vestra Deo.

Bow your heads before God.

Dismissal

℣. Dóminus vobíscum.

The Lord be with you.

℟. Et cum spíritu tuo.

And with thy spirit.

The Deacon (or the Priest) then intones the dismissal:

℣. Ite missa est.

Go, the Mass is ended.

℟. Deo grátias.

Thanks be to God.

¶ *When the Mass is immediately followed by a procession, as on Holy Thursday:*

℣. Benedicámus Dómino.

Let us bless the Lord.

℟. Deo grátias.

Thanks be to God.

Pláceat tibi, sancta Trínitas, obséquium servitútis meæ: et præsta; ut sacrifícium, quod óculis tuæ maiestátis indígnus óbtuli, tibi sit acceptábile, mihíque et ómnibus, pro quibus illud óbtuli, sit, te miseránte, propitiábile. Per Christum Dóminum nostrum. Amen.

May the performance of my homage be pleasing to thee, O Holy Trinity: and grant that the sacrifice which I, though unworthy, have offered up in the sight of thy majesty, may be acceptable to thee, and through thy mercy be a propitiation for me, and all those for whom I have offered it. Through Christ our Lord. Amen.

Final Blessing

Benedícat vos omnípotens Deus, Pater, et Fílius, ✚ et Spíritus Sanctus. ℟. Amen.

May almighty God bless you, the Father, Son and Holy Spirit.

¶ *The blessing is omitted when* Benedicámus Dómino *is said instead of* Ite, missa est, *as on Holy Thursday.*

Last Gospel

℣. Dóminus vobíscum.

℟. Et cum spíritu tuo.

The Lord be with you.

And with thy spirit.

✚ Inítium sancti Evangélii secúndum Ioánnem

℟. Gloria tibi, Domine.

Glory be to thee, O Lord.

Jn 1: 1-14.

In princípio erat Verbum, et Verbum erat apud Deum, et Deus erat Verbum. Hoc erat in princípio apud Deum. Omnia per ipsum facta sunt: et sine ipso factum est nihil, quod factum est: in ipso vita erat, et vita erat lux hóminum: et lux in ténebris lucet, et ténebræ eam non comprehendérunt.

Fuit homo missus a Deo, cui nomen erat Ioánnes. Hic venit in testimónium, ut testimónium perhibéret de lúmine, ut omnes créderent per illum. Non erat ille lux, sed ut testimónium perhibéret de lúmine.

Erat lux vera, quæ illúminat omnem hóminem veniéntem in hunc mundum. In mundo erat, et mundus per ipsum factus est, et mundus eum non cognóvit. In própria venit, et sui eum non recepérunt. Quotquot autem recepérunt eum, dedit eis potestátem fílios Dei fíeri, his, qui credunt in nómine eius: qui non ex san-

In the beginning was the Word, and the Word was with God, and the Word was God. The same was in the beginning with God. All things were made by him, and without him was made nothing that was made. In him was life, and the life was the light of men; and the light shineth in darkness, and the darkness did not comprehend it.

There was a man sent from God, whose name was John. This man came for a witness, to give testimony of the light, that all men might believe through him. He was not the light, but was to give testimony of the light. That was the true light, which enlighteneth every man that cometh into this world.

He was in the world, and the world was made by him, and the world knew him not. He came unto his own, and his own received him not. But as many as received him, he gave them power to be made the sons of God, to them that believe in his name, who are born not of blood, nor of the will of the flesh, nor of the will of man, but of God.

guínibus, neque ex voluntáte carnis, neque ex voluntáte viri, sed ex Deo nati sunt.

(Genuflect)

Et Verbum caro factum est, et habitávit in nobis: et vídimus glóriam eius, glóriam quasi Unigéniti a Patre, plenum grátiæ et veritátis.

℟. Deo grátias.

And the Word was made flesh, and dwelt among us. And we saw his glory, the glory as it were of the only-begotten of the Father, full of grace and truth.

Thanks be to God.

PALM SUNDAY

The Asperges *is not said.*

BLESSING OF PALMS

The sacred ministers are vested in red, with the celebrant wearing a cope instead of a chasuble. As they enter the sanctuary, the following antiphon is sung:

Ant.

VII.

Mt 21: 9

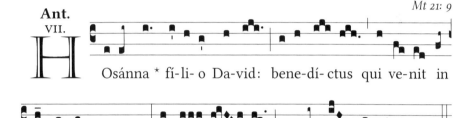

Osánna * fí-li- o Da-vid: bene-dí- ctus qui ve-nit in nómi-ne Dómi-ni. Rex Is- ra- ël: Ho-sánna in excél-sis.

Hosanna to the son of David: blessed is he that cometh in the name of the Lord. O King of Israel: Hosanna in the highest.

Then the celebrant, turned towards the palms and the people, begins:

℣. Dóminus vobíscum.

℟. Et cum spíritu tuo.

Orémus.

B éne✠dic, quǽsumus, Dómine, hos palmárum (*or* olivárum *or* aliárum árborum) ramos: et præsta; ut, quod pópulus tuus in tui veneratiónem hodiérna die corporáliter agit, hoc spirituáliter summa devotióne perfíciat, de hoste victóriam reportándo et opus misericórdiæ summópere diligéndo. Per Dóminum nostrum Iesum Christum.

The Lord be with you.

And with thy spirit.

Let us pray.

Bless, we beseech thee, O Lord, these branches of palm (*or* olive *or* other trees): and grant that what thy people today bodily perform for thy honor, they may perfect spiritually with the utmost devotion, by gaining the victory over the enemy, and ardently loving every work of mercy. Through our Lord Jesus Christ, thy Son, who lives and reigns with thee.

The celebrant sprinkles the palms with holy water, then he blesses incense and censes the palms.

DISTRIBUTION OF PALMS

After the blessing, palms are distributed to the clergy, servers, choir, and to all the faithful. It is customary to kiss the palm and then the celebrant's hand when receiving a blessed palm. During this, the following antiphons and psalms are sung:

1 Ant.
I. f   Mt 21: 9

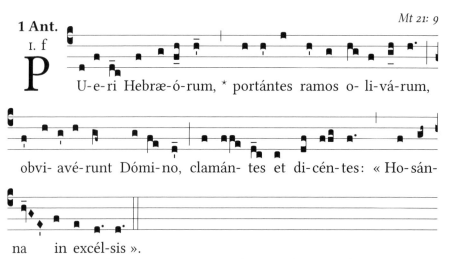

PU-e-ri Hebræ-ó-rum, * portántes ramos o- li-vá-rum,

obvi- avé-runt Dómi-no, clamán- tes et di-cén-tes: « Ho-sán-

na   in excél-sis ».

The children of the Hebrews, carrying olive branches, went forth to meet the Lord, crying aloud and repeating: "Hosanna in the highest."

Psalm 23
℣. 1-2, 7-10.

1. Dómi- ni est terra, et ple-ni- **tú**- do **e**- ius: * orbis terrá-rum, et

uni-vérsi qui há-bi-*tant in* **e**- o. *Flex:* prínci-pes, vestras, †

The earth is the Lord's and the fullness thereof: the world, and all they that dwell therein.

2. Quia ipse super mária fundávit **e**um: * et super flúmina præparávit **e**um.	For he hath founded it upon the seas; and hath prepared it upon the rivers.

Repeat Ant. Púeri *as above.*

7. Attóllite portas, príncipes, vestras, † et elevámini, portæ æternáles: * et introí*bit Rex* **gló**riæ.

Lift up your gates, O ye princes, and be ye lifted up, O eternal gates: and the King of Glory shall enter in.

8. Quis est iste Rex glóriæ? † Dóminus **for**tis et **pot**ens: * Dóminus pot*ens in* **præ**lio.

Who is this King of Glory? the Lord who is strong and mighty: the Lord mighty in battle.

Repeat Ant. Púeri *as above.*

9. Attóllite portas, príncipes, vestras, † et elevámini, portæ æternáles: * et introí*bit Rex* **gló**riæ.

Lift up your gates, O ye princes, and be ye lifted up, O eternal gates: and the King of Glory shall enter in.

10. Quis est **i**ste Rex **gló**riæ? * Dóminus virtútum ipse *est Rex* **gló**riæ.

Who is this King of Glory? the Lord of hosts, he is the King of Glory.

Repeat Ant. Púeri *as above.*

11. Glória **Pa**tri et **Fí**lio, * et Spirí*tui* **San**cto.
12. Sicut erat in princípio, et **nunc**, et **sem**per, * et in sǽcula sæcu*ló*rum. **A**men.

Repeat Ant. Púeri *as above.*

2 Ant.
1. f

Mt 21: 8, 9

PU-e-ri Hebræ-ó-rum * vestiménta prosternébant in vi-

a, et clamábant di-céntes: « Ho-sánna fí-li-o Da-vid: bene-dí-

ctus qui ve-nit in nómi-ne Dómi-ni ».

The children of the Hebrews strewed their garments in the way and cried aloud, repeating: "Hosanna to the son of David: blessed is he that cometh in the name of the Lord."

Psalm 46

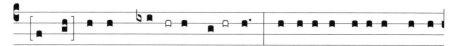

1. Omnes gentes, **pláu**di-te **máni**-bus: * iu-bi-lá-te De-o in vo-ce

exsul*ta-ti-* **ó-** nis.

> O clap your hands, all ye nations: shout unto God with the voice of Joy.

2. Quóniam Dóminus ex**cél**sus, ter**rí**bilis: * Rex magnus super *omnem* **ter**ram.	For the Lord is high, terrible: a great king over all the earth.

Repeat Ant. Púeri *as above.*

3. Subiécit **pópulos no**bis: * et gentes sub pé*dibus* **no**stris.	He hath subdued the people under us; and the nations under our feet.
4. Elégit nobis heredi**tátem su**am: * spéciem Iacob, *quam* di**lé**xit.	He hath chosen for us his inheritance the beauty of Jacob which he hath loved.

Repeat Ant. Púeri *as above.*

5. Ascéndit **Deus** in **iúbilo**: * et Dóminus in *voce* **tu**bæ.	God is ascended with jubilee, and the Lord with the sound of trumpet.
6. P**sál**lite Deo **no**stro, **psál**lite: * psállite Regi *nostro,* **psál**lite.	Sing praises to our God, sing ye: sing praises to our king, sing ye.

Repeat Ant. Púeri *as above.*

7. Quóniam Rex omnis **terræ Deus**: * psállite *sapié*nter.	For God is the king of all the earth: sing ye wisely.
8. Regnábit Deus **super gen**tes: * Deus sedet super sedem *sanctam* **su**am.	God shall reign over the nations: God sitteth on his holy throne.

Repeat Ant. Púeri *as above.*

9. Príncipes populórum congregáti sunt cum **Deo Abraham**: * quóniam dii fortes terræ	The princes of the people are gathered together, with the God of Abraham: for the strong gods of the

veheménter *elevá*ti sunt.

| earth are exceedingly exalted.

Repeat Ant. Púeri *as above.*

10. Glória **Pa**tri et **Fí**lio, * et Spirí*tui* **San**cto.

11. Sicut erat...et **nunc**, et **sem**per, * et in sǽcula sǽcu*lórum.* **A**men.

Repeat Ant. Púeri *as above.*

If these chants are not long enough, they are repeated until the distribution of palms is finished; if the distribution ends first however, the Glória Patri *is sung at once, followed by the antiphon.*

When all have received blessed palms, the celebrant washes his hands; the table and extra palms are removed from the sanctuary.

READING OF THE GOSPEL

The Gospel is now sung in the usual way, with incense and candles.

✚ Sequéntia sancti Evangélii secúndum Matthǽum
Mt 21: 1-9.

In illo témpore: Cum appropinquásset Iesus Ierosólymis, et venísset Béthphage ad montem Olivéti: tunc misit duos discípulos suos, dicens eis: « Ite in castéllum, quod contra vos est, et statim inveniétis ásinam alligátam et pullum cum ea: sólvite et addúcite mihi: et si quis vobis áliquid díxerit, dícite, quia Dóminus his opus habet, et conféstim dimíttet eos ». Hoc autem totum factum est, ut adimplerétur, quod dictum est per Prophétam, dicéntem: Dícite fíliæ Sion: Ecce, Rex tuus venit tibi mansuétus, sedens super ásinam et pullum, fílium subiugális. Eúntes autem discípuli, fecérunt, sicut præcépit illis Iesus. Et adduxérunt ásinam et pullum: et imposuérunt super eos vestiménta sua, et eum désuper sedére fecérunt. Plúrima autem turba stravérunt vestiménta sua in via: álii

At that time, when Jesus drew nigh to Jerusalem, and was come to Bethphage, unto Mount Olivet, then he sent two disciples, saying to them: Go ye into the village that is over against you, and immediately you shall find an ass tied, and a colt with her: loose them and bring them to me. And if any man shall say anything to you, say ye, that the Lord hath need of them: and forthwith he will let them go. Now all this was done that it might be fulfilled which was spoken by the prophet, saying: Tell ye the daughter of Sion: Behold thy King cometh to thee, meek, and sitting upon an ass, and a colt the foal of her that is used to the yoke. And the disciples going, did as Jesus commanded them. And they brought the ass and the colt, and laid their garments upon them, and made him sit thereon. And a very great multitude spread their garments in the way: and others cut

autem cædébant ramos de arbóribus, et sternébant in via: turbæ autem, quæ præcedébant et quæ sequebántur, clamábant, dicéntes: « Hosánna fílio David: benedíctus, qui venit in nómine Dómini ».

boughs from the trees, and strewed them in the way, and the multitudes that went before and that followed, cried, saying: Hosanna to the Son of David: Blessed is he that cometh in the name of the Lord.

THE PROCESSION WITH BLESSED PALMS

The deacon: *All respond:*

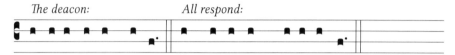

Pro-cedámus in pa-ce. ℟. In nómi-ne Christi. Amen.

Let us go forth in peace.   In the name of Christ. Amen.

As the procession begins, all or some of the following antiphons may be sung:

1

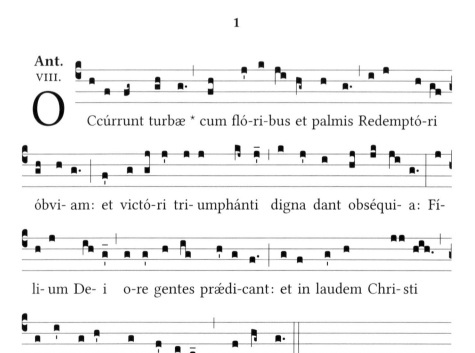

Ant.
VIII.

O

Ccúrrunt turbæ * cum fló-ri-bus et palmis Redemptó-ri

óbvi- am: et victó-ri tri- umphánti digna dant obséqui- a: Fí-

li- um De- i o-re gentes prædi-cant: et in laudem Chri-sti

vo-ces tonant per nú-bi-la: « Ho-sánna ».

The multitude goeth forth to meet our Redeemer with flowers and palms: and payeth the homage due to a triumphant Conqueror: the Gentiles proclaim the Son of God, and their voices thunder through the skies in praise of Christ: "Hosanna."

2

Ant. VII.

CUM Ange-lis et pú- e-ris * fi-dé-les inve-ni- ámur, tri-umpha-tó-ri mortis clamántes: « Ho-sánna in excél-sis ».

Let the faithful join with the Angels and children, singing to the Conqueror of death: "Hosanna in the highest."

3

Ant. IV.

cf. *Jn 12*

TUrba multa, * quæ convéne-rat ad di- em festum, clamá-bat Dómino: « Bene-díctus qui ve-nit in nómi-ne Dómi-ni: Ho-sánna in excél-sis ».

A great multitude, that was met together at the festival, cried out to the Lord: "Blessed is he that cometh in the name of the Lord: Hosanna in the highest."

4

Ant. I.

Lk 19: 37-38 (10th c.)

CŒpé-runt * omnes turbæ descendénti- um gaudén-tes laudá-re De- um vo-ce magna, super ó- mni- bus quas

ví-de-rant virtú-ti-bus, di-céntes: « Be-ne-díctus qui ve-nit Rex

in nómi-ne Dómi-ni; pax in terra, et gló-ri- a in excélsis ».

Near the descent the whole multitude began with joy to praise God with a loud voice, for all the mighty works they had seen, saying: "Blessed be the King who cometh in the name of the Lord; peace on earth, and glory on high."

¶ *In the course of the procession, the following hymn is sung. If possible, the congregation should sing the first lines,* Glória laus, *between the verses.*

Hymn to Christ the King

Choir: *Theodulf, Bishop of Orleans († 821)*
I.

Ló-ri- a, laus et honor ti-bi sit, Rex Christe Redém-

ptor: Cu- i, pu-e- rí-le de-cus prompsit Ho-sánna pi- um.

All repeat: Glória laus.

Glory and honor and praise be to thee, Christ, King and Redeemer: to whom children cried out loving 'Hosannas' with joy.

Choir:

1. Isra-el es tu Rex, Da-ví-dis et íncli-ta pro-les: Nómi-ne qui in

Dómi-ni, Rex bene-dícte, ve-nis. *All:* Glória laus.

Israel's King art thou, King David's magnicent offspring: thou art the blessed King who comest in the name of the Lord.

Choir:

2. Cœtus in ex-cél-sis te laudat cǽ-li-cus omnis, Et mortá-lis

homo, et cuncta cre-á- ta simul. *All:* Glória laus.

Heavenly hosts on high unite in singing thy praises: menkind on earth, and all creation join in.

Choir:

3. Plebs Hebrǽ-a ti- bi cum palmis óbvi- a ve-nit: Cum pre-ce,

vo-to, hymnis, ádsumus ecce ti-bi. *All:* Glória laus.

Bearing palms, Hebrews came crowding to greet thee: see how with prayers and hymns we come to pay thee our vows.

Choir:

4. Hi ti-bi pas-sú-ro solvébant mú-ni- a laudis: Nos ti-bi regnán-

ti pángimus ecce me-los. *All:* Glória laus.

They offered gifts of praise to thee, so near to thy passion: see how we sing this song now to thee reigning on high.

Choir:

5. Hi placu- é-re ti- bi, plá-ce- at de-vó-ti- o nostra: Rex bone,

Rex clemens, cui bona cuncta pla-cent. *All:* Glória laus.

Those thou wert then pleased to accept, now accept our gifts of devotion: O good and merciful King, lover of all that is good.

5

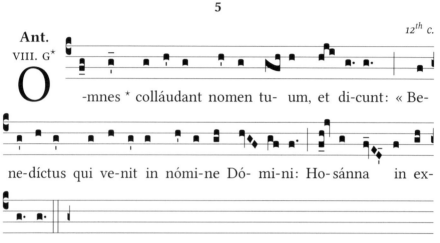

Ant.

VIII. G*

12th c.

O-mnes * colláudant nomen tu- um, et di-cunt: « Be-ne-díctus qui ve-nit in nómi-ne Dó- mi-ni: Ho-sánna   in ex-cél-sis ».

All praise thy name highly and say: "Blessed is he who cometh in the name of the Lord: Hosanna in the highest."

Or, another melody, antiphon **13**, *p.* 241.

Psalm 147

1. Lauda, Ie-rú-sa-lem, **Dóminum:** * lauda De-um *tu-um*, **Si-** on.

O Jerusalem praise our Lord: praise thy God O Sion.

2. Quóniam confortávit seras portárum tuárum: * benedíxit fíliis *tuis* **in** te.

Because he hath strengthened the locks of thy gates: he hath blessed thy children in thee.

3. Qui pósuit fines tuos **pacem:** * et ádipe fruménti *sátiat* te.

Who hath set thy borders peace: and filleth thee with the fat of corn.

4. Qui emíttit elóquium suum **terræ:** * velóciter currit *sermo* **eius.**

Who sendeth forth his speech to the earth: his word runneth swiftly.

5. Qui dat nivem sicut **la**nam: * nébulam sicut cí*nerem* **spar**git.	Who giveth snow as wool: scattereth mist as ashes.
6. Mittit crystállum suam sicut buc**céll**as: * ante fáciem frígoris eius quis *susti*né bit?	He casteth his crystal as morsels: before the face of his cold who shall endure?
7. Emíttet verbum suum et liquefáciet **e**a: * flabit spíritus eius et *fluent* aquæ.	He shall send forth his word, and shall melt them: his spirit shall blow, and waters shall flow.
8. Qui annúntiat verbum suum **Ia**cob: * iustítias et iudícia *sua* **Is**raël.	Who declareth his word to Jacob: his justices, and judgments to Israel.
9. Non fecit táliter omni na-ti**ó**ni: * et iudícia sua non manife*stávit* **e**is.	He hath not done in like manner to any nation: and his judgments he hath not made manifest to them.

10. Glória Patri et **Fí**lio, * et Spirí*tui* **San**cto.

11. Sicut erat...et nunc, et **sem**per, * et in sæcula sæcu*lórum.* **A**men.

Repeat Ant. Omnes colláudant *as above.*

6

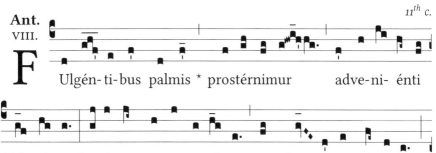

Fulgén-ti-bus palmis * prostérnimur adve-ni- énti

Dó-mi-no: hu- ic omnes occurrámus cum hymnis et cánti-cis,

glo-ri-fi-cántes et di-céntes: « Be-ne-díctus Dó-mi-nus ».

We are strewn with the shining palms before the Lord as he approacheth: let us all run to meet him with hymns and songs, glorify him and say: "Blessed be the Lord."

7

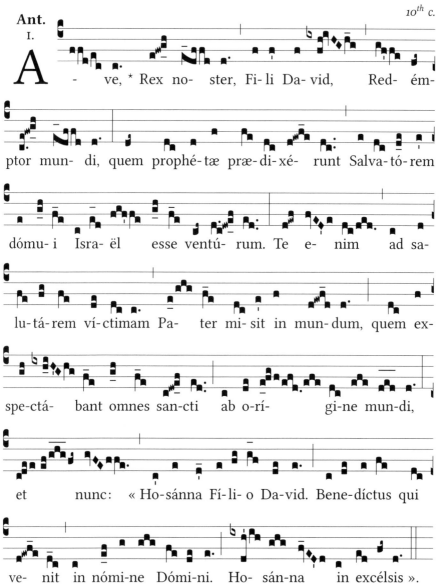

Ave, * Rex noster, Fili David, Redémptor mundi, quem prophétæ prædixérunt Salvatórem dómui Israël esse ventúrum. Te enim ad salutárem víctimam Pater misit in mundum, quem exspectábant omnes sancti ab orígine mundi, et nunc: « Hosánna Fílio David. Benedíctus qui venit in nómine Dómini. Hosánna in excélsis ».

Hail, our King, O Son of David, O world's Redeemer, whom prophets did foretell as the Savior to come of the house of Israel. For the Father sent thee into the world as victim for salvation; from the beginning of the world all the saints awaited thee: "Hosanna now to the Son of David! Blessed be he who cometh in the name of the Lord. Hosanna in the highest."

Additional antiphons in the Appendix, p. 235. In addition, other hymns may be sung in honor of Christ the King, such as Christus vincit, *p. 247.*

When the procession enters the church—as the celebrant goes through the door—the responsory is begun:

Resp.

cf. Jn 12

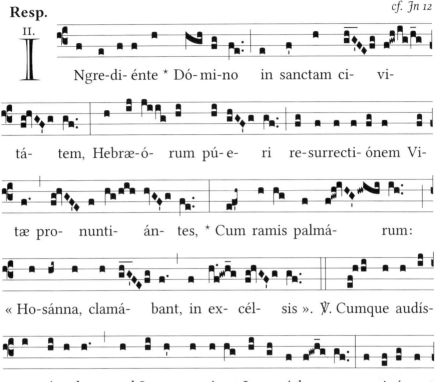

Ngre-di- énte * Dó- mi-no in sanctam ci- vi-tá- tem, Hebræ-ó- rum pú- e- ri re-surrecti- ónem Vi-tæ pro- nunti- án- tes, * Cum ramis palmá- rum: « Ho-sánna, clamá- bant, in ex- cél- sis ». ℣. Cumque audís-set pópu-lus, quod Ie-sus ve-ní-ret Ie-ro-só-ly- mam, ex-i- é-runt

ób- vi- am e- i. * Cum ramis

As our Lord entered the holy city, the Hebrew children, declaring the resurrection of life, * With palm branches, cried out: "Hosanna in the highest." ℣. When the people heard that Jesus was coming to Jerusalem, they went forth to meet him: * With palm branches, cried out: "Hosanna in the highest."

All continue back to their places and finally the celebrant enters the sanctuary and goes up to the altar to conclude the procession:

℣. Dóminus vobíscum.	The Lord be with you.
℟. Et cum spíritu tuo.	And with thy spirit.
Orémus.	Let us pray.

Dómine Iesu Christe, Rex ac Redémptor noster, in cuius honórem, hoc ramos gestántes, solémnes laudes decantávimus: concéde pro-

O Lord Jesus Christ, our King and Redeemer, in whose honor we have borne these palms and gone on praising thee with song and solemnity: mercifully

pítius; ut, quocúmque hi rami de-portáti fúerint, ibi tuæ benedictió-nis grátia descéndat, et quavis dǽ-monum iniquitáte vel illusióne pro-fligáta, déxtera tua prótegat, quos re-démit: Qui vivis et regnas in ómnia sǽcula sæculórum.

℟. Amen.

grant that wheresoever these palms are taken, there the grace of thy blessing may descend; may every wickedness and trick of the demons be frustrated; and may thy right hand protect those it hath redeemed: Who live and reign forever and ever.

The celebrant and sacred ministers change their red vestments for violet Mass vestments.

AT MASS

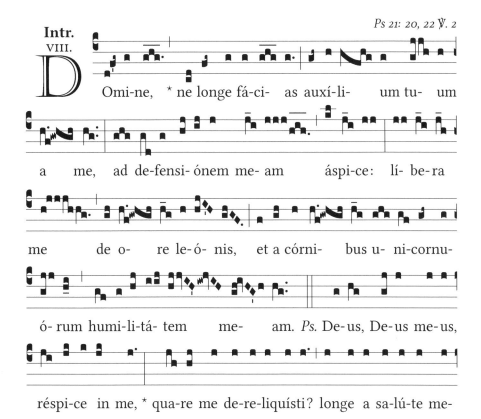

Ps 21: 20, 22 ℣. 2

Intr. VIII.

DOmi-ne, * ne longe fá-ci- as auxí-li- um tu- um a me, ad de-fensi- ónem me- am áspi-ce: lí- be-ra me de o- re le-ó- nis, et a córni- bus u- ni-cornu- ó- rum humi-li-tá- tem me- am. *Ps.* De-us, De-us me-us, réspi-ce in me, * qua-re me de-re-liquísti? longe a sa-lú-te me- a verba de-lictó- rum me- ó-rum. *Repeat:* Dómine, ne longe.

O Lord, remove not thy help to a distance from me, look towards my defense: deliver me from the lion's mouth, and my lowness from the horns of the unicorns. *Ps.* O God, my God, look upon me: why hast thou forsaken me? Far from my salvation are the words of my sins.

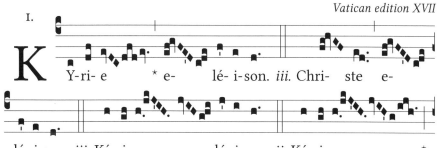

Vatican edition XVII

I.

KY-ri- e * e- lé- i-son. *iii.* Chri- ste e- lé- i-son. *iii.* Ký-ri- e e- lé- i-son. *ii.* Ký-ri- e *

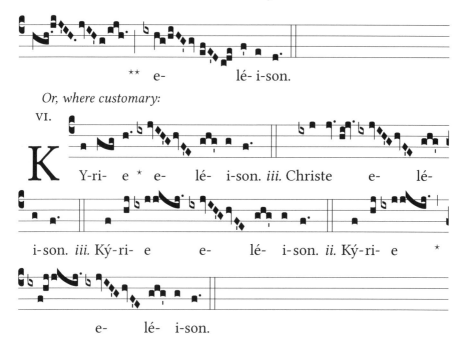

** e- lé- i-son.

Or, where customary:

VI.

Kᵧ-ri- e * e- lé- i-son. *iii.* Christe e- lé-

i-son. *iii.* Ký-ri- e e- lé- i-son. *ii.* Ký-ri- e *

e- lé- i-son.

Collect

Omnípotens sempitérne Deus, qui humáno géneri, ad imitándum humilitátis exémplum, Salvatórem nostrum carnem súmere et crucem subíre fecísti: concéde propítius; ut et patiéntiæ ipsíus habére documénta et resurrectiónis consórtia mereámur. Per eúndem Dóminum.

Almighty and everlasting God, who, to give an example of humility for all mankind to follow, didst will that our Savior should take up our nature and submit to the cross: grant us, we beseech thee, to heed the teachings of example, and so merit a part in his resurrection. Through the same Lord.

Léctio Epístolæ beáti Pauli Apóstoli ad Philippénses
Phil 2: 5-11.

Fratres: Hoc enim sentíte in vobis, quod et in Christo Iesu: qui, cum in forma Dei esset, non rapínam arbitrátus est esse se æquálem Deo: sed semetípsum exinanívit, formam servi accípiens, in similitúdinem hóminum factus, et hábitu invéntus ut homo. Humiliávit semetípsum, factus obœdiens usque ad mortem, mortem autem crucis. Propter quod et Deus

Brethren: For let this mind be in you, which was also in Christ Jesus: who being in the form of God, thought it not robbery to be equal with God: but emptied himself, taking the form of a servant, being made in the likeness of men, and in habit found as a man. He humbled himself, becoming obedient unto death, even to the death of the cross. For which cause God also hath exalted him, and

exaltávit illum: ei donávit illi nomen, quod est super omne nomen: *(here all kneel)* ut in nómine Iesu omne genu flectátur cæléstium, terréstrium et inférnorum: et omnis lingua confiteátur, quia Dóminus Iesus Christus in glória est Dei Patris.

hath given him a name which is above all names: *(here all kneel)* that in the name of Jesus every knee should bow, of those that are in heaven, on earth, and under the earth: and that every tongue should confess that the Lord Jesus Christ is in the glory of God the Father.

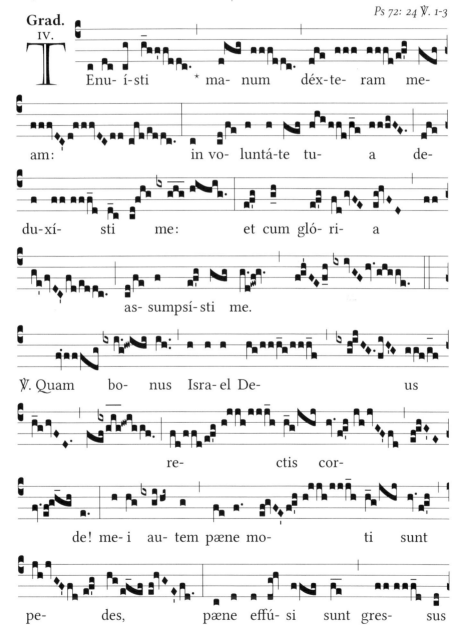

Ps 72: 24 ℣. 1-3

Grad. IV.

Tenuísti * manum déxteram meam: in voluntáte tua deduxísti me: et cum glória assumpsísti me.

℣. Quam bonus Israel Deus rectis corde! mei autem pæne moti sunt pedes, pæne effúsi sunt gressus

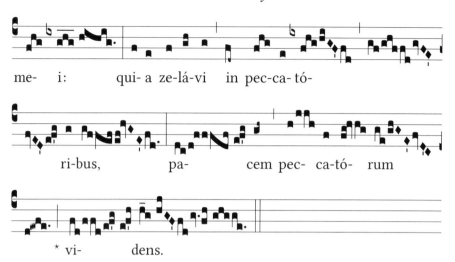

me- i: qui- a ze-lá-vi in pec-ca- tó-
ri-bus, pa- cem pec- ca-tó- rum
* vi- dens.

Thou hast held me by my right hand: and by thy will thou hast conducted me: and with glory thou hast received me. ℣. How good is God to Israel, to them that are of a right heart! But my feet were almost moved, my steps had well nigh slipped: because I had a zeal on occasion of sinners, seeing the peace of sinners.

Tract. II.

Ps 21: 2-9, 18, 19, 22, 24, 32

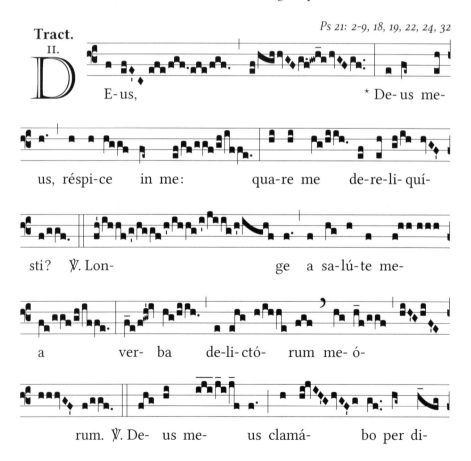

E- us, * De- us me-
us, réspi-ce in me: qua-re me de-re-li- quí-
sti? ℣. Lon- ge a sa-lú-te me-
a ver- ba de-li-ctó- rum me- ó-
rum. ℣. De- us me- us clamá- bo per di-

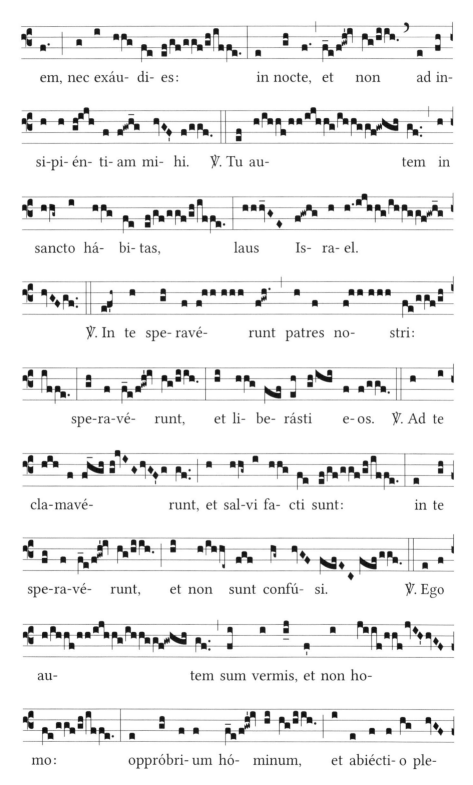

em, nec exáu- di- es: in nocte, et non ad in-

si-pi- én- ti- am mi- hi. ℣. Tu au- tem in

sancto há- bi- tas, laus Is- ra- el.

℣. In te spe- ravé- runt patres no- stri:

spe-ra-vé- runt, et li- be- rásti e- os. ℣. Ad te

cla-mavé- runt, et sal-vi fa- cti sunt: in te

spe-ra-vé- runt, et non sunt confú- si. ℣. Ego

au- tem sum vermis, et non ho-

mo: oppróbri- um hó- minum, et abiécti- o ple-

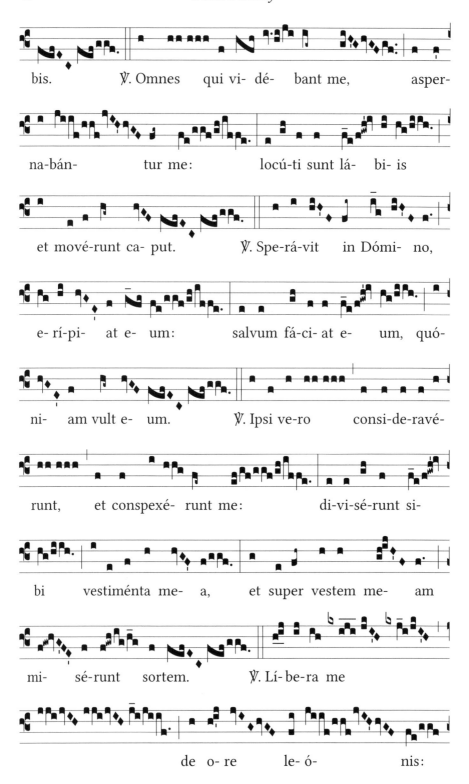

bis. ℣. Omnes qui vi- dé- bant me, asper-

na-bán- tur me: locú-ti sunt lá- bi- is

et mové-runt ca- put. ℣. Spe-rá-vit in Dómi- no,

e- rí-pi- at e- um: salvum fá-ci- at e- um, quó-

ni- am vult e- um. ℣. Ipsi ve-ro consi-de-ravé-

runt, et conspexé- runt me: di-vi-sé-runt si-

bi vestiménta me- a, et super vestem me- am

mi- sé-runt sortem. ℣. Lí-be-ra me

de o- re le- ó- nis:

et a cór-ni- bus uni-cornu- ó- rum hu-

mi- li- tá-tem me- am. ℣. Qui timé-tis Dómi- num, lau-

dá-te e- um: uni-vérsum semen Ia- cob,

magni- fi- cá-te e-um. ℣. Annunti- á-bi- tur Dómi-

no ge-ne-rá-ti- o ventú- ra: et annunti- á-

bunt cæ- li iustí- ti- am e-

ius. ℣. Pó-pu-lo qui nascé- tur, quem fe- cit *

Dó- mi-nus.

My God, my God, look upon me: why hast thou forsaken me? ℣. Far from my salvation, are the words of my sins. ℣. O my God, I cry out by day and thou wilt not hear; and by night, and it shall not be reputed as folly in me. ℣. But thou dwellest in the holy place, the praise of Israel. ℣. In thee have our fathers hoped: they have hoped and thou hast delivered them. ℣. They cried to thee, and they were saved: they trusted in thee, and were not confounded. ℣. But I am a worm, and no man: the reproach of men, and the outcast of the people. ℣. All they that saw me have laughed me to scorn: they have spoken with the lips, and wagged the head. ℣. He hoped in the Lord; let him deliver him: let him save him, seeing he delighteth in him.

℣. But they have looked and stared upon me: they parted my garments amongst them, and upon my vesture they cast lots. ℣. Deliver me from the lion's mouth: and my lowness from the horns of the unicorns. ℣. Ye that fear the Lord, praise him: all ye the seed of Jacob, glorify him. ℣. There shall be declared to the Lord a generation to come: and the heavens shall show forth his justice. ℣. To a people that shall be born, which the Lord hath made.

Or, the Tract may be sung in a Psalm-tone, p. 253.

THE PASSION

It is permitted for the schola to sing, as the "Turba," the words for which notes are given.

Pássio Dómini nostri Iesu Christi secúndum Matthǽum
Mt 26: 36-75; 27: 1-60.

IN illo témpore: Venit Iesus cum discípulis suis in villam, quæ dícitur Gethsémani, et dixit discípulis suis: ✠ Sedéte hic, donec vadam illuc, et orem. **C.** Et assúmpto Petro, et duóbus fíliis Zebedǽi, cœpit contristári et mæstus esse. Tunc ait illis: ✠ Tristis est ánima mea usque ad mortem: sustinéte hic, et vigiláte mecum.

C. Et progréssus pusíllum, prócidit in fáciem suam, orans, et dicens: ✠ Pater mi, si possíbile est, tránseat a me calix iste. Verúmtamen non sicut ego volo, sed sicut tu. **C.** Et venit ad discípulos suos, et invénit eos dormiéntes: et dicit Petro: ✠ Sic non potuístis una hora vigiláre mecum? Vigiláte, et oráte ut non intrétis in tentatiónem. Spíritus quidem promptus est, caro autem infírma. **C.** Iterum secúndo ábiit, et orávit, dicens: ✠ Pater mi, si non potest hic calix transíre, nisi bibam illum, fiat volúntas tua. **C.** Et venit íterum, et invénit eos dormiéntes: erant enim óculi eó-

C. At that time Jesus came with his disciples into a country place which is called Gethsemani; and he said to his disciples: ✠ Sit you here, till I go yonder and pray. **C.** And taking with him Peter and the two sons of Zebedee, He began to grow sorrowful and to be sad. Then he saith to them: ✠ My soul is sorrowful even unto death; stay you here and watch with me.

C. And going a little further, He fell upon his face, praying and saying: ✠ My Father, if it be possible, let this chalice pass from me; nevertheless, not as I will, but as thou wilt. **C.** And he cometh to his disciples, and findeth them asleep. And he saith to Peter: ✠ What! Could you not watch one hour with me? Watch ye, and pray that ye enter not into temptation. The spirit indeed is willing, but the flesh is weak. **C.** Again the second time, He went and prayed, saying: ✠ My Father, if this chalice may not pass away, but I must drink it, Thy will be done. **C.** And he cometh again, and findeth them sleeping, for their eyes were

rum graváti. Et relíctis illis, íterum ábiit, et orávit tértio, eúndem sermónem dicens. Tunc venit ad discípulos suos, et dicit illis: ✠ Dormíte iam, et requiéscite: ecce appropinquávit hora, et Fílius hóminis tradétur in manus peccatórum. Súrgite, eámus: ecce appropinquávit qui me tradet.

heavy. And leaving them, He went again and he prayed the third time, saying the self-same word. Then he cometh to his disciples, and saith to them: ✠ Sleep ye now and take your rest; behold, the hour is at hand, and the Son of Man shall be betrayed into the hands of sinners. Rise, let us go; behold, he is at hand that will betray me.

The apprehension of our Lord.

C. Adhuc eo loquénte, ecce Iudas unus de duódecim venit, et cum eo turba multa cum gládiis et fústibus, missi a princípibus sacerdótum, et senióribus pópuli. Qui autem trádidit eum, dedit illis signum dicens: **S.** Quemcúmque osculátus fúero, ipse est, tenéte eum. **C.** Et conféstim accédens ad Iesum, dixit: **S.** Ave, Rabbi. **C.** Et osculátus est eum. Dixítque illi Iesus: ✠ Amíce, ad quid venísti? **C.** Tunc accessérunt, et manus iniecérunt in Iesum, et tenuérunt eum. Et ecce unus ex his, qui erant cum Iesu, exténdens manum, exémit gládium suum, et percútiens servum príncipis sacerdótum, amputávit aurículam eius. Tunc ait illi Iesus: ✠ Convérte gládium tuum in locum suum. Omnes enim, qui accéperint gládium, gládio períbunt. An putas quia non possum rogáre Patrem meum, et exhibébit mihi modo plus quam duódecim legiónes Angelórum? Quómodo ergo implebúntur Scriptúræ, quia sic opórtet fíeri?

C. In illa hora dixit Iesus turbis: ✠ Tamquam ad latrónem exístis cum gládiis et fústibus comprehén-

As he yet spoke, behold Judas, one of the twelve, came, and with him a great multitude with swords and clubs, sent from the chief priests and the ancients of the people. And he that betrayed him gave them a sign, saying: **S.** Whomsoever I shall kiss, that is he; hold him fast. **C.** And forthwith coming to Jesus, he said: **S.** Hail, Rabbi. **C.** And he kissed him. And Jesus said to him: ✠ Friend, whereto art thou come? **C.** Then they came up and laid hands on Jesus, and held him. And behold one of them that were with Jesus, stretching forth his hand, drew out his sword, and striking the servant of the high priest, cut off his ear. Then Jesus saith to him: ✠ Put up again thy sword into its place; for all that take the sword shall perish with the sword. Thinkest thou that I cannot ask my Father, and he will give me presently more than twelve legions of Angels? How then shall the Scriptures be fulfilled, that so it must be done?

C. In that same hour Jesus said to the multitudes: ✠ You are come out, as it were to a robber, with swords and

dere me: quotídie apud vos sedébam docens in templo, et non me tenuístis. **C.** Hoc autem totum factum est, ut adimpleréntur Scriptúræ prophetárum. Tunc discípuli omnes, relícto eo, fugérunt.

clubs to apprehend me. I sat daily with you, teaching in the temple, and you laid not hands on me. **C.** Now all this was done that the Scriptures of the prophets might be fulfilled. Then the disciples, all leaving him, fled.

The night trial and buffeting

At illi tenéntes Iesum, duxérunt ad Cáipham príncipem sacerdótum, ubi scribæ et senióres convénerant. Petrus autem sequebátur eum a longe, usque in átrium príncipis sacerdótum. Et ingréssus intro, sedébat cum minístris, ut vidéret finem.

But they holding Jesus led him to Caiphas the high priest, where the scribes and the ancients were assembled. And Peter followed him afar off, even to the court of the high priest. And going in, he sat with the servants, that he might see the end.

Príncipes autem sacerdótum, et omne concílium, quærébant falsum testimónium contra Iesum, ut eum morti tráderent: et non invenérunt, cum multi falsi testes accessíssent. Novíssime autem venérunt duo falsi testes, et dixérunt:

And the chief priests and the whole council sought false witness against Jesus, that they might put him to death. And they found none, whereas many false witnesses had come in. And last of all there came two false witnesses; and they said:

S. Hic di-xit: Possum destrú-e-re templum De-i, et post trídu-um
S. This man said, I am able to destroy the temple of God, and after three days

re-ædi-fi-cá-re illud.
to rebuild it.

C. Et surgens princeps sacerdótum, ait illi: **S.** Nihil respóndes ad ea, quæ isti advérsum te testificántur? **C.** Iesus autem tacébat. Et princeps sacerdótum ait illi: **S.** Adiúro te per Deum vivum, ut dicas nobis, si tu es Christus Fílius Dei. **C.** Dicit illi Iesus: ✠ Tu dixísti. Verúmtamen dico vobis, ámodo vidébitis Fílium hóminis sedéntem a dextris

And the high priest, rising up, said to him: **S.** Answerest thou nothing to the things which these witness against thee? **C.** But Jesus held his peace. And the high priest said to him: **S.** I adjure thee by the living God, that thou tell us if thou be the Christ the Son of God. **C.** Jesus saith to him: ✠ Thou hast said it. Nevertheless I say to you, hereafter you shall see the Son of Man sitting on

virtútis Dei, et veniéntem in núbibus cæli. **C.** Tunc princeps sacerdótum scidit vestiménta sua, dicens: **S.** Blasphemávit: quid adhuc egémus téstibus? Ecce nunc audístis blasphémiam: quid vobis vidétur? **C.** At illi respondéntes dixérunt:

the right hand of the power of God, and coming in the clouds of heaven. **C.** Then the high priest rent his garments, saying: **S.** He hath blasphemed; what further need have we of witnesses? Behold, now you have heard the blasphemy. What think you? **C.** But they answering, said:

S. Re- us est mortis.

S. He is guilty of death.

C. Tunc exspuérunt in fáciem eius, et cólaphis eum cecidérunt, álii autem palmas in fáciem eius dedérunt, dicéntes:

C. Then they did spit in his face and buffeted him; and others struck his face with the palms of their hands, saying:

S. Prophe-tíza nobis, Christe, quis est qui te percússit?
S. Prophesy unto us, O Christ, who is he that struck thee?

The three denials of Peter

C. Petrus vero sedébat foris in átrio: et accéssit ad eum una ancílla, dicens: **S.** Et tu cum Iesu Galilǽo eras. **C.** At ille negávit coram ómnibus, dicens: **S.** Néscio quid dicis. **C.** Exeúnte autem illo iánuam, vidit eum ália ancílla, et aít his qui erant ibi: **S.** Et hic erat cum Iesu Nazaréno. **C.** Et íterum negávit cum iuraménto: Quia non novi hóminem. Et post pusíllum accessérunt qui stabant, et dixérunt Petro:

C. But Peter sat without in the court, and there came to him a servant maid, saying: **S.** Thou also wast with Jesus the Galilean. **C.** But he denied it before them all, saying: **S.** I know not what thou sayest. **C.** And as he went out of the gate, another maid saw him, and she saith to them that were there: **S.** This man also was with Jesus of Nazareth. **C.** And again he denied it with an oath: I know not the man. And after a little while, they came that stood by and said to Peter:

S. Ve-re et tu ex il-lis es: nam et loqué-la tu-a mani-féstum te fa-cit.
S. Surely thou also art one of them; for even thy speech doth discover thee.

C. Tunc cœpit detestári, et iuráre quia non novísset hóminem. Et contínuo gallus cantávit. Et recor-

C. Then he began to curse and to swear that he knew not the man; and immediately the cock crew. And Peter

dátus est Petrus verbi Iesu, quod díxerat: Priúsquam gallus cantet, ter me negábis. Et egréssus foras, flevit amáre.

remembered the words of Jesus which he had said: before the cock crow, thou wilt deny me thrice. And going forth, he wept bitterly.

The morning council of the chief priests

Mane autem facto, consílium iniérunt omnes príncipes sacerdótum, et senióres pópuli advérsus Iesum, ut eum morti tráderent. Et vinctum adduxérunt eum, et tradidérunt Póntio Piláto præsidi.

Tunc videns Iudas, qui eum trádidit, quod damnátus esset, pæniténtia ductus, rétulit trigínta argénteos princípibus sacerdótum et senióribus, dicens: **S.** Peccávi, tradens sánguinem iustum. **C.** At illi dixérunt:

And when morning was come, all the chief priests and ancients of the people took counsel against Jesus, that they might put him to death. And they brought him bound, and delivered him to Pontius Pilate the governor.

Then Judas, who betrayed Him, seeing that he was condemned, repenting himself, brought back the thirty pieces of silver to the chief priests and ancients, saying: **S.** I have sinned in betraying innocent blood. **C.** But they said:

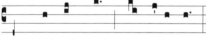

S. Quid ad nos? Tu víde- ris.

S. What is that to us? Look thou to it.

C. Et proiéctis argénteis in templo, recéssit: et ábiens, láqueo se suspéndit. Príncipes autem sacerdótum, accéptis argénteis, dixérunt:

C. And casting down the pieces of silver in the temple, he departed, and went and hanged himself with a halter. But the chief priests having taken the pieces of silver, said:

S. Non li-cet e-os mítte-re in córbonam: qui-a pré-ti-um sángui-nis est.
S. It is not lawful to put them into the corbona, because it is the price of blood.

C. Consílio autem ínito, emérunt ex illis agrum fíguli, in sepultúram peregrinórum. Propter hoc vocátus est ager ille Hacéldama, hoc est, ager sánguinis, usque in hodiérnum diem. Tunc implétum est, quod dictum est per Ieremíam prophétam, dicéntem: Et accepérunt trigínta argénteos prétium appretiáti,

And after they had consulted together, they bought with them the potter's field, to be a burying-place for strangers. For this cause that field was called Haceldama, that is, the field of blood, even to this day. Then was fulfilled that which was spoken by Jeremias the prophet, saying: And they took the thirty pieces of silver, the price of him

quem appretiavérunt a fíliis Israël: et dedérunt eos in agrum fíguli, sicut constítuit mihi Dóminus.

that was prized, whom they prized of the children of Israel: and they gave them unto the potter's field, as the Lord appointed to me.

Our Lord before Pilate

Iesus autem stetit ante præsidem, et interrogávit eum præses, dicens: **S.** Tu es Rex Iudæórum? **C.** Dicit illi Iesus: ✠ Tu dicis. **C.** Et cum accusarétur a princípibus sacerdótum et senióribus, nihil respóndit. Tunc dicit illi Pilátus: **S.** Non audis quanta advérsum te dicunt testimónia? **C.** Et non respóndit ei ad ullum verbum, ita ut mirarétur præses veheménter.

Per diem autem solémnem consúerat præses pópulo dimíttere unum vinctum, quem voluíssent. Habébat autem tunc vinctum insígnem, qui dicebátur Barábbas. Congregátis ergo illis, dixit Pilátus: **S.** Quem vultis dimíttam vobis: Barábbam, an Iesum, qui dícitur Christus? **C.** Sciébat enim quod per invídiam tradidíssent eum. Sedénte autem illo pro tribunáli, misit ad eum uxor eius, dicens: **S.** Nihil tibi et iusto illi: multa enim passa sum hódie per visum propter eum. **C.** Príncipes autem sacerdótum et senióres persuasérunt pópulis, ut péterent Barábbam, Iesum vero pérderent. Respóndens autem præses ait illis: **S.** Quem vultis vobis de duóbus dimítti? **C.** At illi dixérunt:

And Jesus stood before the governor, and the governor asked Him, saying: **S.** Art thou the King of the Jews? **C.** Jesus saith to him: ✠ Thou sayest it. **C.** And when he was accused by the chief priests and ancients, He answered nothing. Then Pilate saith to him: **S.** Dost not thou hear how great testimonies they allege against thee? **C.** And he answered to him never a word, so that the governor wondered exceedingly.

Now upon the solemn day the governor was accustomed to release to the people one prisoner, whom they would. And he had then a notorious prisoner that was called Barabbas. They therefore being gathered together, Pilate said: **S.** Whom will you that I release to you: Barabbas, or Jesus that is called Christ? **C.** For he knew that for envy they had delivered him. And as he was sitting in the place of judgment his wife sent to him, saying: **S.** Have thou nothing to do with that just man, for I have suffered many things this day in a dream because of him. **C.** But the chief priests and ancients persuaded the people that they should ask Barabbas, and make Jesus away. And the governor answering, said to them: **S.** Whither will you of the two to be released unto you? **C.** But they said:

S. Ba- rábbam.

C. Dicit illis Pilátus: **S.** Quid ígitur fáciam de Iesu, qui dícitur Christus? **C.** Dicunt omnes:

S. Cruci- figá- tur.

C. Ait illis præses: **S.** Quid enim mali fecit? **C.** At illi magis clamábant, dicéntes:

S. Cruci- figá- tur.

C. Videns autem Pilátus quia nihil profíceret, sed magis tumúltus fíeret: accépta aqua, lavit manus coram pópulo, dicens: **S.** Innocens ego sum a sánguine iusti huius: vos vidéritis. **C.** Et respóndens univérsus pópulus dixit:

S. Barabbas.

C. Pilate saith to them: **S.** What shall I do then with Jesus that is called Christ? **C.** They all call:

S. Let him be crucified.

C. The governor said to them: **S.** Why, what evil hath he done? **C.** But they cried out the more, saying:

S. Let him be crucified.

C. And Pilate seeing that he prevailed nothing, but that rather a tumult was made, taking water washed his hands before the people, saying: **S.** I am innocent of the blood of this just man; look you to it. **C.** And the whole people answering, said:

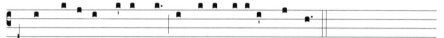

S. Sanguis e-ius super nos, et super fí-li-os nostros.

S. His blood be upon us and upon our children.

C. Tunc dimísit illis Barábbam: Iesum autem flagellátum trádidit eis, ut crucifigerétur.

C. Then he released to them Barabbas, and having scourged Jesus, delivered him unto them to be crucified.

The scourging and crowning with thorns

Tunc mílites præsidis suscipiéntes Iesum in prætórium, congregavérunt ad eum univérsam cohórtem: et exuéntes eum, chlámydem coccíneam circumdedérunt ei: et plecténtes corónam de spinis, posuérunt super caput eius, et arúndinem in déxtera eius. Et genu flexo ante eum, illudébant ei, dicéntes:

Then the soldiers of the governor, taking Jesus into the hall, gathered together unto him the whole band; and stripping him they put a scarlet cloak about him. And platting a crown of thorns they put it upon his head and a reed in his right hand. And bowing the knee before Him, they mocked Him, saying:

S. Ave, Rex Iudæ- órum.

C. Et exspuéntes in eum, accepérunt arúndinem, et percutiébant caput eius. Et postquam illusérunt ei, exuérunt eum chlámyde, et induérunt eum vestiméntis eius, et duxérunt eum ut crucifígerent.

S. Hail, King of the Jews.

C. And spitting upon Him, they took the reed and struck his head. And after they had mocked Him, they took off the cloak from Him, and put on him his own garments, and led him away to crucify him.

The way to Golgotha and the crucifixion

Exeúntes autem, invenérunt hóminem Cyrenǽum, nómine Simónem: hunc angariavérunt, ut tólleret crucem eius. Et venérunt in locum qui dícitur Gólgotha, quod est Calváriæ locus. Et dedérunt ei vinum bíbere cum felle mixtum. Et cum gustásset, nóluit bíbere. Postquam autem crucifixérunt eum, divisérunt vestiménta eius, sortem mitténtes: ut implerétur, quod dictum est per prophétam, dicéntem: Divisérunt sibi vestiménta mea, et super vestem meam misérunt sortem. Et sedéntes, servábant eum. Et imposuérunt super caput eius causam ipsíus scriptam: Hic est Iesus Rex Iudæórum.

Tunc crucifíxi sunt cum eo duo latrónes: unus a dextris, et unus a sinístris. Prætereúntes autem blasphemábant eum, movéntes cápita sua, et dicéntes:

And going out, they found a man of Cyrene, named Simon; him they forced to take up his cross. And they came to the place that is called Golgotha, which is, the place of Calvary. And they gave him wine to drink mingled with gall; and when he had tasted he would not drink. And after they had crucified Him, they divided his garments, casting lots; that it might be fulfilled which was spoken by the prophet, saying: They divided my garments among them, and upon my vesture they cast lots. And they sat and watched him. And they put over his head his cause written: This is Jesus the King of the Jews.

Then were crucified with him two thieves; one on the right hand and one on the left. And they that passed by blasphemed Him, wagging their heads, and saying:

S. Vah, qui déstru- is templum De- i, et in trídu- o illud re- ædí- fi
S. Vah, Thou that destroyest the temple of God and in three days dost rebuild

cas: salva teme-típsum. Si Fí-li-us De-i es, descende de cruce.
it,   save thine own self. If thou be the Son of God, come down from the cross.

C. Simíliter et príncipes sacerdótum illudéntes cum scribis et senióribus, dicébant:

C. In like manner also the chief priests with the scribes and ancients, mocking, said:

S. A-li-os salvos fe-cit, se-ípsum non pot-est salvum fáce-re: si
S. He saved others, himself he cannot save; if he be the king of Israel,

Rex Isra-ël est, descéndat nunc de cruce, et crédimus e-i: confí-dit
let him now come down from the cross, and we will believe him; he trusted

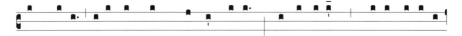

in De-o: líbe-ret nunc, si vult e-um; di-xit enim: Qui-a Fí-li-us
in God, let him now deliver him if he will have him; for he said:

De-i sum.
I am the Son of God.

C. Idípsum autem et latrónes, qui crucifíxi erant cum eo, improperábant ei.

C. And the self-same thing the thieves also, that were crucified with him, reproached him with.

The death of our Lord

A sexta autem hora ténebræ factæ sunt super univérsam terram, usque ad horam nonam. Et circa horam nonam clamávit Iesus voce magna, dicens: ✠ Eli, Eli, lamma sabactháni? **C.** Hoc est: ✠ Deus meus, Deus meus, ut quid dereliquísti me? **C.** Quidam autem illic stantes, et audiéntes, dicébant:

Now from the sixth hour there was a darkness over the whole earth, until the ninth hour. And about the ninth hour, Jesus cried out with a loud voice, saying: ✠ Eli, Eli, lamma sabacthani? **C.** That is: ✠ My God, My God, why hast thou forsaken me? **C.** And some that stood there and heard said:

S. E- lí- am vocat iste.

S. This man calleth Elias.

C. Et contínuo currens unus ex eis, accéptam spóngiam implévit acéto, et impósuit arúndini, et dabat ei bíbere. Céteri vero dicébant:

C. And immediately one of them running took a sponge and filled it with vinegar and and gave him to drink. And the others said:

S. Sine, vide-ámus an véni- at E-lí-as líberans e-um.

S. Let be; let us see whether Elias will come to deliver him.

C. Iesus autem íterum clamans voce magna, emísit spíritum.

C. And Jesus again crying with a loud voice, yielded up the ghost.

(Here a pause is made, and all kneel).

Et ecce velum templi scissum est in duas partes a summo usque deórsum: et terra mota est, et petræ scissæ sunt, et monuménta apérta sunt: et multa córpora sanctórum, qui dormiérant, surrexérunt. Et exeúntes de monuméntis post resurrectiónem eius, venérunt in sanctam civitátem, et apparuérunt multis. Centúrio autem, et qui cum eo erant custodiéntes Iesum, viso terræmótu et his, quæ fiébant, timuérunt valde, dicéntes:

And behold the veil of the temple was rent in two from top even to the bottom; and the earth quaked and the rocks were rent; and the graves were opened, and many bodies of the saints that had slept arose, and coming out of the tombs after his resurrection, came into the holy city, and appeared to many. Now the centurion and they that were with him watching Jesus, having seen the earthquake and the things that were done, were sore afraid, saying:

S. Ve-re Fí-li-us De- i erat iste.

S. Indeed this was the Son of God.

C. Erant autem ibi mulíeres multæ a longe, quæ secútæ erant Iesum a Galilǽa, ministrántes ei: inter quas erat María Magdaléne, et María Iacóbi et Ioseph mater, et mater filiórum Zebedǽi.

C. And there were there many women afar off, who had followed Jesus from Galilee, ministering unto him: among whom was Mary Magdalen, and Mary the mother of James and Joseph, and the mother of the sons of Zebedee.

The burial of Jesus

Cum autem sero factum esset, venit quidam homo dives ab Arimathǽa, nómine Ioseph, qui et ipse discípulus erat Iesu. Hic accéssit ad Pilátum, et pétiit corpus Iesu. Tunc Pilátus iussit reddi corpus. Et accépto córpore, Ioseph invólvit illud in síndone munda. Et pósuit illud in monuménto suo novo, quod excíderat in petra. Et advólvit saxum magnum ad óstium monuménti, et ábiit.	And when it was evening, there came a certain rich man of Arimathea, named Joseph, who also himself was a disciple of Jesus. He went to Pilate and asked the body of Jesus. Then Pilate commanded that the body should be delivered. And Joseph taking the body wrapt it up in a clean linen cloth, and laid it in his own new monument, which he had hewed out in a rock. And he rolled a great stone to the door of the monument and went his way.

Vatican edition I

IV.

Credo in unum De- um, Patrem omnipot-éntem, factó-rem cæ-li et terræ, vi-si-bí-li- um ómni- um, et invi-si-bí- li- um.

Et in unum Dóminum Ie-sum Christum, Fí-li- um De- i uni- gé-ni-tum. Et ex Patre na-tum ante ómni- a sǽ-cu-la. De- um de De- o, lumen de lúmi-ne, De- um ve-rum de De- o ve-ro.

Gé-ni-tum, non factum, consubstanti- á-lem Patri: per quem ó-

mni- a facta sunt. Qui propter nos hómi-nes et propter nostram

sa-lú-tem descéndit de cæ-lis. Et incarná-tus est de Spí-ri-tu

Sancto   ex Ma-rí- a Vírgi-ne: Et homo factus est. Cru-ci-fí-

xus ét-i- am pro no-bis: sub Pónti- o Pi-lá-to   passus, et sepúl-

tus est. Et re-surré-xit térti- a di- e,   secúndum Scriptú-ras.

Et ascéndit in cæ-lum: sedet ad déxte-ram Patris.   Et í-te-rum

ventú-rus est cum gló-ri- a,   iudi-cá-re vi-vos et mórtu- os: cu-

ius regni non e-rit fi-nis.   Et in Spí-ri-tum Sanctum, Dóminum,

et vi-vi-fi-cántem: qui   ex Patre Fi-li- óque pro-cé-dit. Qui

cum Patre et Fí-li- o simul ado-rá-tur, et conglo-ri-fi-cá-tur:

qui locú-tus est per Prophé-tas. Et unam sanctam cathó-li-cam

et apostó-li-cam Ecclé-si- am. Confí-te- or unum baptísma

in remissi- ónem pecca-tó-rum. Et exspécto re- surrecti- ónem

mortu-ó-rum. Et vi-tam ventú-ri sǽ-cu-li. A- men.

Offert.
VIII.

Ps 68: 21-22

I M- propé- ri- um * exspectá- vit cor

me- um, et mi- sé- ri- am: et sustí- nu- i

qui si- mul contrista-ré- tur, et non fu- it: con- so-

lán- tem me quæ- sí- vi, et non invé- ni:

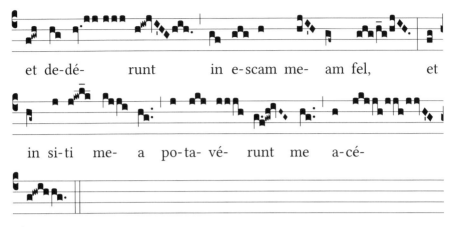

et de-dé- runt in e-scam me- am fel, et

in si-ti me- a po-ta- vé- runt me a-cé-

to.

Insult has broken my heart, and I am weak: I looked for sympathy, but there was none: for comforters, and I found none: rather they put gall in my food, and in my thirst they gave me vinegar to drink.

Secret

Concéde, quǽsumus, Dómine: ut óculis tuæ maiestátis munus oblátum, et grátiam nobis devotiónis obtíneat, et efféctum beátæ perennitátis acquírat. Per Dóminum.

Grant, we beseech thee, O Lord: that the sacrifice we offer in the sight of thy divine majesty, may draw down upon us the grace of holy fervor, and may lead us to the everlasting happiness we hope for. Through our Lord.

Preface
of the Holy Cross.

Vere dignum et iustum est, æquum et salutáre, nos tibi semper et ubíque grátias ágere: Dómine sancte, Pater omnípotens, ætérne Deus: Qui salútem humáni géneris in ligno Crucis constituísti: ut, unde mors oriebátur, inde vita resúrgeret: et, qui in ligno vincébat, in ligno quoque vincerétur: per Christum, Dóminum nostrum. Per quem maiestátem tuam laudant Angeli, adórant Dominatiónes, tremunt Potestátes. Cæli cælorúmque Virtútes ac beáta Séraphim sócia exsultatió-

It is truly meet and just, right and salutary, that we should always, and in all places, give thanks to thee: O holy Lord, Father almighty, eternal God: who didst set the salvation of mankind upon the tree of the cross, so that whence came death, thence also life might rise again: and he that overcame by the tree, on the tree also might be overcome. Through Christ our Lord: through whom the Angels praise thy majesty, the Dominions adore, the Powers tremble. The Heavens, and the Virtues of the heavens, and the blessed Seraphim, do celebrate with

ne concélebrant. Cum quibus et nostras voces ut admítti iúbeas, deprecámur, súpplici confessióne dicéntes: Sanctus...

united joy. In union with whom, we beseech thee, that thou wouldst command our voices also to be admitted, with suppliant confession, saying:

Vatican edition XVII

℣. SAn- ctus, * San- ctus, San- ctus Dóminus De- us Sába- oth. Ple-ni sunt cæ- li et ter-ra gló-ri- a tu- a. Hosánna in excél- sis. Be-ne-díctus qui ve-nit in nómi-ne Dómi-ni. Ho- sánna in excél- sis.

Vatican edition XVII

℣. A -gnus De- i, * qui tol-lis peccá- ta mundi: mi-se-ré-re no- bis. Agnus De- i, * qui tol-lis peccá- ta mundi: mi-se-ré-re no- bis. Agnus De- i, * qui tol- lis peccá- ta mundi: dóna no-bis pa- cem.

Mt 26: 42

Comm.
VIII.

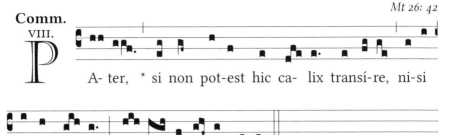

PA- ter, * si non pot-est hic ca- lix transí-re, ni-si

bi-bam il- lum: fi- at vo-lúntas tu- a.

Father, if this chalice may not pass away, but I must drink it: thy will be done.

The antiphon may be repeated between psalm verses during the distribution of Holy Communion:

Psalm 21

℣. *2-3, 5, 7, 13, 17-18, 22-24, 28-31.*

1. De- us, De- us me- us, réspi-ce in me: qua-re me de-re-liquí-

sti? * longe a sa-lú-te me-a verba de-lictó- rum me- ó-rum. *Ant.*

O God my God, look upon me: why hast thou forsaken me? Far from my salvation are the words of my sins.

2. De-us me-us, clamábo per di- em, et non exáudi- es: * et nocte,

et non ad insi-pi- én- ti- am mi-hi. *Ant.*

O my God, I shall cry by day, and thou wilt not hear: and by night, and it shall not be reputed as folly in me.

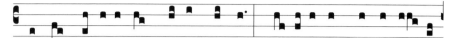

3. In te spe-ravé-runt patres nostri: * spe-ravé-runt, et li-be- rá-

sti e-os. *Ant.*

In thee have our fathers hoped: they have hoped, and thou hast delivered them.

4. E-go autem sum vermis, et non homo: * oppróbri- um hóminum,

et abié- cti- o ple-bis. *Ant.*

But I am a worm, and no man: the reproach of men, and the outcast of the people.

5. Circumdedé-runt me ví-tu-li multi: * tau-ri pingues ob- se-dé-

runt me. *Ant.*

Many calves have surrounded me: fat bulls have besieged me.

6. Fo-dé-runt manus me- as et pedes me- os: * di-nume-ravé-runt

ómni- a ossa me- a. *Ant.*

They have dug my hands and feet. They have numbered all my bones. And they have looked and stared upon me.

7. Salva me ex o-re le-ónis: * et a córni-bus uni-córni- um hu-

mi-li- tá-tem me-am. *Ant.*

Save me from the lion's mouth; and my lowness from the horns of the unicorns.

8. Narrá-bo nomen tu-um frá-tri-bus me- is: * in mé-di- o Ecclé-

si- æ laudá-bo te. *Ant.*

I will declare thy name to my brethren: in the midst of the church will I praise thee.

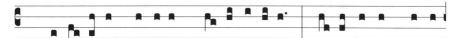

9. Qui timé-tis Dóminum, laudá-te e- um: * u-ni-vérsum semen

Iacob, glo-ri-fi- cá-te e-um. *Ant.*

Ye that fear the Lord, praise him: all ye the seed of Jacob, glorify him.

10. Remi-niscéntur et converténtur ad Dóminum * u-ni-vérsi

fi-nes terræ. *Ant.*

All the ends of the earth shall remember, and shall be converted to the Lord.

11. Et ad-o-rábunt in conspéctu e-ius * u-ni-vérsæ famí-li- æ

Génti- um. *Ant.*

And all the kindreds of the Gentiles shall adore in his sight.

12. Quó-ni- am Dómi-ni est regnum: * et ipse dominá-bi- tur

Génti- um. *Ant.*

For the kingdom is the Lord's; and he shall have dominion over the nations.

13. Mandu-cavé-runt et ado-ravé-runt omnes pingues terræ: * in

conspéctu e-ius cadent omnes qui descén-dunt in terram. *Ant.*

All the fat ones of the earth have eaten and have adored: all they that go down
to the earth shall fall before him.

14. Et á-nima me- a il-li vi-vet: * et semen me- um sér- vi- et

ipsi. *Ant.*

And to him my soul shall live: and my seed shall serve him.

Postcommunion

Per huius, Dómine, operatiónem mystérii: et vítia nostra purgéntur, et iusta desidéria compleántur. Per Dóminum.

May these mysteries, O Lord, work in us: to the subduing of our evil passions, and to the fulfilling of our righteous desires. Through our Lord.

I -te, missa est. ℟. De-o grá-ti- as.

At the end of Mass, the Last Gospel is not said. In other Masses this day, the Gospel from at the blessing of palms is read as the Last Gospel.

MONDAY IN HOLY WEEK

Ps 34: 1-2 ℣. 3

Intr.
IV.

IU- di-ca * Dómi-ne no-céntes me, expúgna impu-

gnán- tes me: apprehénde arma et scu- tum, et exsúr-ge

in adiu-tó- ri- um me- um, Dó-mi- ne, vir-tus sa-

lú- tis me- æ. *Ps.* Effúnde fráme- am, et conclúde advér-

sus e- os qui persequúntur me: * dic ánimæ me- æ: Sa-lus tu-a

ego sum. Iú- di-ca.

Judge thou, O Lord, them that wrong me: overthrow them that fight against me: take hold of arms and shield, and rise up to help me, O Lord, my salvation. *Ps.* Bring out the sword, and shut up the way against them that persecute me: say to my soul: I am thy salvation.

Vatican edition XVIII

IV.

KY- ri- e * e-lé- i-son. *iii.* Christe e- lé- i-son. *iii.* Ký- ri-

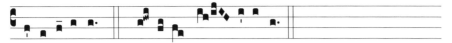

e e-lé- i-son. *ii.* Ký- ri- e * e- lé- i-son.

Collect

D a, quǽsumus, omnípotens Deus: ut, qui in tot advérsis ex nostra infirmitáte defícimus; intercedénte unigéniti Fílii tui passióne respirémus: Qui tecum vivit et regnat.

Grant, we beseech thee, almighty God: that we who fail through our weakness in so many difficulties, may be relieved through the Passion of thine only-begotten Son. Who lives and reigns.

Léctio Isaíæ Prophétæ

Is 50: 5-10.

I n diébus illis: Dixit Isaías: Dóminus Deus apéruit mihi aurem, ego autem non contradíco: retrórsum non ábii. Corpus meum dedi percutiéntibus et genas meas velléntibus: fáciem meam non avérti ab increpántibus et conspuéntibus in me. Dóminus Deus auxiliátor meus, ideo non sum confúsus: ídeo pósui fáciem meam ut petram duríssimam, et scio, quóniam non confúndar. Iuxta est, qui iustíficat me, quis contradícet mihi? Stemus simul, quis est adversárius meus? Accédat ad me. Ecce, Dóminus Deus auxiliátor meus: quis est, qui condémnet me? Ecce, omnes quasi vestiméntum conteréntur, tínea cómedet eos. Quis ex vobis timens Dóminum, áudiens vocem servi sui? Qui ambulávit in ténebris, et non est lumen ei, speret in nómine Dómini, et innitátur super Deum suum.

In those days, Isaias said: The Lord God hath opened my ear, and I do not resist: I have not gone back. I have given my body to the strikers, and my cheeks to them that plucked them: I have not turned away my face from them that rebuked me, and spit upon me. The Lord God is my helper, therefore am I not confounded: therefore have I set my face as a most hard rock, and I know that I shall not be confounded. He is near that justifieth me, who will contend with me? Let us stand together, who is my adversary? Let him come near to me. Behold the Lord God is my helper: who is he that shall condemn me? Lo, they shall all be destroyed as a garment, the moth shall eat them up. Who is there among you that feareth the Lord, that heareth the voice of his servant, that hath walked in darkness, and hath no light? Let him hope in the name of the Lord, and lean upon his God.

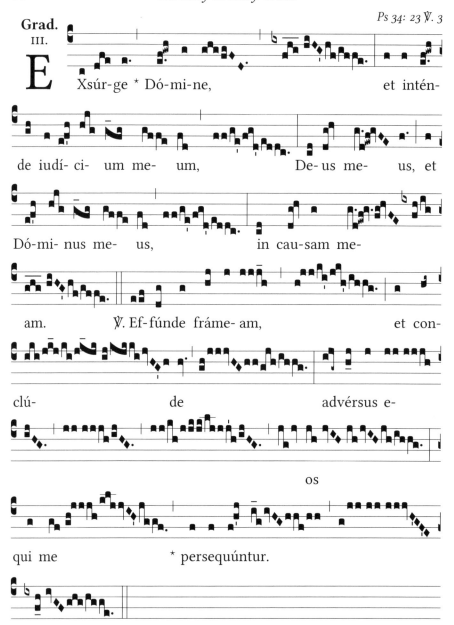

Grad. III.

E Xsúr-ge * Dó-mi-ne, et intén-de iudí-ci-um me-um, De-us me-us, et Dó-mi-nus me-us, in cau-sam me-am. ℣. Ef-fúnde fráme-am, et con-clú-de advérsus e-os qui me * persequúntur.

Ps 34: 23 ℣. 3

Arise, and be attentive to my judgment, to my cause, my God, and my Lord. ℣. Bring out the sword, and shut up the way against them that persecute me.

Tract. II.

D Omi-ne, * non secúndum peccá-

Ps 102: 10

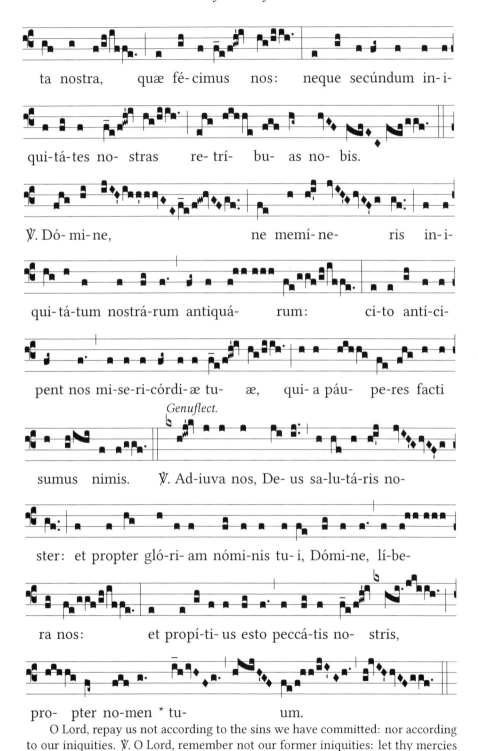

ta nostra, quæ fé-cimus nos: neque secúndum in-i-

qui-tá-tes no- stras re- trí- bu- as no- bis.

℣. Dó- mi- ne, ne memí- ne- ris in-i-

qui-tá-tum nostrá-rum antiquá- rum: ci-to antí-ci-

pent nos mi-se-ri-córdi-æ tu- æ, qui-a páu- pe-res facti

Genuflect.

sumus nimis. ℣. Ad-iuva nos, De- us sa-lu-tá-ris no-

ster: et propter gló-ri- am nómi-nis tu- i, Dómi-ne, lí-be-

ra nos: et propí-ti- us esto peccá-tis no- stris,

pro- pter no-men * tu- um.

O Lord, repay us not according to the sins we have committed: nor according to our iniquities. ℣. O Lord, remember not our former iniquities: let thy mercies speedily prevent us, for we are become exceeding poor. ℣. Help us, O God, our

Savior: and for the glory of thy name, O Lord, deliver us: and forgive us our sins for thy name's sake.

✠ Sequéntia sancti Evangélii secúndum Ioánnem

Jn 12: 1-9.

Ante sex dies Paschæ venit Iesus Bethániam, ubi Lázarus fúerat mórtuus, quem suscitávit Iesus. Fecérunt autem ei cenam ibi: et Martha ministrábat, Lázarus vero unus erat ex discumbéntibus cum eo. María ergo accépit libram unguénti nardi pístici pretiósi, et unxit pedes Iesu, et extérsit pedes eius capíllis suis: et domus impléta est ex odóre unguénti. Dixit ergo unus ex discípulis eius, Iudas Iscariótes, qui erat eum traditúrus: Quare hoc unguéntum non véniit trecéntis denáriis, et datum est egénis? Dixit autem hoc, non quia de egénis pertinébat ad eum, sed quia fur erat, et lóculos habens, ea, quæ mittebántur, portábat. Dixit ergo Iesus: Sínite illam, ut in diem sepultúræ meæ servet illud. Páuperes enim semper habétis vobíscum: me autem non semper habétis. Cognóvit ergo turba multa ex Iudǽis, quia illic est: et venérunt, non propter Iesum tantum, sed ut Lázarum vidérent, quem suscitávit a mórtuis.

Jesus therefore, six days before the Pasch, came to Bethania, where Lazarus had been dead, whom Jesus raised to life. And they made him a supper there: and Martha served: but Lazarus was one of them that were at table with him. Mary therefore took a pound of ointment of right spikenard, of great price, and anointed the feet of Jesus, and wiped his feet with her hair; and the house was filled with the odor of the ointment. Then one of his disciples, Judas Iscariot, he that was about to betray him, said: Why was not this ointment sold for three hundred pence, and given to the poor? Now he said this, not because he cared for the poor; but because he was a thief, and having the purse, carried the things that were put therein. Jesus therefore said: Let her alone, that she may keep it against the day of my burial. For the poor you have always with you; but me you have not always. A great multitude therefore of the Jews knew that he was there; and they came, not for Jesus' sake only, but that they might see Lazarus, whom he had raised from the dead.

The Credo *is not said.*

Offert.
III.

E - ri- pe me * de in- i-mí-cis me- is,   Dó-

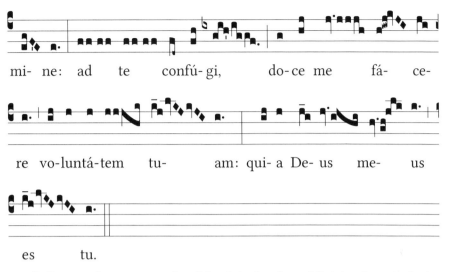

mi- ne: ad te confú- gi, do-ce me fá- ce-

re vo-luntá-tem tu- am: qui- a De- us me- us

es tu.

Deliver me from my enemies, O Lord: to thee have I fled, teach me to do thy will, for thou art my God.

Secret

Hæc sacrifícia nos, omnípotens Deus, poténti virtúte mundátos, ad suum fáciant purióres veníre princípium. Per Dóminum.

May these sacrifices, almighty God, make us, whom thou cleansest by thy mighty power, to approach their source with greater purity. Through our Lord.

Preface of the Holy Cross, p. 13.

Vatican edition XVIII

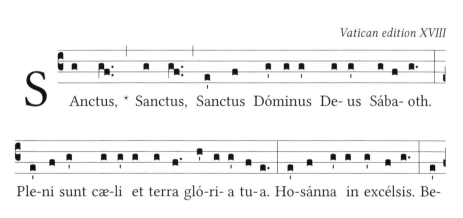

Anctus, * Sanctus, Sanctus Dóminus De- us Sába- oth.

Ple-ni sunt cæ-li et terra gló-ri- a tu-a. Ho-sánna in excélsis. Be-

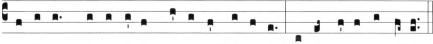

ne-díctus qui ve-nit in nómi-ne Dómi-ni. Ho-sánna in excélsis.

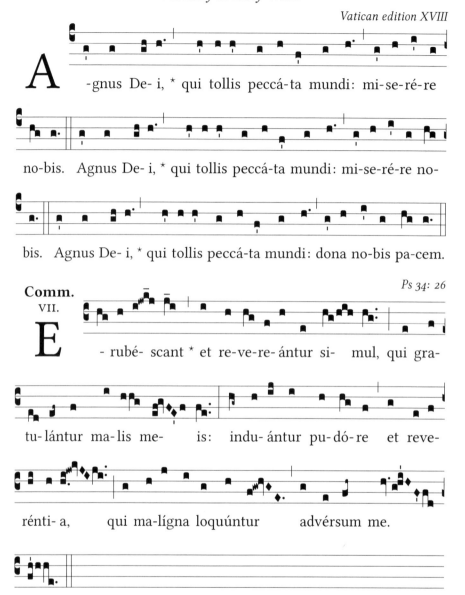

Vatican edition XVIII

A -gnus De- i, * qui tollis peccá-ta mundi: mi-se-ré-re

no-bis. Agnus De- i, * qui tollis peccá-ta mundi: mi-se-ré-re no-

bis. Agnus De- i, * qui tollis peccá-ta mundi: dona no-bis pa-cem.

Comm.
VII.

Ps 34: 26

E - rubé- scant * et re-ve-re-ántur si- mul, qui gra-

tu-lántur ma-lis me- is: indu- ántur pu-dó-re et reve-

rénti- a, qui ma-lígna loquúntur advérsum me.

Let them blush and be ashamed together, who rejoice at my evils: let them be clothed with confusion and shame, who speak great things against me.

Postcommunion

Præbeant nobis, Dómine, divínum tua sancta fervórem: quo eórum páriter et actu delectémur et fructu. Per Dóminum.

Let thy holy mysteries, O Lord, inspire up with divine fervor, that we may delight both in their celebration and in their fruit. Through our Lord.

Prayer over the People

Orémus.	Let us pray.
Humiliáte cápita vestra Deo.	Bow down your heads before God.

Adiuva nos, Deus, salutáris noster: et ad benefícia recolénda, quibus nos instauráre dignátus es, tríbue veníre gaudéntes. Per Dóminum nostrum Iesum Christum.

Help us, O God, our salvation: and grant that we may draw nigh with joy, to keep the memory of those mercies, whereby thou didst deign to restore us to life. Through our Lord Jesus Christ.

IV.

I -te, missa est. ℟. De-o grá-ti- as.

TUESDAY IN HOLY WEEK

Introit. Nos autem gloriári. *p.* 101.

Mass XVIII, Kýrie, eléison, *p.* 68.

Collect

Omnípotens sempitérne Deus: da nobis ita domínicæ passiónis sacraménta perágere; ut indulgéntiam percípere mereámur. Per eúndem Dóminum nostrum.

Almighty and eternal God: grant us so to celebrate thy mysteries of our Lord's passion; that we may deserve to obtain forgiveness. Through the same our Lord Jesus Christ.

Léctio Ieremíæ Prophétæ
Jer 11: 18-20.

In diébus illis: Dixit Ieremías: Dómine, demonstrásti mihi, et cognóvi: tunc ostendísti mihi stúdia eórum. Et ego quasi agnus mansuétus, qui portátur ad víctimam: et non cognóvi, quia cogitavérunt super me consília, dicéntes: Mittámus lignum in panem eius, et eradámus eum de terra vivéntium, et nomen eius non memorétur ámplius. Tu autem, Dómine Sábaoth, qui iúdicas iuste et probas renes et corda, vídeam ultió-

In those days, Jeremias said: But thou, O Lord, hast shown me, and I have known: then thou showedst me their doings. And I was as a meek lamb, that is carried to be a victim: and I knew not that they had devised counsels against me, saying: Let us put wood on his bread, and cut him off from the land of the living, and let his name be remembered no more. But thou, O Lord of Sabaoth, who judgest justly, and triest the reins and hearts, let me see thy revenge on them:

nem tuam ex eis: tibi enim revelávi | for to thee I have revealed my cause.
causam meam, Dómine, Deus meus.

Grad.
III.

E-go au- tem, * dum mi- hi mo- lé- sti es-

sent, indu- é- bam me ci- lí- ci- o,

et humi-li- á- bam in ie-iú- ni- o ánimam

me- am: et o-rá- ti- o me- a

in si-nu me- o con- ver- té- tur, ℣. Iú- di- ca Dó-

mi- ne no-céntes me, expú- gna

impu-gnán- tes me: apprehén-de ar- ma et scu-

tum, et exsúr- ge

in ad- iu-tó- ri- um * mi- hi.

Ps 34: 13 ℣. 34: 1-2

But as for me, when they were troublesome to me, I was clothed with haircloth,

and I humbled my soul with fasting: and my prayer shall be turned into my bosom. ℣. Judge thou, O Lord, them that wrong me: overthrow them that fight against me: take hold of arms and shield, and rise up to help me.

The Passion is sung in the same manner as on Palm Sunday.

Pássio Dómini nostri Iesu Christi secúndum Marcum
Mk 14: 32-72; 15: 1-46.

IN illo témpore: Iesus et discípuli eius véniunt in prǽdium, cui nomen Gethsémani. Et ait discípulis suis: ✠ Sedéte hic donec orem. **C.** Et assúmit Petrum, et Iacóbum, et Ioánnem secum: et cœpit pavére, et tædére. Et ait illis: ✠ Tristis est ánima mea usque ad mortem: sustinéte hic, et vigiláte. **C.** Et cum processísset páululum, prócidit super terram: et orábat, ut si fíeri posset, transíret ab eo hora: et dixit:

✠ Abba, Pater, ómnia tibi possibília sunt, transfer cálicem hunc a me: sed non quod ego volo, sed quod tu. **C.** Et venit, et invénit eos dormiéntes. Et ait Petro: ✠ Simon, dormis? non potuísti una hora vigiláre? Vigiláte, et oráte, ut non intrétis in tentatiónem. Spíritus quidem promptus est, caro vero infírma. **C.** Et íterum ábiens orávit, eúndem sermónem dicens. Et revérsus, dénuo invénit eos dormiéntes (erant enim óculi eórum graváti) et ignorábant quid respondérent ei.

Et venit tértio, et ait illis: ✠ Dormíte iam, et requiéscite. Súfficit: venit hora: ecce Fílius hóminis tradétur in manus peccatórum. Súrgite, eámus: ecce qui me tradet, prope est. **C.** Et, adhuc eo loquénte, venit Iudas Iscariótes, unus de duódecim, et

C. In those days: Jesus and his disciples came to a farm called Gethsemani. And he saith to his disciples: ✠ Sit you here, while I pray. **C.** And he taketh Peter and James and John with him; and he began to fear and to be heavy. And he saith to them: ✠ My soul is sorrowful even unto death; stay you here, and watch. **C.** And when he was gone forward a little, he fell flat on the ground; and he prayed, that if it might be, the hour might pass from him. And he saith:

✠ Abba, Father, all things are possible to thee: remove this chalice from me; but not what I will, but what thou wilt. **C.** And he cometh, and findeth them sleeping. And he saith to Peter: ✠ Simon, sleepest thou? couldst thou not watch one hour? Watch ye, and pray that you enter not into temptation. The spirit indeed is willing, but the flesh is weak. **C.** And going away again, he prayed, saying the same words. And when he returned, he found them again asleep, (for their eyes were heavy,) and they knew not what to answer him.

And he cometh the third time, and saith to them: ✠ Sleep ye now, and take your rest. It is enough: the hour is come: behold the Son of man shall be betrayed into the hands of sinners. Rise up, let us go. Behold, he that will betray me is at hand. **C.** And while he was yet speak-

cum eo turba multa cum gládiis et lignis, a summis sacerdótibus et scribis et senióribus. Déderat autem tráditor eius signum eis, dicens: **S.** Quemcúmque osculátus fúero, ipse est, tenéte eum, et dúcite caute. **C.** Et cum venísset, statim accédens ad eum, ait: **S.** Ave, Rabbi. **C.** Et osculátus est eum.

At illi manus iniecérunt in eum, et tenuérunt eum. Unus autem quidam de circumstántibus, edúcens gládium, percússit servum summi sacerdótis: et amputávit illi aurículam. Et respóndens Iesus, ait illis: ✝ Tamquam ad latrónem exístis cum gládiis et lignis comprehéndere me? cotídie eram apud vos in templo docens, et non me tenuístis. Sed ut impleántur Scriptúræ. **C.** Tunc discípuli eius relinquéntes eum, omnes fugérunt. Adoléscens autem quidam sequebátur eum amíctus síndone super nudo: et tenuérunt eum. At ille, reiécta síndone, nudus profúgit ab eis.

Et adduxérunt Iesum ad summum sacerdótem: et convenérunt omnes sacerdótes et scribæ et senióres. Petrus autem a longe secútus est eum usque intro in átrium summi sacerdótis: et sedébat cum minístris ad ignem, et calefaciébat se. Summi vero sacerdótes, et omne concílium, quærébant advérsus Iesum testimónium, ut eum morti tráderent, nec inveniébant. Multi enim testimónium falsum dicébant advérsus

ing, cometh Judas Iscariot, one of the twelve: and with him a great multitude with swords and staves, from the chief priests and the scribes and the ancients. And he that betrayed him, had given them a sign, saying: **S.** Whomsoever I shall kiss, that is he; lay hold on him, and lead him away carefully. **C.** And when he was come, immediately going up to him, he saith: **S.** Hail, Rabbi. **C.** And he kissed him.

But they laid hands on him, and held him. And one of them that stood by, drawing a sword, struck a servant of the chief priest, and cut off his ear. And Jesus answering, said to them: ✝ Are you come out as to a robber, with swords and staves to apprehend me? I was daily with you in the temple teaching, and you did not lay hands on me. But that the scriptures may be fulfilled. **C.** Then his disciples leaving him, all fled away. And a certain young man followed him, having a linen cloth cast about his naked body; and they laid hold on him. But he, casting off the linen cloth, fled from them naked.

And they brought Jesus to the high priest; and all the priests and the scribes and the ancients assembled together. And Peter followed him from afar off, even into the court of the high priest; and he sat with the servants at the fire, and warmed himself. And the chief priests and all the council sought for evidence against Jesus, that they might put him to death, and found none. For many bore false witness against him, and their evidences were not agreeing. And some

eum: et conveniéntia testimónia non erant. Et quidam surgéntes, falsum testimónium ferébant advérsus eum, dicéntes: **S.** Quóniam nos audívimus eum dicéntem: Ego dissólvam templum hoc manufáctum, et per tríduum áliud non manufáctum ædificábo. **C.** Et non erat convéniens testimónium illórum. Et exsúrgens summus sacérdos in médium, interrogávit Iesum, dicens: **S.** Non respóndes quidquam ad ea, quæ tibi obiciúntur ab his? **C.** Ille autem tacébat, et nihil respóndit. Rursum summus sacérdos interrogábat eum, et dixit ei: **S.** Tu es Christus Fílius Dei benedícti? **C.** Iesus autem dixit illi: ✠ Ego sum: et vidébitis Fílium hóminis sedéntem a dextris virtútis Dei, et veniéntem cum núbibus cæli. **C.** Summus autem sacérdos, scindens vestiménta sua, ait: **S.** Quid adhuc desiderámus testes? Audístis blasphémiam: quid vobis vidétur? **C.** Qui omnes condemnavérunt eum esse reum mortis.

Et cœpérunt quidam conspúere eum, et veláre fáciem eius, et cólaphis eum cædere, et dícere ei: **S.** Prophetíza. **C.** Et minístri álapis eum cædébant.

Et cum esset Petrus in átrio deórsum, venit una ex ancíllis summi sacerdótis: et cum vidísset Petrum calefaciéntem se, aspíciens illum, ait: **S.** Et tu cum Iesu Nazaréno eras. **C.** At ille negávit, dicens: **S.** Neque scio, neque novi quid dicas. **C.** Et éxiit foras ante átrium, et gallus can-

rising up, bore false witness against him, saying: **S.** We heard him say, I will destroy this temple made with hands, and within three days I will build another not made with hands. **C.** And their witness did not agree. And the high priest rising up in the midst, asked Jesus, saying: **S.** Answerest thou nothing to the things that are laid to thy charge by these men? **C.** But he held his peace, and answered nothing. Again the high priest asked him, and said to him: **S.** Art thou the Christ the Son of the blessed God? **C.** And Jesus said to him: ✠ I am. And you shall see the Son of man sitting on the right hand of the power of God, and coming with the clouds of heaven. **C.** Then the high priest rending his garments, saith: **S.** What need we any further witnesses? You have heard the blasphemy. What think you? **C.** Who all condemned him to be guilty of death.

And some began to spit on him, and to cover his face, and to buffet him, and to say unto him: **S.** Prophesy. **C.** And the servants struck him with the palms of their hands.

Now when Peter was in the court below, there cometh one of the maidservants of the high priest. And when she had seen Peter warming himself, looking on him she saith: **S.** Thou also wast with Jesus of Nazareth. **C.** But he denied, saying: **S.** I neither know nor understand what thou sayest. **C.** And he went forth

távit. Rursus autem cum vidísset illum ancílla, cœpit dícere circumstántibus: Quia hic ex illis est. At ille íterum negávit. Et post pusíllum rursus qui astábant, dicébant Petro: **S.** Vere ex illis es: nam et Galilǽus es. **C.** Ille autem cœpit anathematizáre, et iuráre: Quia néscio hóminem istum, quem dícitis. Et statim gallus íterum cantávit. Et recordátus est Petrus verbi, quod díxerat ei Iesus: Priúsquam gallus cantet bis, ter me negábis. Et cœpit flere.

Et conféstim mane consílium faciéntes summi sacerdótes, cum senióribus et scribis, et univérso concílio, vinciéntes Iesum, duxérunt, et tradidérunt Piláto. Et interrogávit eum Pilátus: **S.** Tu es Rex Iudæórum? **C.** At ille respóndens, ait illi: ✠ Tu dicis. **C.** Et accusábant eum summi sacerdótes in multis. Pilátus autem rursum interrogávit eum, dicens: **S.** Non respóndes quidquam? vide in quantis te accúsant. **C.** Iesus autem ámplius nihil respóndit, ita ut mirarétur Pilátus.

Per diem autem festum solébat dimíttere illis unum ex vinctis, quemcúmque petiíssent. Erat autem, qui dicebátur Barábbas, qui cum seditiósis erat vinctus, qui in seditióne fécerat homicídium. Et cum ascendísset turba, cœpit rogáre, sicut semper faciébat illis. Pilátus autem respóndit eis, et dixit: **S.** Vultis dimíttam vobis Regem Iudæórum? **C.** Sciébat enim quod per invídiam tradidíssent

before the court; and the cock crew. And again a maidservant seeing him, began to say to the standers by: **S.** This is one of them. **C.** But he denied again. And after a while they that stood by said again to Peter: **S.** Surely thou art one of them; for thou art also a Galilean. **C.** But he began to curse and to swear, saying: I know not this man of whom you speak. And immediately the cock crew again. And Peter remembered the word that Jesus had said unto him: Before the cock crow twice, thou shalt thrice deny me. And he began to weep.

And straightway in the morning, the chief priests holding a consultation with the ancients and the scribes and the whole council, binding Jesus, led him away, and delivered him to Pilate. And Pilate asked him: **S.** Art thou the king of the Jews? **C.** But he answering, saith to him: ✠ Thou sayest it. **C.** And the chief priests accused him in many things. And Pilate again asked him, saying: **S.** Answerest thou nothing? Behold in how many things they accuse thee. **C.** But Jesus still answered nothing, so that Pilate wondered.

Now on the festival day he was wont to release unto them one of the prisoners, whomsoever they demanded. And there was one called Barabbas, who was put in prison with some seditious men, who in the sedition had committed murder. And when the multitude was come up, they began to desire that he would do, as he had ever done unto them. And Pilate answered them, and said: **S.** Will you that I release to you

eum summi sacerdótes. Pontífices autem concitavérunt turbam, ut magis Barábbam dimítteret eis. Pilátus autem íterum respóndens, ait illis: **S.** Quid ergo vultis fáciam Regi Iudæórum? **C.** At illi íterum clamavérunt: **S.** Crucifíge eum. **C.** Pilátus vero dicébat illis: **S.** Quid enim mali fecit? **C.** At illi magis clamábant: **S.** Crucifíge eum. **C.** Pilátus autem volens pópulo satisfácere, dimísit illis Barábbam, et trádidit Iesum flagéllis cæsum, ut crucifigerétur.

Mílites autem duxérunt eum in átrium prætórii, et cónvocant totam cohórtem, et índuunt eum púrpura, et impónunt ei plecténtes spíneam corónam. Et cœpérunt salutáre eum: Ave, Rex Iudæórum. Et percutiébant caput eius arúndine: et conspuébant eum, et ponéntes génua, adorábant eum. Et postquam illusérunt ei, exuérunt illum púrpura, et induérunt eum vestiméntis suis: et edúcunt illum, ut crucifígerent eum. Et angariavérunt prætereúntem quémpiam, Simónem Cyrenǽum, veniéntem de villa, patrem Alexándri et Rufi, ut tólleret crucem eius.

Et perdúcunt illum in Gólgotha locum, quod est interpretátum Calváriæ locus. Et dabant ei bíbere myrrhátum vinum: et non accépit. Et crucifigéntes eum, divisérunt vestiménta eius, mitténtes sortem super eis, quis quid tólleret. Erat autem hora

the king of the Jews? **C.** For he knew that the chief priests had delivered him up out of envy. But the chief priests moved the people, that he should rather release Barabbas to them. And Pilate again answering, saith to them: **S.** What will you then that I do to the king of the Jews? **C.** But they again cried out: **S.** Crucify him. **C.** And Pilate saith to them: **S.** Why, what evil hath he done? **C.** But they cried out the more: **S.** Crucify him. **C.** And so Pilate being willing to satisfy the people, released to them Barabbas, and delivered up Jesus, when he had scourged him, to be crucified.

And the soldiers led him away into the court of the palace, and they called together the whole band: And they clothe him with purple, and platting a crown of thorns, they put it upon him. And they began to salute him: Hail, king of the Jews. And they struck his head with a reed: and they did spit on him. And bowing their knees, they adored him. And after they had mocked him, they took off the purple from him, and put his own garments on him, and they led him out to crucify him. And they forced one Simon a Cyrenian who passed by, coming out of the country, the father of Alexander and of Rufus, to take up his cross.

And they bring him into the place called Golgotha, which being interpreted is, The place of Calvary. And they gave him to drink wine mingled with myrrh; but he took it not. And crucifying him, they divided his garments, casting lots upon them, what every man should take.

tértia: et crucifixérunt eum. Et erat títulus causæ eius inscríptus: Rex Iudæórum. Et cum eo crucifígunt duos latrónes: unum a dextris, et álium a sinístris eius.

Et impléta est Scriptúra, quæ dicit: Et cum iníquis reputátus est. Et prætereúntes blasphemábant eum, movéntes cápita sua, et dicéntes: **S.** Vah, qui déstruis templum Dei, et in tribus diébus reædíficas: salvum fac temetípsum, descéndens de cruce. **C.** Simíliter et summi sacerdótes illudéntes, ad altérutrum cum scribis dicébant: **S.** Alios salvos fecit, seípsum non potest salvum fácere. Christus Rex Israël descéndat nunc de cruce, ut videámus, et credámus. **C.** Et qui cum eo crucifíxi erant conviciabántur ei. Et facta hora sexta, ténebræ factæ sunt per totam terram, usque in horam nonam. Et hora nona exclamávit Iesus voce magna, dicens: ✠ Eloi, Eloi, lamma sabacthání? **C.** Quod est interpretátum: ✠ Deus meus, Deus meus, ut quid dereliquísti me? **C.** Et quidam de circumstántibus audiéntes, dicébant: **S.** Ecce Elíam vocat. **C.** Currens autem unus, et implens spóngiam acéto, circumponénsque cálamo, potum dabat ei, dicens: **S.** Sínite, videámus si véniat Elías ad deponéndum eum. **C.** Iesus autem emíssa voce magna exspirávit.

And it was the third hour, and they crucified him. And the inscription of his cause was written over: The King of the Jews. And with him they crucify two thieves; the one on his right hand, and the other on his left.

And the scripture was fulfilled, which saith: And with the wicked he was reputed. And they that passed by blasphemed him, wagging their heads, and saying: **S.** Vah, thou that destroyest the temple of God, and in three days buildest it up again; Save thyself, coming down from the cross. **C.** In like manner also the chief priests mocking, said with the scribes one to another: **S.** He saved others; himself he cannot save. Let Christ the king of Israel come down now from the cross, that we may see and believe. **C.** And they that were crucified with him reviled him. And when the sixth hour was come, there was darkness over the whole earth until the ninth hour. And at the ninth hour, Jesus cried out with a loud voice, saying: ✠ Eloi, Eloi, lamma sabacthani? **C.** Which is, being interpreted, My God, my God, why hast thou forsaken me? And some of the standers by hearing, said: **S.** Behold he calleth Elias. **C.** And one running and filling a sponge with vinegar, and putting it upon a reed, gave him to drink, saying: **S.** Stay, let us see if Elias come to take him down. **C.** And Jesus having cried out with a loud voice, gave up the ghost.

(Here a pause is made, and all kneel).

Et velum templi scissum est in duo, a summo usque deórsum. Vi-

And the veil of the temple was rent in two, from the top to the bot-

dens autem centúrio, qui ex advérso stabat, quia sic clamans exspirásset, ait: **S.** Vere hic homo Fílius Dei erat. **C.** Erant autem et mulíeres de longe aspiciéntes: inter quas erat María Magdaléne, et María Iacóbi minóris, et Ioseph mater, et Salóme: et cum esset in Galilǽa, sequebántur eum, et ministrábant ei, et áliæ multæ, quæ simul cum eo ascénderant Ierosólymam.

Et cum iam sero esset factum (quia erat Parascéve, quod est ante sábbatum) venit Ioseph ab Arimathǽa, nóbilis decúrio, qui et ipse erat exspéctans regnum Dei, et audácter introívit ad Pilátum, et pétiit corpus Iesu. Pilátus autem mirabátur si iam obiísset. Et accersíto centurióne, interrogávit eum si iam mórtuus esset. Et cum cognovísset a centurióne, donávit corpus Ioseph. Ioseph autem mercátus síndonem, et depónens eum invólvit síndone, et pósuit eum in monuménto, quod erat excísum de petra, et advólvit lápidem ad óstium monuménti.

tom. And the centurion who stood over against him, seeing that crying out in this manner he had given up the ghost, said: **S.** Indeed this man was the Son of God. **C.** And there were also women looking on afar off: among whom was Mary Magdalen, and Mary the mother of James the less and of Joseph, and Salome: who also when he was in Galilee followed him, and ministered to him, and many other women that came up with him to Jerusalem.

And when evening was now come, (because it was the Parasceve, that is, the day before the sabbath,) Joseph of Arimathea, a noble counselor, who was also himself looking for the kingdom of God, came and went in boldly to Pilate, and begged the body of Jesus. But Pilate wondered that he should be already dead. And sending for the centurion, he asked him if he were already dead. And when he had understood it by the centurion, he gave the body to Joseph. And Joseph buying fine linen, and taking him down, wrapped him up in the fine linen, and laid him in a sepulcher which was hewed out of a rock. And he rolled a stone to the door of the sepulcher.

The Credo *is not said.*

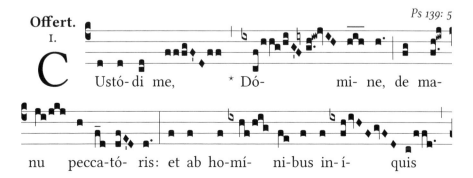

Offert. I.

Ps 139: 5

Custó-di me, * Dó-mi-ne, de manu peccató-ris: et ab ho-mí-ni-bus in-í-quis

é-ri- pe me, Dó- mi- ne.

Keep me, O Lord, from the hand of the wicked: and from unjust men deliver me, O Lord

Secret

Sacrifícia nos, quǽsumus, Dómine, propénsius ista restáurent: quæ medicinálibus sunt institúta ieiúniis. Per Dóminum.

May these sacrifices, we beseech thee, O Lord, speedily restore us: which are observed along with health-giving fasts. Through our Lord.

Preface of the Holy Cross, p. 13.

Sanctus *and* Agnus Dei, *p. 73.*

Comm.
v.

Ps 68: 13-14

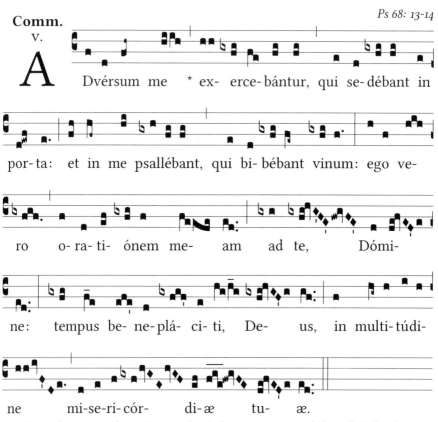

ADvérsum me * ex- erce-bántur, qui se-débant in por-ta: et in me psallébant, qui bi- bébant vinum: ego ve- ro o- ra- ti- ónem me- am ad te, Dómi- ne: tempus be- ne-plá- ci- ti, De- us, in multi-túdi- ne mi-se-ri-cór- di-æ tu- æ.

They that sat in the gate were busied against me: and they that drank wine made me their song: but as for me, my prayer is to thee, O Lord: for the time of thy good pleasure, O God, in the multitude of thy mercy.

Postcommunion

Sanctificatiónibus tuis, omnípotens Deus: et vítia nostra curéntur, et remédia nobis sempitérna provéniant. Per Dóminum.

By thy holy mysteries, almighty God: may our vices be cured, and everlasting healing be granted to us. Through our Lord Jesus Christ.

Prayer over the People

Orémus.

Humiliáte cápita vestra Deo.

Tua nos misericórdia, Deus, et ab omni subreptióne vetustátis expúrget, et capáces sanctæ novitátis effíciat. Per Dóminum.

Let us pray.

Bow down your heads before God.

May thy mercy, O God, cleanse us from all traces of our old nature, and enable us to be formed anew unto holiness. Through our Lord.

Ite, missa est, *p. 75.*

WEDNESDAY IN HOLY WEEK

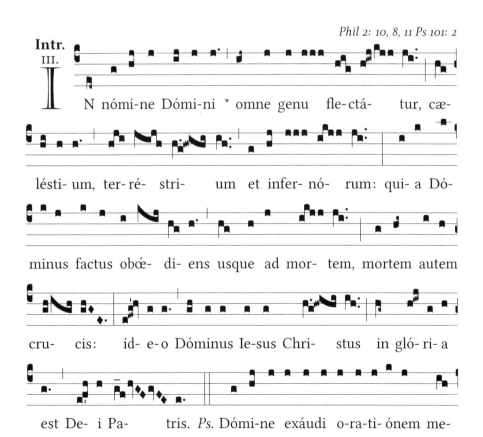

Phil 2: 10, 8, 11 Ps 101: 2

IN nómi-ne Dómi-ni * omne genu fle-ctá- tur, cæ-lésti- um, ter-ré- stri- um et infer-nó- rum: qui-a Dóminus factus obœ- di- ens usque ad mor- tem, mortem autem cru- cis: íd-e-o Dóminus Ie-sus Chri- stus in gló-ri-a est De- i Pa- tris. *Ps.* Dómi-ne exáudi o-ra-ti-ónem me-

am: * et clamor me-us ad te vé-ni- at. In nómi-ne.

In the name of Jesus let every knee bow of those that are in heaven, on earth, and under the earth: and let every tongue confess that the Lord Jesus Christ is in the glory of God the Father. *Ps.* O Lord, our Lord, how wonderful is thy name in the whole earth.

Mass XVIII, Kýrie, eléison, *p.* 68.

After Kýrie, eléison:

Orémus.	Let us pray.
Flectámus génua.	Let us kneel.
Leváte.	Arise.

Prayer

Præsta, quǽsumus, omnípotens Deus: ut, qui nostris excéssibus incessánter afflígimur, per unigéniti Fílii tui passiónem liberémur: Qui tecum vivit et regnat in unitáte Spíritus Sancti, Deus.

Grant, we beseech thee, almighty God: that we who are continually afflicted by reason of our waywardness, may be delivered by the passion of thine only-begotten Son: Who lives and reigns with thee in the unity of the Holy Spirit.

Léctio Isaíæ Prophétæ
Is 62: 11; 63: 1-7.

Hæc dicit Dóminus Deus: Dícite fíliæ Sion: Ecce Salvátor tuus venit: ecce, merces eius cum eo. Quis est iste, qui venit de Edom, tinctis véstibus de Bosra? Iste formósus in stola sua, grádiens in multitúdine fortitúdinis suæ. Ego, qui loquor iustítiam, et propugnátor sum ad salvándum. Quare ergo rubrum est induméntum tuum, et vestiménta tua sicut calcántium in torculári? Tórcular calcávi solus, et de géntibus non est vir mecum: calcávi eos in furóre meo, et conculcávi eos in ira mea: et aspérsus est sanguis eórum super vestiménta mea, et ómnia in-

Thus saith the Lord God: Tell the daughter of Sion: Behold thy Savior cometh: behold his reward is with him, and his work before him. Who is this that cometh from Edom, with dyed garments from Bosra, this beautiful one in his robe, walking in the greatness of his strength. I, that speak justice, and am a defender to save. Why then is thy apparel red, and thy garments like theirs that tread in the winepress? I have trodden the winepress alone, and of the Gentiles there is not a man with me: I have trampled on them in my indignation, and have trodden them down in my wrath, and their blood is sprinkled upon my garments,

duménta mea inquinávi. Dies enim ultiónis in corde meo, annus redemptiónis meæ venit. Circumspéxi, et non erat auxiliátor: quæsívi, et non fuit, qui adiuváret: et salvávit mihi bráchium meum, et indignátio mea ipsa auxiliáta est mihi. Et conculcávi pópulos in furóre meo, et inebriávi eos in indignatióne mea, et detráxi in terram virtútem eórum. Miseratiónum Dómini recordábor, laudem Dómini super ómnibus, quæ réddidit nobis Dóminus, Deus noster.

and I have stained all my apparel. For the day of vengeance is in my heart, the year of my redemption is come. I looked about, and there was none to help: I sought, and there was none to give aid: and my own arm hath saved for me, and my indignation itself hath helped me. And I have trodden down the people in my wrath, and have made them drunk in my indignation, and have brought down their strength to the earth. I will remember the tender mercies of the Lord, the praise of the Lord for all the things that the Lord hath bestowed upon us.

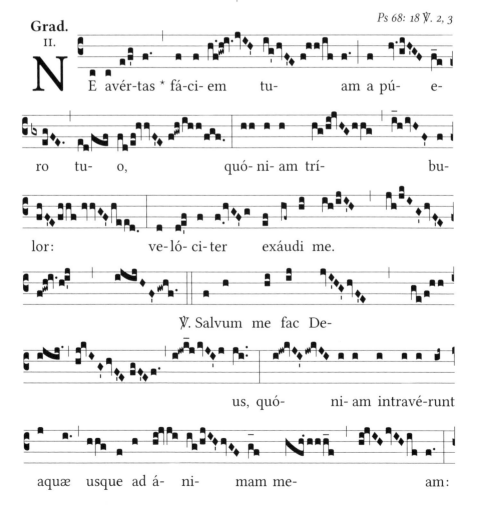

in- fí- xus sum in li- mo pro- fún- di, et

non est * substánti- a.

And turn not away thy face from thy servant, for I am in trouble, hear me speedily. ℣. Save me, O God, for the waters are come in even unto my soul: I stick fast in the mire of the deep, and there is no sure standing.

Collect

Deus, qui pro nobis Fílium tuum Crucis patíbulum subíre voluísti, ut inimíci a nobis expélleres potestátem: concéde nobis fámulis tuis; ut resurrectiónis grátiam consequámur. Per eúndem Dóminum nostrum Iesum Christum.

O God, who didst will that thy Son should submit, for our sake, to the yoke of the Cross, that the power of the enemy might be driven away grant us, thy servants; to obtain the grace of the resurrection. Through the same our Lord Jesus Christ.

Léctio Isaíæ Prophétæ
Is 53: 1-12.

In diébus illis: Dixit Isaías: Dómine, quis crédidit audítui nostro? et bráchium Dómini cui revelátum est? Et ascéndet sicut virgúltum coram eo, et sicut radix de terra sitiénti: non est spécies ei neque decor: et vídimus eum, et non erat aspéctus, et desiderávimus eum: despéctum et novíssimum virórum, virum dolórum, et sciéntem infirmitátem: et quasi abscónditus vultus eius et despéctus, unde nec reputávimus eum. Vere languóres nostros ipse tulit, et dolóres nostros ipse portávit: et nos putávimus eum quasi leprósum, et percússum a Deo, et humiliátum. Ipse autem vulnerátus est propter ini-

In those days, Isaias said: Who hath believed our report? And to whom is the arm of the Lord revealed? And he shall grow up as a tender plant before him, and as a root out of a thirsty ground: there is no beauty in him, nor comeliness: and we have seen him, and there was no sightliness, that we should be desirous of him: Despised, and the most abject of men, a man of sorrows, and acquainted with infirmity: and his look was as it were hidden and despised, whereupon we esteemed him not. Surely he hath borne our infirmities and carried our sorrows: and we have thought him as it were a leper, and as one struck by God and afflicted. But he was wounded

quitátes nostras, attrítus est propter scélera nostra: disciplína pacis nostræ super eum, et livóre eius sanáti sumus. Omnes nos quasi oves errávimus, unusquísque in viam suam declinávit: et pósuit Dóminus in eo iniquitátem ómnium nostrum. Oblátus est, quia ipse vóluit, et non apéruit os suum: sicut ovis ad occisiónem ducétur, et quasi agnus coram tondénte se obmutéscet, et non apériet os suum. De angústia et de iudício sublátus est: generatiónem eius quis enarrábit? quia abscíssus est de terra vivéntium: propter scelus pópuli mei percússi eum. Et dabit ímpios pro sepultúra, et dívitem pro morte sua: eo quod iniquitátem non fécerit, neque dolus fúerit in ore eius. Et Dóminus vóluit contérere eum in infirmitáte: si posúerit pro peccáto ánimam suam, vidébit semen longǽvum, et volúntas Dómini in manu eius dirigétur. Pro eo, quod laborávit ánima eius, vidébit, et saturábitur: in sciéntia sua iustificábit ipse iustus servus meus multos, et iniquitátes eórum ipse portábit. Ideo dispértiam ei plúrimos: et fórtium dívidet spólia, pro eo, quod trádidit in mortem ánimam suam, et cum scelerátis reputátus est: et ipse peccáta multórum tulit, et pro transgressóribus rogávit.

for our iniquities, he was bruised for our sins: the chastisement of our peace was upon him, and by his bruises we are healed. All we like sheep have gone astray, every one hath turned aside into his own way: and the Lord hath laid on him the iniquity of us all. He was offered because it was his own will, and he opened not his mouth: he shall be led as a sheep to the slaughter, and shall be dumb as a lamb before his shearer, and he shall not open his mouth. He was taken away from distress, and from judgment: who shall declare his generation? because he is cut off out of the land of the living: for the wickedness of my people have I struck him. And he shall give the ungodly for his burial, and the rich for his death: because he hath done no iniquity, neither was there deceit in his mouth. And the Lord was pleased to bruise him in infirmity: if he shall lay down his life for sin, he shall see a long-lived seed, and the will of the Lord shall be prosperous in his hand. Because his soul hath labored, he shall see and be filled: by his knowledge shall this my just servant justify many, and he shall bear their iniquities. Therefore will I distribute to him very many, and he shall divide the spoils of the strong, because he hath delivered his soul unto death, and was reputed with the wicked: and he hath borne the sins of many, and hath prayed for the transgressors.

Ps 101: 2-5, 14

Tract.

II.

D Omi- ne, * ex-áu- di o- ra-

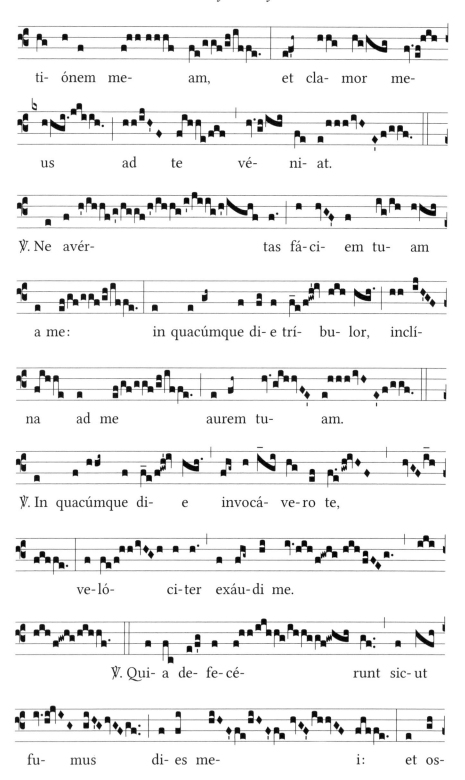

ti- ónem me- am, et cla- mor me-

us ad te vé- ni- at.

℣. Ne avér- tas fá-ci- em tu- am

a me: in quacúmque di- e trí- bu- lor, inclí-

na ad me aurem tu- am.

℣. In quacúmque di- e invocá- ve-ro te,

ve-ló- ci-ter exáu-di me.

℣. Qui- a de- fe-cé- runt sic- ut

fu- mus di- es me- i: et os-

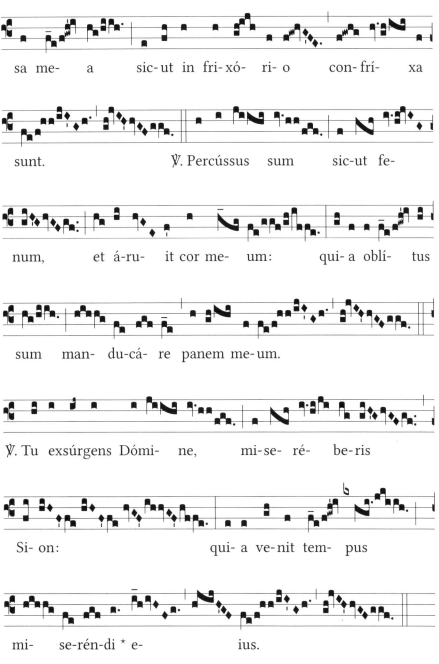

sa me- a sic-ut in fri- xó- ri- o con- frí- xa

sunt. ℣. Percússus sum sic-ut fe-

num, et á-ru- it cor me- um: qui- a oblí- tus

sum man- du-cá- re panem me-um.

℣. Tu exsúrgens Dómi- ne, mi-se- ré- be-ris

Si- on: qui- a ve-nit tem- pus

mi- se-rén-di * e- ius.

Hear, O Lord, my prayer, and let my cry come to thee. ℣. Turn not away thy face from me: in the day when I am in trouble, incline thy ear to me. ℣. In what day soever I shall call upon thee, hear me speedily. ℣. For my days are vanished like smoke: and my bones are grown dry like fuel for the fire. ℣. I am smitten as grass, and my heart is withered: because I forgot to eat my bread. ℣. Thou shalt arise and have mercy on Sion: for it is time to have mercy on it, for the time is come.

The Passion is sung in the same manner as on Palm Sunday.

Pássio Dómini nostri Iesu Christi secúndum Lucam

Lk 22: 39-71; 23: 1-53.

IN illo témpore: Egréssus Iesus ibat secúndum consuetúdinem in montem Olivárum. Secúti sunt autem illum et discípuli. Et cum pervenísset ad locum, dixit illis: ✠ Oráte, ne intrétis in tentatiónem. C. Et ipse avúlsus est ab eis, quantum iactus est lápidis, et pósitis génibus orábat, dicens: ✠ Pater, si vis, transfer cálicem istum a me: verúmtamen non mea volúntas, sed tua fiat. C. Appáruit autem illi Angelus de cælo, confórtans eum. Et factus in agonía, prolíxius orábat. Et factus est sudor eius, sicut guttæ sánguinis decurréntis in terram. Et cum surrexísset ab oratióne, et venísset ad discípulos suos, invénit eos dormiéntes præ tristítia. Et ait illis: ✠ Quid dormítis? súrgite, oráte, ne intrétis in tentatiónem.

C. Adhuc eo loquénte, ecce turba: et qui vocabátur Iudas, unus de duódecim, antecedébat eos: et appropinquávit Iesu, ut osculárétur eum. Iesus autem dixit illi: ✠ Iuda, ósculo Fílium hóminis tradis? C. Vidéntes autem hi, qui circa ipsum erant, quod futúrum erat, dixérunt ei: S. Dómine, si percútimus in gladio? C. Et percússit unus ex illis servum príncipis sacerdótum, et amputávit aurículam eius déxteram. Respóndens autem Iesus, ait: ✠ Sínite usque huc. C. Et cum tetigísset aurículam eius, saná-

C. In those days: Going out, Jesus went, according to his custom, to the mount of Olives. And his disciples also followed him. And when he was come to the place, he said to them: ✠ Pray, lest ye enter into temptation. C. And he was withdrawn away from them a stone's cast; and kneeling down, he prayed, Saying: ✠ Father, if thou wilt, remove this chalice from me: but yet not my will, but thine be done. C. And there appeared to him an angel from heaven, strengthening him. And being in an agony, he prayed the longer. And his sweat became as drops of blood, trickling down upon the ground. And when he rose up from prayer, and was come to his disciples, he found them sleeping for sorrow. And he said to them: ✠ Why sleep you? arise, pray, lest you enter into temptation.

C. As he was yet speaking, behold a multitude; and he that was called Judas, one of the twelve, went before them, and drew near to Jesus, for to kiss him. And Jesus said to him: ✠ Judas, dost thou betray the Son of man with a kiss? C. And they that were about him, seeing what would follow, said to him: S. Lord, shall we strike with the sword? C. And one of them struck the servant of the high priest, and cut off his right ear. But Jesus answering, said: ✠ Suffer ye thus far. C. And when he had touched his ear, he healed him. And Jesus said to

vit eum. Dixit autem Iesus ad eos, qui vénerant ad se, príncipes sacerdótum et magistrátus templi et senióres: ✠ Quasi ad latrónem exístis cum gládiis et fústibus? Cum cotídie vobíscum fúerim in templo, non extendístis manus in me: sed hæc est hora vestra et potéstas tenebrárum.

C. Comprehendéntes autem eum, duxérunt ad domum príncipis sacerdótum: Petrus vero sequebátur a longe. Accénso autem igne in médio átrii, et circumsedéntibus illis, erat Petrus in médio eórum. Quem cum vidísset ancílla quædam sedéntem ad lumen, et eum fuísset intúita, dixit: **S.** Et hic cum illo erat. **C.** At ille negávit eum, dicens: **S.** Múlier, non novi illum. **C.** Et post pusíllum álius videns eum, dixit: **S.** Et tu de illis es. **C.** Petrus vero ait: **S.** O homo, non sum. **C.** Et intervállo facto quasi horæ uníus, álius quidam affirmábat, dicens: **S.** Vere et hic cum illo erat: nam et Galilǽus est. **C.** Et ait Petrus: **S.** Homo, néscio, quid dicis. **C.** Et contínuo adhuc illo loquénte cantávit gallus. Et convérsus Dóminus respéxit Petrum. Et recordátus est Petrus verbi Dómini, sicut díxerat: Quia priúsquam gallus cantet, ter me negábis. Et egréssus foras Petrus flevit amáre.

Et viri, qui tenébant illum, illudébant ei, cædéntes. Et velavérunt eum et percutiébant fáciem eius: et interrogábant eum, dicéntes: **S.** Prophetíza, quis est, qui te percússit? **C.** Et alia multa blasphemántes dicé-

the chief priests, and magistrates of the temple, and the ancients, that were come unto him: ✠ Are ye come out, as it were against a thief, with swords and clubs? When I was daily with you in the temple, you did not stretch forth your hands against me: but this is your hour, and the power of darkness.

C. And apprehending him, they led him to the high priest's house. But Peter followed afar off. And when they had kindled a fire in the midst of the hall, and were sitting about it, Peter was in the midst of them. Whom when a certain servant maid had seen sitting at the light, and had earnestly beheld him, she said: **S.** This man also was with him. **C.** But he denied him, saying: **S.** Woman, I know him not. **C.** And after a little while, another seeing him, said: **S.** Thou also art one of them. **C.** But Peter said: **S.** O man, I am not. **C.** And after the space, as it were of one hour, another certain man affirmed, saying: **S.** Of a truth, this man was also with him; for he is also a Galilean. **C.** And Peter said: **S.** Man, I know not what thou sayest. **C.** And immediately, as he was yet speaking, the cock crew. And the Lord turning looked on Peter. And Peter remembered the word of the Lord, as he had said: Before the cock crow, thou shalt deny me thrice. And Peter going out, wept bitterly.

And the men that held him, mocked him, and struck him. And they blindfolded him, and smote his face. And they asked him, saying: **S.** Prophesy, who is it that struck thee? **C.** And blaspheming, many other things they said against him.

bant in eum. Et ut factus est dies, convenérunt senióres plebis et príncipes sacerdótum et scribæ, et duxérunt illum in concílium suum, dicéntes: **S.** Si tu es Christus, dic nobis. **C.** Et ait illis: ✠ Si vobis díxero, non credétis mihi: si autem et interrogávero, non respondébitis mihi, neque dimittétis. **S.** Ex hoc autem erit Fílius hóminis sedens a dextris virtútis Dei. **C.** Dixérunt autem omnes: **S.** Tu ergo es Fílius Dei? **C.** Qui ait: ✠ Vos dícitis, quia ego sum. **C.** At illi dixérunt: **S.** Quid adhuc desiderámus testimónium? Ipsi enim audívimus de ore eius.

C. Et surgens omnis multitúdo eórum, duxérunt illum ad Pilátum. Cœpérunt autem illum accusáre, dicéntes: **S.** Hunc invénimus subverténtem gentem nostram, et prohibéntem tribúta dare Cǽsari, et dicéntem se Christum regem esse. **C.** Pilátus autem interrogávit eum, dicens: **S.** Tu es Rex Iudæórum? **C.** At ille respóndens, ait: ✠ Tu dicis. **C.** Ait autem Pilátus ad príncipes sacerdótum et turbas: **S.** Nihil invénio causæ in hoc hómine. **C.** At illi invalescébant, dicéntes: **S.** Cómmovet pópulum, docens per univérsam Iudǽam, incípiens a Galilǽa usque huc.

C. Pilátus autem áudiens Galilǽam, interrogávit, si homo Galilǽus esset. Et ut cognóvit, quod de Heródis potestáte esset, remísit eum ad Heródem, qui et ipse Ierosólymis erat illis diébus. Heródes autem, viso Iesu, gavísus est valde. Erat enim cú-

And as soon as it was day, the ancients of the people, and the chief priests and scribes, came together; and they brought him into their council, saying: **S.** If thou be the Christ, tell us. **C.** And he saith to them: ✠ If I shall tell you, you will not believe me. And if I shall also ask you, you will not answer me, nor let me go. But hereafter the Son of man shall be sitting on the right hand of the power of God. **C.** Then said they all: **S.** Art thou then the Son of God? **C.** Who said: ✠ You say that I am. **C.** And they said: **S.** What need we any further testimony? for we ourselves have heard it from his own mouth.

C. And the whole multitude of them rising up, led him to Pilate. And they began to accuse him, saying: **S.** We have found this man perverting our nation, and forbidding to give tribute to Caesar, and saying that he is Christ the king. **C.** And Pilate asked him, saying: **S.** Art thou the king of the Jews? **C.** But he answering, said: ✠ Thou sayest it. **C.** And Pilate said to the chief priests and to the multitudes: **S.** I find no cause in this man. **C.** But they were more earnest, saying: **S.** He stirreth up the people, teaching throughout all Judea, beginning from Galilee to this place.

C. But Pilate hearing Galilee, asked if the man were of Galilee? And when he understood that he was of Herod's jurisdiction, he sent him away to Herod, who was also himself at Jerusalem, in those days. And Herod, seeing Jesus, was very glad; for he was desirous of

piens ex multo témpore vidére eum, eo quod audíerat multa de eo, et sperábat signum áliquod vidére ab eo fíeri. Interrogábat autem eum multis sermónibus. At ipse nihil illi respondébat. Stabant autem príncipes sacerdótum et scribæ, constánter accusántes eum. Sprevit autem illum Heródes cum exércitu suo: et illúsit indútum veste alba, et remísit ad Pilátum. Et facti sunt amíci Heródes et Pilátus in ipsa die: nam ántea inimíci erant ad ínvicem. Pilátus autem, convocátis princípibus sacerdótum et magistrátibus et plebe, dixit ad illos: **S.** Obtulístis mihi hunc hóminem, quasi averténtem pópulum, et ecce, ego coram vobis intérrogans, nullam causam invéni in hómine isto ex his, in quibus eum accusátis. Sed neque Heródes: nam remísi vos ad illum, et ecce, nihil dignum morte actum est ei. Emendátum ergo illum dimíttam.

C. Necésse autem habébat dimíttere eis per diem festum, unum. Exclamávit autem simul univérsa turba, dicens: **S.** Tolle hunc, et dimítte nobis Barábbam. **C.** Qui erat propter seditiónem quandam fáciam in civitáte et homicídium missus in cárcerem. Iterum autem Pilátus locútus est ad eos, volens dimíttere Iesum. At illi succlamábant, dicéntes: **S.** Crucifíge, crucifíge eum. **C.** Ille autem tértio dixit ad illos: **S.** Quid enim mali fecit iste? Nullam causam mortis invénio in eo: corrípiam ergo illum et dimíttam. **C.** At illi instábant vóci-

a long time to see him, because he had heard many things of him; and he hoped to see some sign wrought by him. And he questioned him in many words. But he answered him nothing. And the chief priests and the scribes stood by, earnestly accusing him. And Herod with his army set him at nought, and mocked him, putting on him a white garment, and sent him back to Pilate. And Herod and Pilate were made friends, that same day; for before they were enemies one to another. And Pilate, calling together the chief priests, and the magistrates, and the people, Said to them: **S.** You have presented unto me this man, as one that perverteth the people; and behold I, having examined him before you, find no cause in this man, in those things wherein you accuse him. No, nor Herod neither. For I sent you to him, and behold, nothing worthy of death is done to him. I will chastise him therefore, and release him.

C. Now of necessity he was to release unto them one upon the feast day. **C.** But the whole multitude together cried out, saying: **S.** Away with this man, and release unto us Barabbas: **C.** Who, for a certain sedition made in the city, and for a murder, was cast into prison. And Pilate again spoke to them, desiring to release Jesus. But they cried again, saying: **S.** Crucify him, crucify him. **C.** And he said to them the third time: **S.** Why, what evil hath this man done? I find no cause of death in him. I will chastise him therefore, and let him go. **C.** But they were instant with loud

bus magnis, postulántes, ut crucifigerétur. Et invalescébant voces eórum. Et Pilátus adiudicávit fíeri petitiónem eórum. Dimísit autem illis eum, qui propter homicídium et seditiónem missus fúerat in cárcerem, quem petébant: Iesum vero trádidit voluntáti eórum.

Et cum dúcerent eum, apprehendérunt Simónem quedam Cyrenénsem, veniéntem de villa: et imposuérunt illi crucem portáre post Iesum. Sequebátur autem illum multa turba pópuli, et mulíerum, quæ plangébant et lamentabántur eum. Convérsus autem ad illas Iesus dixit: ✠ Filiæ Ierúsalem, nolíte flere super me, sed super vos ipsas flete et super fílios vestros. Quóniam ecce vénient dies, in quibus dicent: Beátæ stériles, et ventres, qui non genuérunt, et úbera, quæ non lactavérunt. Tunc incípient dícere móntibus: Cádite super nos; et cóllibus: Operíte nos. Quia si in víridi ligno hæc fáciunt, in árido quid fiet? **C.** Ducebántur autem et alii duo nequam cum eo, ut interficeréntur. Et postquam venérunt in locum, qui vocátur Calváriæ, ibi crucifixérunt eum: et latrónes, unum a dextris et álterum a sinístris. Iesus autem dicébat: ✠ Pater, dimítte illis: non enim sciunt, quid fáciunt.

C. Dividéntes vero vestiménta eius, misérunt sortes. Et stabat pópulus spectans, et deridébant eum príncipes cum eis, dicéntes: **S.** Alios salvos fecit: se salvum fáciat, si hic est

voices, requiring that he might be crucified; and their voices prevailed. And Pilate gave sentence that it should be as they required. And he released unto them him who for murder and sedition, had been cast into prison, whom they had desired; but Jesus he delivered up to their will.

And as they led him away, they laid hold of one Simon of Cyrene, coming from the country; and they laid the cross on him to carry after Jesus. And there followed him a great multitude of people, and of women, who bewailed and lamented him. But Jesus turning to them, said: ✠ Daughters of Jerusalem, weep not over me; but weep for yourselves, and for your children. For behold, the days shall come, wherein they will say: Blessed are the barren, and the wombs that have not borne, and the paps that have not given suck. Then shall they begin to say to the mountains: Fall upon us; and to the hills: Cover us. For if in the green wood they do these things, what shall be done in the dry? And there were also two other malefactors led with him to be put to death. **C.** And when they were come to the place which is called Calvary, they crucified him there; and the robbers, one on the right hand, and the other on the left. And Jesus said: ✠ Father, forgive them, for they know not what they do.

C. But they, dividing his garments, cast lots. And the people stood beholding, and the rulers with them derided him, saying: **S.** He saved others; let him save himself, if he be Christ, the elect of

Christus Dei eléctus. **C.** Illudébant autem ei et mílites accedéntes, et acétum offeréntes ei, et dicéntes: **S.** Si tu es Rex Iudæórum, salvum te fac.

C. Erat autem et superscríptio scripta super eum lítteris græcis et latínis et hebráicis: Hic est Rex Iudæórum. Unus autem de his, qui pendébant, latrónibus, blasphemábat eum, dicens: **S.** Si tu es Christus, salvum fac temetípsum, et nos. **C.** Respóndens autem alter increpábat eum, dicens: **S.** Neque tu times Deum, quod in eadem damnatióne es. Et nos quidem iuste, nam digna factis recípimus: hic vero nihil mali gessit. **C.** Et dicébat ad Iesum: **S.** Dómine, meménto mei, cum véneris in regnum tuum. **C.** Et dixit illi Iesus: ✝ Amen, dico tibi: Hódie mecum eris in paradíso. **C.** Erat autem fere hora sexta, et ténebræ factæ sunt in univérsam terram usque in horam nonam. Et obscurátus est sol: et velum templi scissum est médium. Et clamans voce magna Iesus, ait: ✝ Pater, in manus tuas comméndo spíritum meum. **C.** Et hæc dicens, exspirávit.

God. **C.** And the soldiers also mocked him, coming to him, and offering him vinegar, And saying: **S.** If thou be the king of the Jews, save thyself.

C. And there was also a superscription written over him in letters of Greek, and Latin, and Hebrew: This is the King of the Jews. And one of those robbers who were hanged, blasphemed him, saying: **S.** If thou be Christ, save thyself and us. **C.** But the other answering, rebuked him, saying: **S.** Neither dost thou fear God, seeing thou art condemned under the same condemnation? And we indeed justly, for we receive the due reward of our deeds; but this man hath done no evil. And he said to Jesus: Lord, remember me when thou shalt come into thy kingdom. **C.** And Jesus said to him: ✝ Amen I say to thee, this day thou shalt be with me in paradise. **C.** And it was almost the sixth hour; and there was darkness over all the earth until the ninth hour. And the sun was darkened, and the veil of the temple was rent in the midst. And Jesus crying out with a loud voice, said: ✝ Father, into thy hands I commend my spirit. **C.** And saying this, he gave up the ghost.

(Here a pause is made, and all kneel).

Videns autem centúrio quod factum fúerat, glorificávit Deum, dicens: **S.** Vere hic homo iustus erat. **C.** Et omnis turba eórum, qui simul áderant ad spectáculum istud et vidébant, quæ fiébant, percutiéntes péctora sua revertebántur. Stabant autem

Now the centurion, seeing what was done, glorified God, saying: **S.** Indeed this was a just man. **C.** And all the multitude of them that were come together to that sight, and saw the things that were done, returned striking their breasts. And all his acquaintance, and

omnes noti eius a longe, et mulíeres, quæ secútæ eum erant a Galilǽa, hæc vidéntes.

    Et ecce, vir nómine Ioseph, qui erat decúrio, vir bonus et iustus: hic non consénserat consílio et áctibus eórum, ab Arimathǽa civitáte Iudǽæ, qui exspectábat et ipse regnum Dei. Hic accéssit ad Pilátum et pétiit corpus Iesu: et depósitum invólvit síndone, et pósuit eum in monuménto excíso, in quo nondum quisquam pósitus fúerat.

the women that had followed him from Galilee, stood afar off, beholding these things.

    And behold there was a man named Joseph, who was a counselor, a good and just man, (the same had not consented to their counsel and doings) of Arimathea, a city of Judea; who also himself looked for the kingdom of God. This man went to Pilate, and begged the body of Jesus. And taking him down, he wrapped him in fine linen, and laid him in a sepulcher that was hewed in stone, wherein never yet any man had been laid.

The Credo *is not said.*

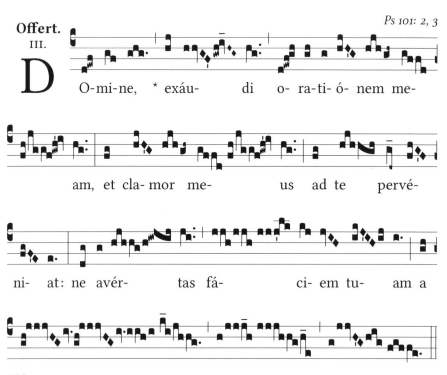

Offert.
III.

DO-mi-ne, * exáudi o- ra-ti-ó- nem me- am, et cla- mor me- us ad te pervé- ni- at: ne avér- tas fá- ci- em tu- am a me.

Ps 101: 2, 3

    Hear, O Lord, my prayer, and let my cry come to thee: turn not away thy face from me.

Secret

Súscipe, quǽsumus, Dómine, munus oblátum, et dignánter operáre: ut, quod passiónis Fílii tui, Dómini nostri, mystério gérimus, piis afféctibus consequámur. Per eúndem Dóminum nostrum Iesum Christum.

Accept, we beseech thee, O Lord, the gift we offer, and graciously effect: that what we celebrate in mystery of the passion of thy Son, we may by holy dispositions obtain. Through the same our Lord Jesus Christ, thy Son, who lives and reigns.

Preface of the Holy Cross, p. 13; Sanctus and Agnus Dei, p. 73.

Ps 101: 10, 13-14

Comm.

II.

Potum me- um * cum fle- tu tempe- rá-bam: qui- a é- le- vans al- li- sísti me: et e- go sic-ut fenum á- ru- i: tu autem, Dó-mi- ne, in æ-tér-num pérma- nes: tu exsúrgens mi-se-ré-be-ris Si- on, qui- a ve-nit tempus mi-se-réndi e- ius.

I mingled my drink with weeping: for having lifted me up thou hast thrown me down, and I am withered like grass: but thou, O Lord, endurest for ever: thou shalt arise and have mercy on Sion, for the time is come to have mercy on it.

Postcommunion

Largíre sénsibus nostris, omnípotens Deus: ut, per temporálem Fílii tui mortem, quam mystéria veneránda testántur, vitam te nobis dedísse perpétuam confidámus. Per eúndem Dóminum.

Grant to us, almighty God, to feel confident: that through the temporal death of thy Son, which these venerable mysteries testify, thou hast given us eternal life. Through the same our Lord Jesus Christ, thy Son.

Prayer over the People

Orémus.

Humiliáte cápita vestra Deo.

Réspice, quǽsumus, Dómine, super hanc famíliam tuam, pro qua Dóminus noster Iesus Christus non dubitávit mánibus tradi nocéntium, et Crucis subíre torméntum: Qui tecum vivit et regnat.

Ite, missa est, *p. 75.*

Let us pray.

Bow down your heads before God.

Look down we beseech thee, O Lord, on this thy family, for whose sake our Lord Jesus Christ refused not to yield himself into the hands of the wicked, and to suffer the torments of the Cross: Who lives and reigns with thee.

HOLY THURSDAY

The Introit antiphon is begun during the procession into the church.

Cf. Gal 6: 14 ℣. Ps 66: 2

Intr.
IV.

NOS au- tem * glo-ri-á-ri opór- tet, in cru-ce Dó-mi-ni nostri Ie- su Chri- sti: in quo est sa-lus, vi- ta, et re- surré-cti- o no- stra: per quem salvá-ti, et li-be-rá- ti su- mus. *Ps.* De- us mi-se-re-á-tur nostri, et be-ne-dí-cat no-bis: * illúmi-net vultum su-um super nos, et mi-se-re-á- tur nostri. Nos au- tem.

But it behooves us to glory in the cross of our Lord Jesus Christ: in whom is our salvation, life, and resurrection: by whom we are saved and delivered. *Ps.* May God have mercy on us, and bless us: may he cause the light of his countenance to shine upon us; and may he have mercy on us.

Additional verses, ad libitum:

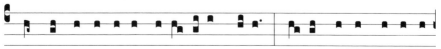

2. Ut cognoscámus in terra vi- am tu-am: * in ómni-bus génti-bus

sa-lu-tá-re tu-um. Nos au- tem.

That we may know thy way upon earth, thy salvation among all nations.

3. Confi-te- ántur ti-bi pó-pu-li, De- us: * confi-te- ántur ti-bi pó-

pu-li omnes. Nos au- tem.

Let the peoples praise thee, O God; let all the peoples praise thee.

¶ *Ordinary chants from Mass IV, as below, or from Mass IX, p. 259.*

Vatican edition IV

I.

K Y-ri- e * e- lé- i-son. *iii.* Christe

e- lé- i-son. *iii.* Ký-ri- e e- lé- i-son. *ii.*

Ký-ri- e * ** e- lé- i-son.

Vatican edition IV

IV.

G Ló- ri- a in excélsis De- o. Et in terra pax homí-ni-

bus bonæ vo-luntá-tis. Laudámus te. Be-ne-dí-cimus te. Ado-

rá-mus te. Glo-ri-fi-cá- mus te. Grá-ti- as á-gimus ti-bi

propter magnam gló-ri- am tu- am. Dómi-ne De- us, Rex cæ-lé-

stis, De- us Pa- ter omní-pot-ens. Dómi-ne Fi-li u-ni-gé-

ni-te Ie- su Chri- ste. Dómi-ne De-us, Agnus De- i, Fí-

li- us Pa- tris. Qui tollis peccá-ta mundi, mi-se-ré-re no-bis.

Qui tollis peccá-ta mundi, súsci-pe depre-ca-ti- ónem nostram.

Qui se-des ad déxte-ram Patris, mi-se-ré-re no-bis. Quó-ni- am

tu so-lus sanctus. Tu so-lus Dóminus. Tu so-lus Altíssimus,

Ie- su Chri- ste. Cum San-cto Spí- ri- tu, in gló-ri- a

De- i Pa- tris. A- men.

Collect

Deus, a quo et Iudas reátus sui pœnam, et confessiónis suæ latro prǽmium sumpsit, concéde nobis tuæ propitiatiónis efféctum: ut, sicut in passióne sua Iesus Christus, Dóminus noster, divérsa utrísque íntulit stipéndia meritórum; ita nobis, abláto vetustátis erróre, resurrectiónis suæ grátiam largiátur: Qui tecum vivit et regnat.

O God, who didst doom Judas to the punishment of his crime, and richly reward the thief for his confession, grant to us the full effect of thy clemency: that, as our Lord Jesus Christ, in his passion, gave to each retribution according to his merits, so, upon absolving our past sins, he may bestow on us the grace of his resurrection: Who lives and reigns with thee.

Léctio Epístolæ beáti Pauli Apóstoli ad Corínthios
1 Cor 11: 20-32.

Fratres: Conveniéntibus vobis in unum, iam non est Domínicam cenam manducáre. Unusquísque enim suam cenam præsúmit ad manducándum. Et álius quidem ésurit: álius autem ébrius est. Numquid domos non habétis ad manducándum et bibéndum? aut ecclésiam Dei contémnitis, et confúnditis eos, qui non habent? Quid dicam vobis? Laudo vos? In hoc non laudo. Ego enim accépi a Dómino quod et trádidi vobis, quóniam Dóminus Iesus, in qua nocte tradebátur, accépit panem, et grátias agens fregit, et dixit: « Accípite, et manducáte: hoc est corpus meum, quod pro vobis tradétur: hoc fácite in meam commemoratiónem ». Simíliter et cálicem, postquam cenávit, dicens: « Hic calix novum Testaméntum est in meo sánguine: hoc fá-

Brethren: When you come therefore into one place, it is not now to eat the Lord's supper. For every one taketh before his own supper to eat. And one indeed is hungry and another is drunk. What, have you not houses to eat and to drink in? Or despise ye the church of God and put them to shame that have not? What shall I say to you? Do I praise you? In this I praise you not. For I have received of the Lord that which I also delivered unto you, that the Lord Jesus, the same night in which he was betrayed, took bread, and giving thanks, broke and said: Take ye and eat: This is my body, which shall be delivered for you. This do for the commemoration of me. In like manner also the chalice, after he had supped, saying: This chalice is the new testament in my blood. This do ye, as often as you shall drink, for the com-

cite, quotiescúmque bibétis, in meam commemoratiónem ». Quotiescúmque enim manducábitis panem hunc et cálicem bibétis: mortem Dómini annuntiábitis, donec véniat. Itaque quicúmque manducáverit panem hunc vel bíberit cálicem Dómini indígne, reus erit córporis et sánguinis Dómini. Probet autem seípsum homo: et sic de pane illo edat et de cálice bibat. Qui enim mandúcat et bibit indígne, iudícium sibi mandúcat et bibit: non diiúdicans corpus Dómini. Ideo inter vos multi infírmi et imbecílles, et dórmiunt multi. Quod si nosmetípsos diiudicarémus, non útique iudicarémur. Dum iudicámur autem, a Dómino corrípimur, ut non cum hoc mundo damnémur.

memoration of me. For as often as you shall eat this bread and drink the chalice, you shall show the death of the Lord, until he come. Therefore, whosoever shall eat this bread, or drink the chalice of the Lord unworthily, shall be guilty of the body and the blood of the Lord. But let a man prove himself; and so let him eat of that bread and drink of the chalice. For he that eateth and drinketh unworthily, eateth and drinketh judgment to himself, not discerning the body of the Lord. Therefore are there many infirm and weak among you: and many sleep. But if we would judge ourselves, we should not be judged. But whilst we are judged, we are chastised by the Lord, that we be not condemned with this world.

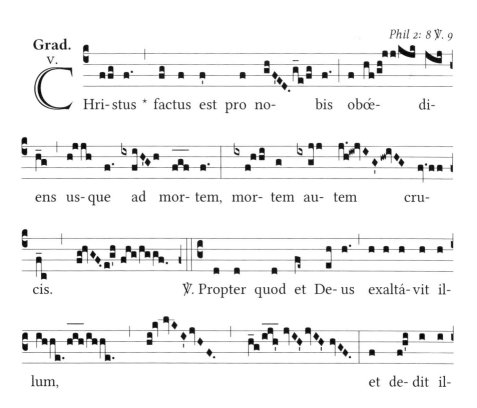

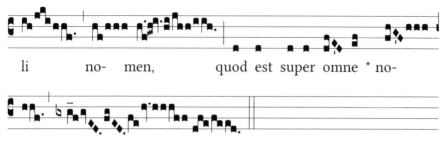

li no- men, quod est super omne * no-

men.

Christ became obedient for us unto death, even to the death of the cross. ℣. For which cause God also exalted him and hath given him a name which is above all names.

✠ Sequéntia sancti Evangélii secúndum Ioánnem

Jn 13: 1-15.

A nte diem festum Paschæ, sciens Iesus, quia venit hora eius, ut tránseat ex hoc mundo ad Patrem: cum dilexísset suos, qui erant in mundo, in finem diléxit eos. Et cena facta, cum diábolus iam misísset in cor, ut tráderet eum Iudas Simónis Iscarió-tæ: sciens, quia ómnia dedit ei Pater in manus, et quia a Deo exívit, et ad Deum vadit: surgit a cena et ponit vestiménta sua: et cum accepísset línteum, præcínxit se. Deínde mittit aquam in pelvim, et cœpit laváre pedes discipulórum, et extérgere línteo, quo erat præcínctus. Venit ergo ad Simónem Petrum. Et dicit ei Petrus: « Dómine, tu mihi lavas pedes? » Respóndit Iesus et dixit ei: « Quod ego fácio, tu nescis modo, scies autem póstea ». Dicit ei Petrus: « Non lavábis mihi pedes in ætérnum ». Respóndit ei Iesus: « Si non lávero te, non habébis partem mecum ». Dicit ei Simon Petrus: « Dómine, non tantum pedes meos, sed et manus et caput ». Dicit ei Iesus: « Qui lotus est, non índiget

Before the festival-day of the Pasch, Jesus knowing that his hour was come, that he should pass out of this world to the Father, having loved his own who were in the world. He loved them unto the end. And when supper was done (the devil having now put into the heart of Judas, the son of Simon the Iscariot, to betray him), knowing that the Father had given him all things into his hands and that he came from God and goeth to God: he riseth from supper and layeth aside his garments and, having taken a towel, girded himself. After that, he putteth water into a basin and began to wash the feet of the disciples and to wipe them with the towel wherewith he was girded. He cometh therefore to Simon Peter. And Peter saith to him: Lord, dost thou wash my feet? Jesus answered and said to him: What I do, thou knowest not now: but thou shalt know hereafter. Peter saith to him: Thou shalt never wash my feet. Jesus answered him: If I wash thee not, thou shalt have no part with me. Simon Peter saith to him: Lord, not

nisi ut pedes lavet, sed est mundus totus. Et vos mundi estis, sed non omnes ». Sciébat enim, quisnam esset, qui tráderet eum: proptérea dixit: Non estis mundi omnes. Postquam ergo lavit pedes eórum et accépit vestiménta sua: cum recubuísset íterum, dixit eis: « Scitis, quid fécerim vobis? Vos vocátis me Magíster et Dómine: et bene dícitis: sum étenim. Si ergo ego lavi pedes vestros, Dóminus et Magíster: et vos debétis alter altérius laváre pedes. Exémplum enim dedi vobis, ut, quemádmodum ego feci vobis, ita et vos faciátis ».

only my feet, but also my hands and my head. Jesus saith to him: He that is washed needeth not but to wash his feet, but is clean wholly. And you are clean, but not all. For he knew who he was that would betray him; therefore he said: You are not all clean. Then after he had washed their feet and taken his garments, being set down again, he said to them: Know you what I have done to you? You call me Master and Lord. And you say well; for so I am. If then I being your Lord and Master, have washed your feet, you also ought to wash one another's feet. For I have given you an example, that as I have done to you, so you do also.

The Credo *is not said.*

THE WASHING OF FEET

¶ *May take place during Mass after the sermon, or outside of Mass.*

As the men are brought forward for the ceremony, the choir begins to sing the antiphons below. When the washing of feet is nearly ended, the 8th antiphon Ubi cáritas *with its verses is begun, omitting the rest if necessary.*

1 Ant.
III.

Jn 13: 34 ℣. 118: 1

M Andá-tum novum do vo-bis: * ut di-li-gá-tis ínvi-cem, sic-ut di-lé-xi vos, di-cit Dóminus. *Ps.* Be-á-ti immacu-lá-ti in vi- a: * qui ámbu-lant in le- ge Dómi-ni.

Repeat Ant. Mandátum novum.

A new commandment I give unto you: That you love one another, as I have loved you, saith the Lord. *Ps.* Blessed are the undefiled in the way: who walk in the law of the Lord.

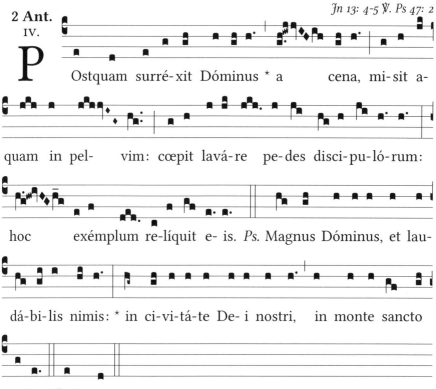

2 Ant.
IV.

Jn 13: 4-5 ℣. Ps 47: 2

POstquam surré-xit Dóminus * a cena, mi-sit a-quam in pel-vim: cœpit lavá-re pe-des disci-pu-ló-rum: hoc exémplum re-líquit e-is. *Ps.* Magnus Dóminus, et lau-dá-bi-lis nimis: * in ci-vi-tá-te De-i nostri, in monte sancto e-ius. Postquam.

After our Lord was risen from supper, he put water into a basin: and began to wash the feet of his disciples: to whom he gave this example. *Ps.* Great is the Lord, and exceedingly to be praised: in the city of our God, in his holy mountain.

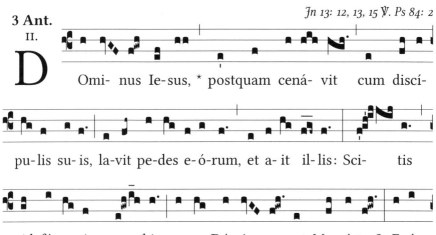

3 Ant.
II.

Jn 13: 12, 13, 15 ℣. Ps 84: 2

DOmi-nus Ie-sus, * postquam cená-vit cum discí-pu-lis su-is, la-vit pe-des e-ó-rum, et a-it il-lis: Sci-tis quid fé-ce-rim vo-bis, e-go Dómi-nus et Ma-gíster? Exém-

plum de-di vo- bis, ut et vos i- ta fa-ci- á-tis. *Ps.* Be-ne-di-xí-

sti Dómi-ne terram tu- am: * a-vertísti capti-vi-tá-tem Ia-cob.

Repeat Ant. Dóminus Iesus.

Our Lord Jesus, after he had supped with his disciples, washed their feet, and said to them: Know you what I your Lord and Master have done to you? I have given you an example, that ye also may do likewise. *Ps.* Thou hast blessed, O Lord, thy land: thou hast turned away the captivity of Jacob.

4 Ant. *Jn 13: 6-7 ℣. 8*

Omi-ne, * tu mi-hi la-vas pe-des? Respóndit Ie-sus, et di-xit e- i: Si non láve-ro ti-bi pe-des, non habé-bis partem me-cum. ℣. Ve-nit ergo ad Simónem Petrum, * et di-xit e- i Petrus. Dómi-ne. ℣. Quod ego fá-ci- o, tu nescis modo: *

sci- es autem póste-a. Dómi-ne.

Lord, dost thou wash my feet? Jesus answered and said to them: If I shall not wash thy feet, thou shalt have no part with me. ℣. He came to Simon Peter, and Peter said to him: Lord, dost thou wash my feet? Jesus answered and said to them: If I shall not wash thy feet, thou shalt have no part with me. ℣. What I do, thou knowest not now; but thou shalt know hereafter.

5 Ant.
IV.

Jn 13: 14 ℣. Ps 48: 2

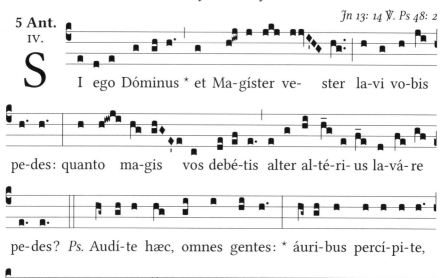

S I ego Dóminus * et Ma-gíster ve- ster la-vi vo-bis

pe-des: quanto ma-gis vos debé-tis alter al-té-ri- us la-vá- re

pe-des? *Ps.* Audí-te hæc, omnes gentes: * áuri-bus percí-pi-te,

qui ha-bi-tá-tis orbem. Si ego.

If I your Lord and Master, have washed your feet: how much more ought you to wash one another's feet? *Ps.* Hear these things, all ye nations: give ear, ye that inhabit the world.

6 Ant.
VII.

Jn 13: 35

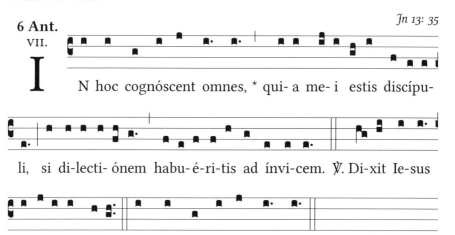

I N hoc cognóscent omnes, * qui- a me- i estis discípu-

li, si di-lecti- ónem habu- é-ri-tis ad ínvi-cem. ℣. Di-xit Ie-sus

discípu-lis su- is. In hoc cognóscent omnes.

By this shall all men know that you are my disciples, if you have love one for another. ℣. Said Jesus to his disciples.

7 Ant.
VII.

1 Cor 13: 13

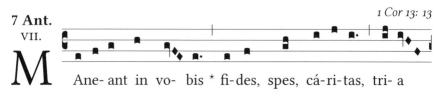

M Ane- ant in vo- bis * fi-des, spes, cá-ri-tas, tri- a

hæc: ma-ior autem ho-rum est cá-ri-tas. ℣. Nunc autem manent

fi-des, spes, cá-ri-tas, tri- a hæc: * ma-ior autem ho-rum est cá-

ri- tas. Máne-ant in vo- bis.

Let these three, faith, hope, and charity, remain in you: but the greatest of these is charity. ℣. And now there remain faith, hope and charity, these three: but the greatest of these is charity.

The following antiphon should not be omitted; it is sung towards the end of the ceremony, omitting some of the above antiphons if necessary.

8 Ant.

VI.

Cf. 1 Jn 2: 3-4

U -bi cá-ri- tas et a-mor, De-us i-bi est. ℣. Congregá-

vit nos in u-num Christi amor. ℣. Exsultémus, et in i-pso

iucundémur. ℣. Time- ámus, et amémus De-um vi-vum. ℣. Et ex

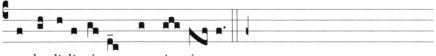

corde di-li-gámus nos sin-cé- ro.

Where charity and love are, there is God. ℣. The love of Christ has gathered us together. ℣. Let us rejoice in him and be glad. ℣. Let us fear and love the living God. ℣. And let us love one another with a sincere heart.

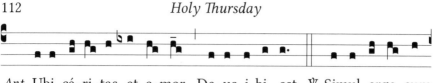

Ant. Ubi cá-ri-tas et a-mor, De-us i-bi est. ℣. Simul ergo cum

in u-num congregámur: ℣. Ne nos mente di-vi-dámur cave-á-

mus. ℣. Cessent iúrgi-a ma-lígna, cessent li-tes. ℣. Et in mé-di-o

nostri sit Christus De-us.

Where charity and love are, there is God. ℣. When, therefore, we are assembled together. ℣. Let us take heed, that we be not divided in mind. ℣. Let malicious quarrels and contentions cease. ℣. And let Christ our God dwell among us.

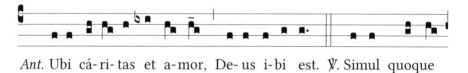

Ant. Ubi cá-ri-tas et a-mor, De-us i-bi est. ℣. Simul quoque

cum be-á-tis vi-de-ámus. ℣. Glo-ri-ánter vul-tum tú-um, Chri-

ste De-us: ℣. Gáudi-um, quod est imménsum, atque probum.

℣. Sǽcu-la per infi-ní-ta sæcu-ló-rum. A-men.

Where charity and love are, there is God. ℣. Let us also with the blessed see. ℣. Thy face in glory, O Christ our God. ℣. There to possess immeasurable and happy joy. ℣. For infinite ages of ages. Amen.

When the feet-washing is finished, the celebrant washes his hands, puts on his chasuble, goes before the altar and says the Pater noster *in silence, until:*

℣. Et ne nos indúcas in tentatiónem.

And lead us not into temptation.

℟. Sed líbera nos a malo.

But deliver us from evil.

℣. Tu mandásti mandáta tua, Dómine.

Thou hast commanded thy commandments, O Lord.

℟. Custodíri nimis.

To be exactly observed.

℣. Tu lavásti pedes discipulórum tuórum.

Thou hast washed the feet of thy disciples.

℟. Opera mánuum tuárum ne despícias.

Despise not the work of thy hands.

℣. Dómine, exáudi oratiónem meam.

O Lord, hear my prayer.

℟. Et clamor meus ad te véniat.

And let my cry come unto thee.

℣. Dóminus vobíscum.

The Lord be with you.

℟. Et cum spíritu tuo.

And with thy spirit.

Orémus.

Let us pray.

Adésto, Dómine, quǽsumus, offício servitútis nostræ: et quia tu discípulis tuis pedes laváre dignátus es, ne despícias ópera mánuum tuárum, quæ nobis retinénda mandásti: ut, sicut hic nobis, et a nobis exterióra abluúntur inquinaménta; sic a te ómnium nostrum interióra lavéntur peccáta. Quod ipse præstáre dignéris, qui vivis et regnas Deus: per ómnia sǽcula sæculórum.

Be present, O Lord, we beseech thee, at the performance of our service: and since thou didst vouchsafe to wash the feet of thy disciples, despise not the work thine own hands did, which thou hast commanded us to retain: that as here the outward stains are washed away by us and from us; so the inward sins of us all may be blotted out by thee. Which do thou vouchsafe to grant, who livest and reignest, one God, forever and ever.

℟. Amen.

Mass then proceeds as usual. Where the foot washing is done outside of Mass, the order given above is followed.

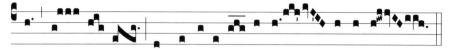

ar, sed vi- vam, et narrábo ó- pe-ra Dómi-ni.

The right hand of the Lord hath wrought strength, the right hand of the Lord hath exalted me: I shall not die, but live, and shall declare the works of the Lord.

Secret

Ipse tibi, quǽsumus, Dómine sancte, Pater omnípotens, ætérne Deus, sacrifícium nostrum reddat accéptum, qui discípulis suis in sui commemoratiónem hoc fíeri hodiérna traditióne monstrávit, Iesus Christus, Fílius tuus, Dóminus noster: Qui tecum vivit et regnat.

We beseech thee, O holy Lord, Father almighty, everlasting God, that he himself may render our sacrifice acceptable to thee, who, by the tradition of this day, taught his disciples to do this in remembrance of him, Jesus Christ, thy Son, our Lord: Who lives and reigns with thee.

Preface of the Holy Cross, p. 13.

Vatican edition IV

VIII.

S An- ctus, * Sanctus, San- ctus Dóminus De-us Sá- ba-

oth. Ple-ni sunt cæ-li et terra gló- ri- a tu- a. Ho- sánna

in ex- cél- sis. Bene-díctus qui ve-nit in nómi-ne Dó-

mi-ni. Ho- sánna in ex- cél- sis.

Or, Sanctus, *from Mass IX, p.* 261

Canon of the Mass

The Canon begins as usual, p. 15, until:

Communicántes, et diem sacratíssimum celebrántes, quo Dóminus noster Iesus Christus pro nobis est tráditus: sed et memóriam venerántes, in primis gloriósæ semper Vírginis Maríæ, Genetrícis eiúsdem Dei et Dómini nostri Iesu Christi: sed et beáti Ioseph, eiúsdem Vírginis Sponsi, et beatórum Apostolórum ac Mártyrum tuórum, Petri et Pauli, Andréæ, Iacóbi, Ioánnis, Thomæ, Iacóbi, Philíppi, Bartholomǽi, Matthǽi, Simónis et Thaddǽi: Lini, Cleti, Cleméntis, Xysti, Cornélii, Cypriáni, Lauréntii, Chrysógoni, Ioánnis et Pauli, Cosmæ et Damiáni: et ómnium Sanctórum tuórum; quorum méritis precibúsque concédas, ut in ómnibus protectiónis tuæ muniámur auxílio. Per eúndem Christum, Dñum nostrum. Amen.

In communion with, and celebrating the most sacred day on which our Lord Jesus Christ was handed over for our sake: and also honoring in the first place the memory of the glorious ever Virgin Mary, Mother of our Lord and God Jesus Christ: as also of the blessed Joseph, her spouse, and thy blessed Apostles and Martyrs Peter and Paul, Andrew, James, John, Thomas, James, Philip, Bartholomew, Matthew, Simon, and Thaddeus: Linus, Cletus, Clement, Sixtus, Cornelius, Cyprian, Lawrence, Chrysogonus, John and Paul, Cosmas and Damian, and of all thy saints, through whose merits and prayers, grant that we may in all things be defended by thy protecting help. Through the same Christ our Lord. Amen.

Hanc ígitur oblatiónem servitútis nostræ, sed et cunctæ famíliæ tuæ, quam tibi offérimus ob diem, in qua Dóminus noster Iesus Christus trádidit discípulis suis Córporis et Sánguinis sui mystéria celebránda: quǽsumus, Dómine, ut placátus accípias: diésque nostros in tua pace dispónas, atque ab ætérna damnatióne nos éripi, et in electórum tuórum iúbeas grege numerári. Per eúndem Christum Dñum nostrum. Amen.

We therefore, beseech thee, O Lord, to be appeased and accept this oblation of our service, as also of thy whole family, which we make unto thee in memory of the day on which our Lord Jesus Christ handed on the mysteries of his Body and Blood for his disciples to celebrate: dispose our days in thy peace, command us to be delivered from eternal damnation, and to be numbered in the flock of thy elect. Through the same Christ our Lord. Amen.

Quam oblatiónem tu, Deus, in ómnibus, quǽsumus, bene✠díctam, adscríp✠tam, ra✠tam, rationábilem, acceptabilémque fácere digné-

Which oblation do thou, O God, vouchsafe in all respects, to make blessed, approved, ratified, reasonable and acceptable; that it may become for us the Body

ris: ut nobis Cor✠pus, et San✠guis fiat dilectíssimi Fílii tui, Dómini nostri Iesu Christi.

Qui prídie, quam pro nostra omniúmque salúte paterétur, hoc est hódie, accépit panem in sanctas ac venerábiles manus suas, et elevátis óculis in cælum ad te Deum, Patrem suum omnipoténtem, tibi grátias agens, bene✠díxit, fregit, dedítque discípulis suis, dicens: Accípite, et manducáte ex hoc omnes.

Hoc est enim Corpus meum.

and Blood of thy most beloved Son Jesus Christ our Lord.

Who, the day before he suffered for our salvation and that of all men, that is, on this day, took bread into his most sacred and venerable hands and with his eyes lifted up towards heaven, unto thee, God, his almighty Father, giving thanks to thee, did bless, break and give to his disciples, saying: Take and eat ye all of this.

For this is my Body.

The Canon continues, as in the Ordinary of the Mass, p. 17.

At the Agnus Dei, *the response each time is* miserére nobis:

VI.

Vatican edition IV*

A -gnus De- i, * qui tollis peccá-ta mundi: mi-se-ré-

re no- bis. Agnus De- i, * qui tollis peccá-ta mundi: mi-se-

ré- re no- bis. Agnus De- i, * qui tollis peccá-ta mundi:

mi-se-ré- re no- bis.

Or, Agnus Dei, *from Mass IX, p. 261*

Today the kiss of peace, the prayer Dómine Iesu Christe, qui dixísti, *and the confession are omitted.*

Jn 13: 12, 13, 15

Comm.

II.

DOmi- nus Ie-sus, * postquam cená- vit cum discí-

pu-lis su- is, la-vit pe-des e-ó-rum, et a- it il-lis: Sci- tis

quid fé-ce-rim vo- bis, e-go Dómi- nus et Ma-gíster? Exém-

plum de-di vo- bis, ut et vos i- ta fa-ci- á-tis.

The Lord Jesus, after he had supped with his disciples, washed their feet, and said to them: Know you what I, your Lord and Master, have done to you? I gave you an example, that you also may do likewise.

During the distribution of Holy Communion, the antiphon Dóminus Iesus *may be sung with psalm verses, as notated below, or as in the Appendix, p. 262.*

Psalm 22

1. Dómi-nus re-git me, et ni-hil mi-hi dé- e-rit: * in loco páscu-æ

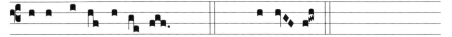

i-bi me col-lo-cá-vit. *Repeat Ant.* Domi- nus.

The Lord ruleth me, and I shall want nothing: he hath set me in a place of pasture.

2. Su-per aquam re-fecti- ó-nis educá-vit me, * á-nimam me-am

convér-tit.   *Ant.*

He hath brought me up, on the water of refreshment, he hath converted my
soul.

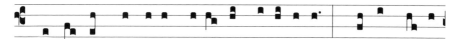

3. De- dú- xit me super sémi- tas iustí- ti- æ, * propter nomen

su- um.   *Ant.*

He hath led me on the paths of justice, for his own name's sake.

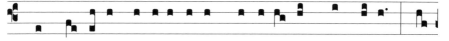

4. Nam, et si ambu-láve-ro in mé-di- o   umbræ mortis: * non

timébo ma-la, quóni- am tu mecum es.   *Ant.*

For though I should walk in the midst of the shadow of death: I will fear no
evils, for thou art with me.

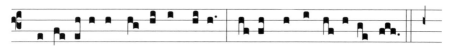

5. Virga tu-a, et bá-cu-lus tu-us: * ipsa me conso-lá-ta sunt.   *Ant.*

Thy rod and thy staff: they have comforted me.

6. Pa-rá-sti in conspéctu me- o mensam, * advérsus e- os, qui

trí-bu-lant me. *Ant.*

Thou hast prepared a table before me, against them that afflict me.

7. Impinguásti in ó-le- o caput me- um: * et ca-lix me- us in-é-

bri- ans quam præclá-rus est! *Ant.*

Thou hast anointed my head with oil: and my chalice which inebriateth me, how goodly is it!

8. Et mi-se-ri-córdi- a tu-a subsequé-tur me * ómni-bus di- ébus

vi-tæ me- æ. *Ant.*

And thy mercy will follow me all the days of my life.

9. Et ut inhá-bi-tem in domo Dómi-ni, * in longi-túdi-nem di-

é-rum. *Ant.*

And that I may dwell in the house of the Lord, unto length of days.

Psalm 150

1. Laudá-te Dóminum in sanctis e-ius: * laudá-te e-um in firma-

ménto virtú-tis e- ius.   *Ant.*

Praise ye the Lord in his holy places: praise ye him in the firmament of his power.

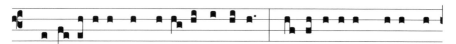

2. Laudá-te e-um in virtú-ti-bus e-ius: * laudá-te e-um secúndum

multi-túdi-nem magni-tú-di-nis e- ius.   *Ant.*

Praise ye him for his mighty acts: praise ye him according to the multitude of his greatness.

3. Laudá-te e-um in sono tubæ: * laudá-te e-um in psalté-ri- o,

et cítha-ra.   *Ant.*

Praise him with sound of trumpet: praise him with psaltery and harp.

4. Laudá-te e-um in týmpa-no, et cho-ro: * laudá-te e-um in

chordis, et órga-no.   *Ant.*

Praise him with timbrel, and choir: praise him with strings and organs.

5. Laudá-te e-um in cýmba-lis be-ne-sonánti-bus: laudá-te e-

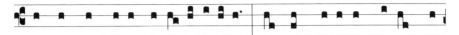

um in cýmba-lis iu-bi-la-ti-ónis: * omnis spí-ri-tus laudet Dó-

mi-num. *Ant.*

Praise him on high sounding cymbals: praise him on cymbals of joy: let every spirit praise the Lord.

Postcommunion

Refécti vitálibus aliméntis, quæsumus, Dómine, Deus noster: ut, quod témpore nostræ mortalitátis exséquimur, immortalitátis tuæ múnere consequámur. Per Dóminum.

Strengthened with life-giving food, we beseech thee, O Lord, our God: that what we do in our mortal life may bring us to the reward of life immortal with thee. Through our Lord.

The deacon sings the dismissal:

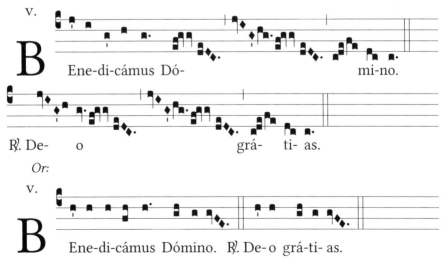

v.

B Ene-di-cámus Dó- mi-no.

℟. De- o grá- ti- as.

Or:

v.

B Ene-di-cámus Dómino. ℟. De-o grá-ti- as.

Or, from the Mass Ordinary: Mass IV, p. 269; Mass IX, p. 261.

The Last Gospel is omitted, and the sacred ministers immediately prepare for the procession.

SOLEMN TRANSLATION AND RESERVATION
OF THE BLESSED SACRAMENT

During the procession of the Blessed Sacrament, the hymn Pange, lingua *is sung, as below, until the verse* Tantum ergo; *if necessary, the hymn is repeated from the second verse. But if the procession is very long, other hymns, psalms, or canticles may be sung.*

When the celebrant arrives at the altar of repose, the ciborium is placed on the altar; all kneel as the Blessed Sacrament is incensed and Tantum ergo *is sung.*

Hymn

III.

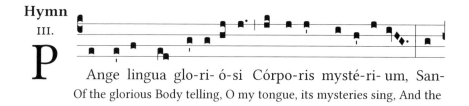

P Ange lingua glo-ri- ó-si Córpo-ris mysté-ri- um, San-
Of the glorious Body telling, O my tongue, its mysteries sing, And the

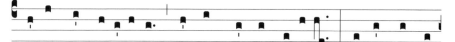

gui-nísque pre-ti- ó-si, Quem in mundi pré-ti- um Fructus ventris
Blood, all price excelling, Which the world's eternal King, In a noble womb

gene-ró-si Rex effú-dit génti- um. 2. No-bis da-tus, no-bis na-
once dwelling Shed for the world's ransoming. Given for us, descending,

tus Ex intácta Vírgi-ne, Et in mundo conversá-tus, Sparso
Of a Virgin to proceed, Man with man in converse blending, Scattered he the

verbi sémi-ne, Su- i mo-ras inco-lá-tus Mi-ro clau-sit ór-di-ne.
Gospel seed, Till his sojourn drew to ending, Which he closed in wondrous deed.

3. In suprémæ nocte cenæ Recúmbens cum frátri-bus,   Observá-
At the last great Supper lying Circled by his brethren's band, Meekly with the

ta lege plene Ci-bis in legá-li-bus, Ci-bum turbæ du-odénæ
law complying, First he finished its command Then, immortal Food supplying,

Se dat su- is má-ni-bus. 4. Verbum ca-ro, panem ve-rum Verbo
Gave himself with his own hand. Word made Flesh, by word he maketh Very

carnem éffi-cit: Fitque Sanguis Christi me-rum, Et si sensus
bread his Flesh to be; man in wine Christ's Blood partaketh: And if senses

dé-fi-cit. Ad firmándum cor sincé-rum So-la fi-des súf-fi-cit.
fail to see, Faith alone the true heart waketh To behold the mystery.

¶ *As the Blessed Sacrament is being incensed on the altar of reposition:*

5. Tantum ergo Sacraméntum Vene-rémur cérnu- i: Et antí-
Therefore we, before him bending, This great Sacrament revere;   Types and

quum documéntum Novo cedat rí-tu- i: Præstet fi-des supplemén-
shadows have their ending, For the newer rite is here; Faith, our outward sense

tum Sénsu-um de- féctu- i. 6. Ge-ni-tó-ri, Ge-ni-tóque Laus et iu-
befriending, makes the inward vision clear. Glory let us give, and blessing To

bi-lá-ti- o,   Sa-lus, honor, virtus quoque Sit et bene-dícti- o:
the Father and the Son; Honor, might and praise addressing, While eternal

Pro-cedénti ab utróque Compar sit lau-dá-ti- o.   A-men.
ages run; Ever too his love confessing, Who, from both, with both is one.

All adore the Blessed Sacrament, and after a little while, the celebrant,
sacred ministers, and servers return to the sacristy in silence.

THE STRIPPING OF THE ALTARS

The celebrant and sacred ministers remove their vestments. Returning to
the high altar, the celebrant says the following antiphon in a clear voice:

Ant. Divisérunt sibi vestiménta mea: et super vestem meam misé-runt sortem.	They parted my garments amongst them; and upon my vesture they cast lots.

He then intones the psalm, recited not chanted, which is then taken up at
the asterisk by the clergy and choir:

1. Deus, Deus meus, réspice in me: quare me dereliquísti? * longe a sa-lúte mea verba delictórum meórum.	O God my God, look upon me: why hast thou forsaken me? Far from my salvation are the words of my sins.

℣. *2 and the rest, p. 168 (recited on one note).*

Or, according to the alternate psalter, as in the Missale Romanum:

Ant. Dívidunt sibi vestiménta mea, et de veste mea mittunt sortem.
Ps. Deus meus, Deus meus, quare me dereliquísti? *

After stripping all altars in the church, excepting the altar of repose, the sacred ministers return to the high altar. The psalm is cut off at this point, and the celebrant repeats the antiphon, as above. All return to the sacristy.

Compline immediately follows in choir, recited without lit candles or chant. During the Triduum, Glória Patri *is omitted from the Office. At the ending of each Psalm, Canticle, and Prayer, the last syllable drops a single tone (la-sol).*

COMPLINE

Compline begins with the officiant's Confíteor.

Afterwards, all others reply:

Misereátur tui omnípotens Deus, et, dimíssis peccátis tuis, perdúcat te ad vitam ætérnam. ℞. Amen.

Confíteor Deo omnipoténti, beátæ Maríæ semper Vírgini, beáto Michaéli Archángelo, beáto Ioánni Baptístæ, sanctis Apóstolis Petro et Paulo, ómnibus Sanctis, et tibi pater: quia peccávi nimis cogitatióne, verbo et ópere: mea culpa, mea culpa, mea máxima culpa. Ideo precor beátam Maríam semper Vírginem, beátum Michaélem Archángelum, beátum Ioánnem Baptístam, sanctos Apóstolos Petrum et Paulum, omnes Sanctos, et te pater, oráre pro me ad Dóminum Deum nostrum.

May the almighty God have mercy upon thee, forgive thee thy sins, and bring thee to life everlasting.

I confess to almighty God, to blessed Mary ever Virgin, to blessed Michael the Archangel, to blessed John the Baptist, to the holy Apostles Peter and Paul, to all the saints, and to thee, father, that I have sinned exceedingly in thought, word and deed: through my fault, through my fault, through my most grievous fault. Therefore I beseech blessed Mary, ever Virgin, blessed Michael the Archangel, blessed John the Baptist, the holy Apostles Peter and Paul, all the saints, and thee, father, to pray for me to the Lord our God.

The officiant:

Misereátur vestri omnípotens Deus, et, dimíssis peccátis vestris, perdúcat vos ad vitam ætérnam. ℞. Amen.

Indulgéntiam, ✠ absolutiónem, et remissiónem peccatórum nostrórum tríbuat nobis omnípotens et miséricors Dóminus. ℞. Amen.

May the almighty God have mercy upon you, forgive you your sins, and bring you to life everlasting.

May the almighty and merciful Lord grant us pardon, absolution, and remission of our sins.

Psalm 4

1. Cum invocárem exaudívit me Deus iustítiæ meæ, * in tribulatióne dilatásti mihi.

When I called upon him, the God of my justice heard me: when I was in distress, thou hast enlarged me.

2. Miserére mei, * et exáudi oratiónem meam.

Have mercy on me: and hear my prayer.

3. Fílii hóminum, úsquequo gravi corde? * ut quid dilígitis vanitátem, et quǽritis mendácium?

O ye sons of men, how long will you be dull of heart? Why do you love vanity, and seek after lying?

4. Et scitóte quóniam mirificávit Dóminus sanctum suum; * Dóminus exáudiet me cum clamávero ad eum.

Know ye also that the Lord hath made his holy one wonderful: the Lord will hear me when I shall cry unto him.

5. Irascímini, et nolíte peccá-re; † quæ dícitis in córdi-bus vestris, * in cubílibus vestris compungímini.

Be ye angry, and sin not: the things you say in your hearts, be sorry for them upon your beds.

6. Sacrificáte sacrifícium iustí-tiæ, † et speráte in Dómino. * Multi dicunt: Quis osténdit nobis bona?

Offer up the sacrifice of justice, and trust in the Lord. Many say: Who showeth us good things?

7. Signátum est super nos lumen vultus tui, Dómine: * dedísti lætítiam in corde meo.

The light of thy countenance, O Lord, is signed upon us: thou hast given gladness in my heart.

8. A fructu fruménti, vini, et ólei sui * multiplicáti sunt.

By the fruit of their corn, their wine, and oil, they are multiplied.

9. In pace in idípsum * dórmiam, et requiéscam.

In peace in the selfsame I will sleep, and I will rest:

10. Quóniam tu, Dómine, sin-guláriter in spe * constituísti me.

For thou, O Lord, singularly hast settled me in hope.

Psalm 90

1. Qui hábitat in adiutório Altíssimi, * in protectióne Dei cæli commorábitur.	He that dwelleth in the aid of the most High, shall abide under the protection of the God of Jacob.
2. Dicet Dómino: Suscéptor meus es tu, et refúgium meum: * Deus meus sperábo in eum.	He shall say to the Lord: Thou art my protector, and my refuge: my God, in him will I trust.
3. Quóniam ipse liberávit me de láqueo venántium, * et a verbo áspero.	For he hath delivered me from the snare of the hunters: and from the sharp word.
4. Scápulis suis obumbrábit tibi: * et sub pennis eius sperábis.	He will overshadow thee with his shoulders: and under his wings thou shalt trust.
5. Scuto circúmdabit te véritas eius: * non timébis a timóre noctúrno.	His truth shall compass thee with a shield: thou shalt not be afraid of the terror of the night.
6. A sagítta volánte in die, † a negótio perambulánte in ténebris: * ab incúrsu, et dæmónio meridiáno.	Of the arrow that flieth in the day, of the business that walketh about in the dark: of invasion, or of the noonday devil.
7. Cadent a látere tuo mille, † et decem míllia a dextris tuis: * ad te autem non appropinquábit.	A thousand shall fall at thy side, and ten thousand at thy right hand: but it shall not come nigh thee.
8. Verúmtamen óculis tuis considerábis: * et retributiónem peccatórum vidébis.	But thou shalt consider with thy eyes: and shalt see the reward of the wicked.
9. Quóniam tu es, Dómine, spes mea: * Altíssimum posuísti refúgium tuum.	Because thou, O Lord, art my hope: thou hast made the most High thy refuge.
10. Non accédet ad te malum: * et flagéllum non appropinquábit tabernáculo tuo.	There shall no evil come to thee: nor shall the scourge come near thy dwelling.

11. Quóniam Angelis suis man-
dávit de te: * ut custódiant te in
ómnibus viis tuis.

For he hath given his angels charge
over thee; to keep thee in all thy
ways.

12. In mánibus portábunt te: *
ne forte offéndas ad lápidem
pedem tuum.

In their hands they shall bear thee
up: lest thou dash thy foot against a
stone.

13. Super áspidem, et basilíscum
ambulábis: * et conculcábis
leónem et dracónem.

Thou shalt walk upon the asp and
the basilisk: and thou shalt trample
under foot the lion and the dragon.

14. Quóniam in me sperávit,
liberábo eum: * prótegam
eum, quóniam cognóvit nomen
meum.

Because he hoped in me I will deliver
him: I will protect him because he
hath known my name.

15. Clamábit ad me, et ego
exáudiam eum: † cum ipso sum
in tribulatióne: * erípiam eum
et glorificábo eum.

He shall cry to me, and I will hear
him: I am with him in tribulation, I
will deliver him, and I will glorify
him.

16. Longitúdine diérum replébo
eum: * et osténdam illi salutáre
meum.

I will fill him with length of days;
and I will show him my salvation.

Psalm 133

1. Ecce nunc benedícite Dóminum, * omnes servi Dó-
mini:

Behold now bless ye the Lord, all ye
servants of the Lord:

2. Qui statis in domo Dómini, *
in átriis domus Dei nostri.

Who stand in the house of the Lord,
in the courts of the house of our
God.

3. In nóctibus extóllite manus
vestras in sancta, * et benedícite
Dóminum.

In the nights lift up your hands to
the holy places, and bless ye the
Lord.

4. Benedícat te Dóminus ex
Sion, * qui fecit cælum et
terram.

May the Lord out of Sion bless thee,
he that made heaven and earth.

Canticle of Simeon

1. Nunc dimíttis servum tuum, Dómine, * secúndum verbum tuum in pace.

Lord, now lettest thou thy servant depart in peace, according to thy word.

2. Quia vidérunt óculi mei * salutáre tuum.

For mine eyes have seen: thy salvation.

3. Quod parásti * ante fáciem ómnium populórum.

Which thou hast prepared: before the face of all peoples.

4. Lumen ad revelatiónem géntium, * et glóriam plebis tuæ Israël.

To be a light, to lighten the Gentiles: and to be the glory of thy people Israel.

Then all kneel, and recite the verse:

℣. Christus * factus est pro nobis obœdiens usque ad mortem.

Christ became, for us, obedient unto death.

On Good Friday, add:

Mortem autem crucis.

Even the death of the cross.

Silently, Pater noster... *Then, the officiant says in a clear voice:*

Vísita, quǽsumus, Dómine, habitatiónem istam, et omnes insídias inimíci ab ea lónge repélle: Angeli tui sancti hábitent in ea, qui nos in pace custódiant; et benedíctio tua sit super nos semper. *Silently:* Per Dóminum.

Visit, we beseech thee, O Lord, this house and family, and drive from it all the snares of the enemy: may thy holy angels dwell herein, who may keep us in peace; and may thy blessing be always upon us. Through our Lord.

Then all arise and leave in silence.

GOOD FRIDAY

THE SOLEMN AFTERNOON LITURGY

The procession into the church is made in silence. The celebrant and sacred ministers prostrate themselves before the altar, and all others go to their places to kneel and bow. All pray in silence for a little while.

PART I: THE LESSONS AND PASSION

Then the celebrant alone stands and sings:

Prayer

Deus, qui peccáti véteris hereditáriam mortem, in qua posteritátis genus omne succésserat, Christi tui, Dómini nostri, passióne solvísti: da, ut, confórmes eídem facti; sicut imáginem terrénæ natúræ necessitáte portávimus, ita imáginem cæléstis grátiæ sanctificatióne portémus. Per eúndem Christum Dóminum nostrum.

℟. Amen.

O God, who by the passion of thy Christ, our Lord, abolished the death inherited, by each succeeding generation, from ancient sin: grant that, being conformed to him, we have borne the image of the man of earth, by the law of nature, so by the sanctification of grace, we may bear the image of the Man of heaven. Through the same Christ our Lord.

After this, all get up and go to their places. A lector, or one of the sacred ministers, sings the first lesson (without title or conclusion) while all sit.

First Lesson
Os (Hos) 6: 1-6.

Hæc dicit Dóminus: In tribulatióne sua mane consúrgent ad me: Veníte, et revertámur ad Dóminum: quia ipse cepit, et sanábit nos: percútiet, et curábit nos. Vivificábit nos post duos dies: in die tértia suscitábit nos, et vivémus in conspéctu eius. Sciémus, sequemúrque, ut cognoscámus Dóminum: quasi dilúculum præparátus est egrés-

Thus saith the Lord: In their affliction they will rise early to me: Come, and let us return to the Lord, for he hath taken us, and he will heal us: he will strike, and he will cure us. He will revive us after two days: on the third day he will raise us up and we shall live in his sight. We shall know and we shall follow on, that we may know the Lord. His going forth is prepared as the morning light

sus eius, et véniet quasi imber nobis temporáneus et serótinus terræ.

Quid fáciam tibi, Ephraim? Quid fáciam tibi, Iuda? misericórdia vestra quasi nubes matutína: et quasi ros mane pertránsiens. Propter hoc dolávi in prophétis, occídi eos in verbis oris mei: et iudícia tua quasi lux egrediéntur. Quia misericórdiam vólui, et non sacrifícium, et sciéntiam Dei, plus quam holocáusta.

and he will come to us as the early and the latter rain to the earth.

What shall I do to thee, O Ephraim? What shall I do to thee, O Juda? Your mercy is as a morning cloud and as the dew that goeth away in the morning. For this reason have I hewed them by the Prophets, I have slain them by the words of my mouth: and thy judgments shall go forth as the light. For I desired mercy and not sacrifice: and the knowledge of God more than holocausts.

Responsory

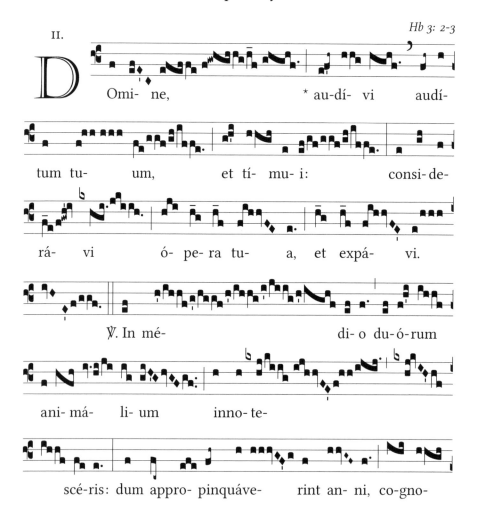

Hb 3: 2-3

Dómine, * audívi audítum tuum, et tímui: considerávi ópera tua, et expávi.

℣. In médio duórum animálium innotescéris: dum appropinquáverint anni, cogno-

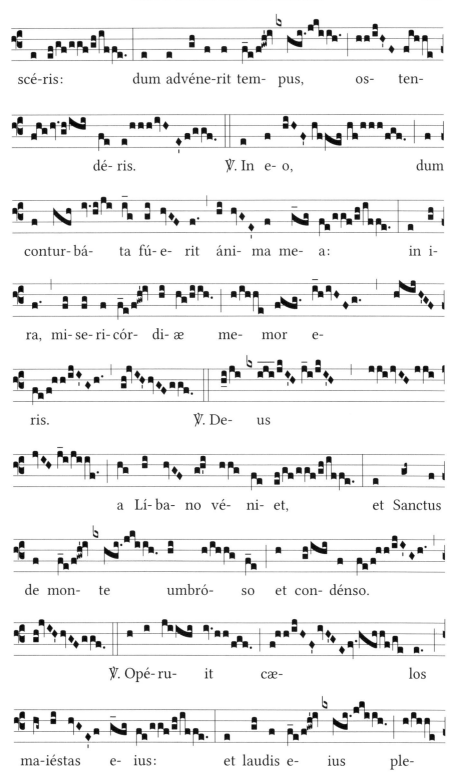

scé-ris: dum advéne-rit tem- pus, os- ten-

dé- ris. ℣. In e- o, dum

contur-bá- ta fú- e- rit áni- ma me- a: in i-

ra, mi-se-ri-cór- di- æ me- mor e-

ris. ℣. De- us

a Lí- ba- no vé- ni- et, et Sanctus

de mon- te umbró- so et con- dénso.

℣. Opé-ru- it cæ- los

ma-iéstas e- ius: et laudis e- ius ple-

na est * ter- ra.

O Lord, I have heard thy hearing and was afraid: I have considered thy works and trembled. ℣. In the midst of two animals thou shalt be made known: when the years shall draw nigh thou shalt be known: when the time shall come, thou shalt be manifested. ℣. When my soul shall be in trouble, thou wilt remember mercy, even in thy wrath. ℣. God will come from Libanus, and the Holy One from the shady and thickly covered mountain. ℣. His majesty covered the heavens: and the earth is full of his praise.

After the Responsory, all rise.

The celebrant: Orémus.	Let us pray.
The deacon: Flectámus génua.	Let us kneel.

All kneel for little while.

The deacon: Leváte.	Arise.

The celebrant:

Deus, a quo et Iudas reátus sui pœnam, et confessiónis suæ latro præmium sumpsit, concéde nobis tuæ propitiatiónis efféctum: ut, sicut in passióne sua Iesus Christus, Dóminus noster, divérsa utrísque íntulit stipéndia meritórum; ita nobis, abláto vetustátis erróre, resurrectiónis suæ grátiam largiátur: Qui tecum vivit et regnat.

O God, who didst doom Judas to the punishment of his crime, and richly reward the thief for his confession, grant to us the full effect of thy clemency: that, as our Lord Jesus Christ, in his passion, gave to each retribution according to his merits, so, upon absolving our past sins, he may bestow on us the grace of his resurrection: Who lives and reigns with thee.

Second Lesson
Ex 12: 1-11.

In diébus illis: Dixit Dóminus ad Móysen et Aaron in terra Ægýpti: « Mensis iste vobis princípium ménsium primus erit in ménsibus anni. Loquímini ad univérsum cœtum filiórum Israël, et dícite eis: Décima die mensis huius tollat unusquísque agnum per famílias et domos suas. Sin autem minor est núme-

In those days: The Lord said to Moses and Aaron in the land of Egypt: This month shall be to you the beginning of months: it shall be the first in the months of the year. Speak ye to the whole assembly of the children of Israel, and say to them: On the tenth day of this month let every man take a lamb by their families and houses. But if the num-

rus, ut suffícere possit ad vescéndum agnum, assúmet vicínum suum, qui iunctus est dómui suæ, iuxta númerum animárum, quæ suffícere possunt ad esum agni. Erit autem agnus absque mácula, másculus, annículus: iuxta quem ritum tollétis et hædum. Et servábitis eum usque ad quartam décimam diem mensis huius: immolabítque eum univérsa multitúdo filiórum Israël ad vésperam. Et sument de sánguine eius, ac ponent super utrúmque postem et in superlimináribus domórum, in quibus cómedent illum. Et edent carnes nocte illa assas igni, et ázymos panes cum lactúcis agréstibus. Non comedétis ex eo crudum quid nec coctum aqua, sed tantum assum igni: caput cum pédibus eius et intestínis vorábitis. Nec remanébit quidquam ex eo usque mane. Si quid resíduum fúerit, igne comburétis. Sic autem comedétis illum: Renes vestros accingétis, et calceaménta habébitis in pédibus, tenéntes báculos in mánibus, et comedétis festinánter: est enim Phase id est tránsitus Dómini ».

ber be less than may suffice to eat the lamb, be shall take unto him his neighbor that joineth to his house, according to the number of souls which may be enough to eat the lamb. And it shall be a lamb without blemish, a male, of one year: according to which rite also you shall take a kid. And you shall keep it until the fourteenth day of this month: and the whole multitude of the children of Israel shall sacrifice it in the evening. And they shall take of blood thereof, and put it upon both the side posts, and on the upper door posts of the houses, wherein they shall eat it. And they shall eat the flesh that night roasted at the fire: and unleavened bread with wild lettuce. You shall not eat thereof any thing raw, nor boiled in water, but only roasted at the fire. You shall eat the head with the feet and entrails thereof. Neither shall there remain any thing of it until morning. If there be any thing left, you shall burn it with fire. And thus you shall eat it: You shall gird your reins, and you shall have shoes on your feet, holding staves in your hands, and you shall eat in haste; for it is the Phase that is the Passage of the Lord.

Resp.

Ps 139: 2-10, 14

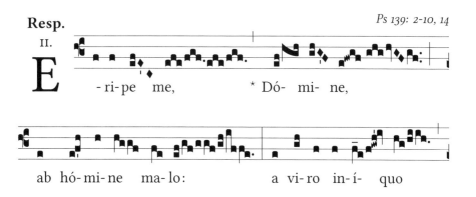

E- ri-pe me, * Dó- mi- ne, ab hó-mi-ne ma-lo: a vi-ro in-í- quo

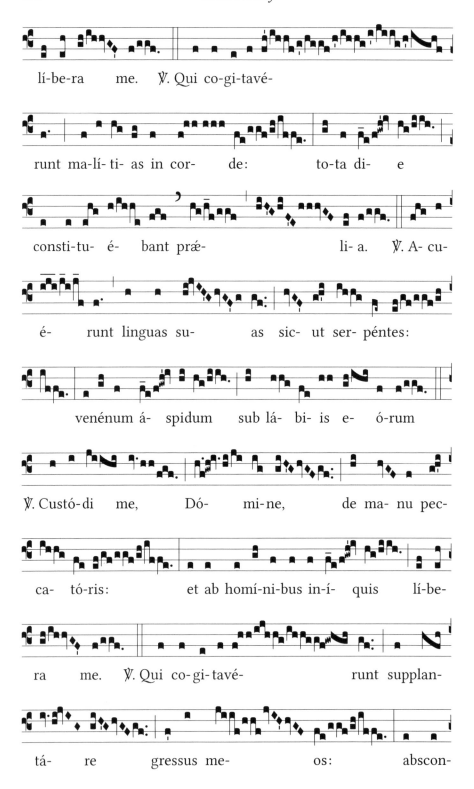

lí-be-ra me. ℣. Qui co-gi-tavé-

runt ma-lí- ti- as in cor- de: to-ta di- e

consti-tu- é- bant præ- li- a. ℣. A- cu-

é- runt linguas su- as sic- ut ser- péntes:

venénum á- spidum sub lá- bi- is e- ó-rum

℣. Custó-di me, Dó- mi-ne, de ma- nu pec-

ca- tó-ris: et ab homí-ni-bus in-í- quis lí-be-

ra me. ℣. Qui co-gi-tavé- runt supplan-

tá- re gressus me- os: abscon-

dé-runt su-pér- bi lá- que- um mi- hi. ℣. Et

fu- nes extendé- runt in láque-

um pé-di-bus me- is: iuxta i-ter scán- da-lum

posu- é- runt mi- hi. ℣. Di-xi Dómi- no: De-

us me- us es tu: exáudi, Dó- mi-ne, vo-

cem o-ra-ti- ónis me-æ. ℣. Dómi-ne, Dómi- ne virtus

sa-lú-tis me- æ: obúmbra caput me- um

in di- e bel- li. ℣. Ne tra-das me

a de-si-dé-ri- o me- o pecca-tó-

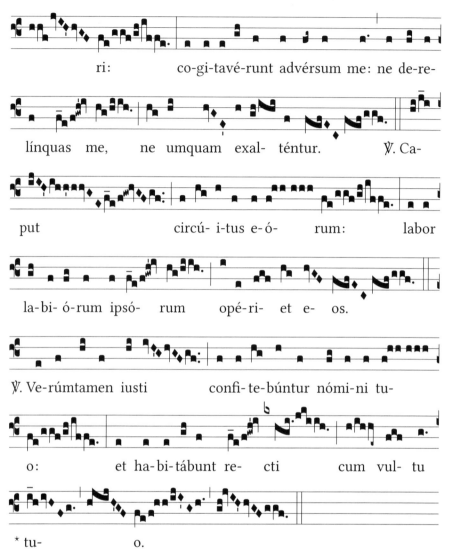

ri: co-gi-tavé-runt advérsum me: ne de-re-

línquas me, ne umquam exal- téntur. ℣. Ca-

put   circú- i-tus e-ó- rum: labor

la-bi- ó-rum ipsó- rum opé-ri- et e- os.

℣. Ve-rúmtamen iusti confi- te-búntur nómi-ni tu-

o: et ha-bi-tábunt re- cti cum vul- tu

* tu-   o.

Deliver me, O Lord, from the evil man: rescue me from the unjust man. ℣. Who have devised iniquities in their hearts: all the day long they designed battles. ℣. They have sharpened their tongues like a serpent: the venom of asps is under their lips. ℣. Keep me, O Lord, from the hand of the wicked: and from unjust men deliver me. Who have proposed to supplant my steps. ℣. The proud have hidden a net for me. And they have stretched out cords for a snare: they have laid for me a stumbling-block by the wayside. ℣. I said to the Lord: Thou art my God: hear, O Lord, the voice of my supplication. ℣. O Lord, Lord, the strength of my salvation: thou hast overshadowed my head in the day of battle. ℣. Give me not up, O Lord, from my desire to the wicked: they have plotted against me; do not thou forsake me, lest they should triumph. ℣. The head of them compassing me about: the labor of their lips shall overwhelm them. ℣. But as for the just, they shall give glory to thy name: and the upright shall dwell with thy countenance.

After the Responsory, the Passion is sung. It is permitted for the schola to sing, as the "Turba," the words for which notes are given.

Pássio Dómini nostri Iesu Christi secúndum Ioánnem

Jn 18: 1-40; 19: 1-42.

Arrest of Jesus

IN illo témpore: Egréssus est Iesus cum discípulis suis trans torréntem Cedron, ubi erat hortus, in quem introívit ipse, et discípuli eius. Sciébat autem et Iudas, qui tradébat eum, locum: quia frequénter Iesus convénerat illuc cum discípulis suis. Iudas ergo, cum accepísset cohórtem, et a pontifícibus et pharisǽis minístros, venit illuc cum latérnis, et fácibus, et armis. Iesus ítaque sciens ómnia, quæ ventúra erant super eum, procéssit, et dixit eis: ✠ Quem quǽritis? **C.** Respondérunt ei:

At that time Jesus went forth with his disciples over the brook Cedron, where there was a garden, into which he entered with his disciples. And Judas also, who betrayed him, knew the place: because Jesus had often resorted thither together with his disciples. Judas therefore having received a band of soldiers and servants from the chief priests and the Pharisees, cometh thither with lanterns and torches and weapons. Jesus therefore, knowing that all things that should come upon him, went forth and said to them: ✠ Whom seek ye? **C.** They answered him:

S. Iesum Nazarénum.

C. Dicit eis Iesus: ✠ Ego sum. **C.** Stabat autem et Iudas, qui tradébat eum, cum ipsis. Ut ergo dixit eis: Ego sum: abiérunt retrórsum, et cecidérunt in terram. Iterum ergo interrogávit eos: ✠ Quem quǽritis? **C.** Illi autem dixérunt:

S. Jesus of Nazareth.

C. Jesus saith to them: ✠ I am he. **C.** And Judas also, who betrayed him, stood with them. As soon therefore as he had said to them: I am he; they went backward and fell to the ground. Again therefore he asked them: ✠ Whom seek ye? **C.** And they said:

S. Iesum Nazarénum.

C. Respóndit Iesus: ✠ Dixi vobis, quia ego sum: si ergo me quǽritis, sínite hos abíre. **C.** Ut implerétur sermo, quem dixit: Quia quos dedísti mihi, non pérdidi ex eis quemquam. Simon ergo Petrus habens gládium edúxit eum: et percússit pon-

S. Jesus of Nazareth.

C. Jesus answered: ✠ I have told you that I am he. If therefore you seek me, let these go their way; **C.** That the word might be fulfilled which he said: Of them whom thou hast given me, I have not lost anyone. Then Simon Peter, having a sword, drew it and struck the ser-

tíficis servum: et abscídit aurículam eius déxteram. Erat autem nomen servo Malchus. Dixit ergo Iesus Petro: ✠ Mitte gládium tuum in vagínam. Cálicem, quem dedit mihi Pater, non bibam illum?

C. Cohors ergo, et tribúnus, et minístri Iudæórum comprehendérunt Iesum, et ligavérunt eum. Et adduxérunt eum ad Annam primum, erat enim socer Cáiphæ, qui erat póntifex anni illíus. Erat autem Cáiphas, qui consílium déderat Iudæis: Quia éxpedit unum hóminem mori pro pópulo. Sequebátur autem Iesum Simon Petrus, et álius discípulus. Discípulus autem ille erat notus pontífici, et introívit cum Iesu in átrium pontíficis. Petrus autem stabat ad óstium foris. Exívit ergo discípulus álius, qui erat notus pontífici, et dixit ostiáriæ: et introdúxit Petrum. Dicit ergo Petro ancílla ostiária: **S.** Numquid et tu ex discípulis es hóminis istíus? **C.** Dicit ille: **S.** Non sum. **C.** Stabant autem servi et minístri ad prunas, quia frigus erat, et calefaciébant se: erat autem cum eis et Petrus stans, et calefáciens se. Póntifex ergo interrogávit Iesum de discípulis suis, et de doctrína eius. Respóndit ei Iesus: ✠ Ego palam locútus sum mundo: ego semper dócui in synagóga et in templo, quo omnes Iudæi convéniunt: et in occúlto locútus sum nihil. Quid me intérrogas? intérroga eos, qui audiérunt quid locutus sim ipsis: ecce hi sciunt quæ díxerim ego. **C.** Hæc autem cum dixísset, unus assístens ministrórum dedit álapam Iesu, dicens: **S.** Sic respóndes pontífici? **C.** Respóndit ei Ie-

vant of the high priest and cut off his right ear. And the name of the servant was Malchus. Jesus therefore said to Peter: ✠ Put up thy sword in the scabbard. The chalice which my Father hath given me, shall I not drink it?

C. Then the band and the tribune and the servants of the Jews took Jesus, and bound him. And they led him away to Annas first, for he was father-in-law to Caiphas, who was the high priest that year. Now Caiphas was he who had given the counsel to the Jews: that it was expedient that one man should die for the people. And Simon Peter followed Jesus: and so did another disciple. And that disciple was known to the high priest and went in with Jesus into the court of the high priest. But Peter stood at the door without. The other disciple therefore, who was known to the high priest, went out and spoke to the portress and brought in Peter. The maid therefore that was portress saith to Peter: **S.** Art not thou also one of this man's disciples? **C.** He saith: **S.** I am not. **C.** Now the servants and ministers stood at a fire of coals, because it was cold, and warmed themselves. And with them was Peter, also, standing and warming himself. The high priest therefore asked Jesus of his disciples and of his doctrine. Jesus answered him: ✠ I have spoken openly to the world. I have always taught in the synagogue and in the temple, whither all the Jews resort: and in secret I have spoken nothing. Why asketh thou me? Ask them who have heard what I have spoken unto them. Behold they know what things I have said. **C.** And when he had said these things, one of the servants, standing by, gave Je-

sus: ✠ Si male locútus sum, testimónium pérhibe de malo: si autem bene, quid me cædis? **C.** Et misit eum Annas ligátum ad Cáipham pontíficem. Erat autem Simon Petrus stans, et calefáciens se. Dixérunt ergo ei:

sus a blow, saying: **S.** Answerest thou the high priest so? **C.** Jesus answered him: ✠ If I have spoken evil, give testimony of the evil; but if well, why strikest thou me? **C.** And Annas sent him bound to Caiphas the high priest. And Simon Peter was standing and warming himself. They said therefore to him:

S. Numquid et tu ex discípu-lis e-ius es?
S. Art not thou also one of his disciples?

C. Negávit ille, et dixit: **S.** Non sum. **C.** Dicit ei unus ex servis pontíficis, cognátus eius, cuius abscídit Petrus aurículam: **S.** Nonne ego te vidi in horto cum illo? **C.** Iterum ergo negávit Petrus: et statim gallus cantávit.

C. He denied it and said: **S.** I am not. **C.** One of the servants of the high priest a kinsman to him whose ear Peter cut off saith to him: **S.** Did I not see thee in the garden with him? **C.** Again therefore Peter denied; and immediately the cock crew.

Before Pilate

Addúcunt ergo Iesum a Cáipha in prætórium. Erat autem mane: et ipsi non introiérunt in prætórium, ut non contaminaréntur, sed ut manducárent Pascha. Exívit ergo Pilátus ad eos foras, et dixit: **S.** Quam accusatiónem affértis advérsus hóminem hunc? **C.** Respondérunt, et dixérunt ei:

Then they led Jesus from Caiphas to the governor's hall. And it was morning; and they went not into the hall, that they might not be defiled, but that they might eat the Pasch. Pilate therefore went out to them, and said: **S.** What accusation bring you against this man? **C.** They answered and said to him:

S. Si non esset hic ma-le-fáctor, non ti-bi tradi-dissémus e-um.
S. If he were not a malefactor, we would not have delivered him up to thee.

C. Dixit ergo eis Pilátus: **S.** Accípite eum vos, et secúndum legem vestram iudicáte eum. **C.** Dixérunt ergo ei Iudǽi:

C. Pilate therefore said to them: **S.** Take him you, and judge him according to your law. **C.** The Jews therefore said to him:

S. Nobis non li-cet interfí-ce-re quemquam.

S. It is not lawful for us to put any man to death.

C. Ut sermo Iesu implerétur, quem dixit, signíficans qua morte esset moritúrus. Introívit ergo íterum in prætórium Pilátus, et vocávit Iesum, et dixit ei: **S.** Tu es Rex Iudæórum? **C.** Respóndit Iesus: ✠ A temetípso hoc dicis, an álii dixérunt tibi de me? **C.** Respóndit Pilátus: **S.** Numquid ego Iudǽus sum? Gens tua et pontífices tradidérunt te mihi: quid fecísti? **C.** Respóndit Iesus: ✠ Regnum meum non est de hoc mundo. Si ex hoc mundo esset regnum meum, minístri mei útique decertárent ut non tráderer Iudǽis: nunc autem regnum meum non est hinc. **C.** Dixit ítaque ei Pilátus: **S.** Ergo rex es tu? **C.** Respóndit Iesus: ✠ Tu dicis, quia Rex sum ego. Ego in hoc natus sum, et ad hoc veni in mundum, ut testimónium perhíbeam veritáti: omnis qui est ex veritáte, audit vocem meam. **C.** Dicit ei Pilátus: **S.** Quid est véritas? **C.** Et cum hoc dixísset, íterum exívit ad Iudǽos, et dicit eis: **S.** Ego nullam invénio in eo causam. Est autem consuetúdo vobis ut unum dimíttam vobis in Pascha: vultis ergo dimíttam vobis Regem Iudæórum? **C.** Clamavérunt ergo rursum omnes, dicéntes:

C. That the word of Jesus might be fulfilled, which he said, signifying what death he should die. Pilate therefore went into the hall again and called Jesus and said to him: **S.** Art thou the King of the Jews? **C.** Jesus answered: ✠ Sayest thou this thing of thyself, or have others told it thee of me? **C.** Pilate answered: **S.** Am I a Jew? Thine own nation and the chief priests have delivered the up to me. What hast thou done? **C.** Jesus answered: ✠ My kingdom is not of this world. If my kingdom were of this world, my servants would certainly strive that I should not be delivered to the Jews: but now my kingdom is not from hence. **C.** Pilate therefore said to him: **S.** Art thou a King then? **C.** Jesus answered: ✠ Thou sayest I am a king. For this was I born, and for this came I into the world; that I should give testimony of the truth. Every one that is of the truth heareth my voice. **C.** Pilate saith to him: **S.** What is truth? **C.** And when he had said this, he went out again to the Jews and saith to them: **S.** I find no cause in him. But you have a custom that I should release one unto you at the Pasch. Will you, therefore, that I release unto you the King of the Jews? **C.** Then cried they all again, saying:

S. Non hunc, sed Barábbam.

S. Not this man, but Barabbas.

C. Erat autem Barábbas latro. Tunc ergo apprehéndit Pilátus Iesum,

C. Now Barabbas was a robber. Then therefore Pilate took Jesus and

et flagellávit. Et mílites plecténtes corónam de spinis, imposuérunt cápiti eius: et veste purpúrea circumdedérunt eum. Et veniébant ad eum, et dicébant:

scourged him. And the soldiers platting a crown of thorns, put it upon his head; and they put on him a purple garment. And they came to him and said:

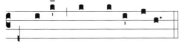

S. Ave, Rex Iudæ- órum.

S. Hail, King of the Jews.

C. Et dabant ei álapas. Exívit ergo íterum Pilátus foras, et dicit eis: **S.** Ecce addúco vobis eum foras, ut cognoscátis, quia nullam invénio in eo causam. **C.** (Exívit ergo Iesus portans corónam spíneam, et purpúreum vestiméntum.) Et dicit eis: **S.** Ecce homo. **C.** Cum ergo vidíssent eum pontífices et minístri, clamábant, dicéntes:

C. And they gave him blows. Pilate therefore went forth again and saith to them: **S.** Behold, I bring him forth unto you, that you may know that I find no cause in him. **C.** Jesus therefore came forth, bearing the crown of thorns and the purple garment. And he saith to them: **S.** Behold the man. **C.** When the chief priests, therefore, and the servants had seen him, they cried out, saying:

S. Cruci-fíge, cruci-fíge e-um.

S. Crucify him, crucify him.

C. Dicit eis Pilátus: **S.** Accípite eum vos, et crucifígite: ego enim non invénio in eo causam. **C.** Respondérunt ei Iudǽi:

C. Pilate saith to them: **S.** Take him you, and crucify him; for I find no cause in him. **C.** The Jews answered him:

S. Nos legem habémus, et secúndum legem debet mo- ri, qui- a
S. We have a law, and according to the law he ought to die,

Fí-li-um De- i se fe-cit.
because he made himself the Son of God.

C. Cum ergo audísset Pilátus hunc sermónem, magis tímuit. Et ingréssus est prætórium íterum: et dixit ad Iesum: **S.** Unde es tu? **C.** Iesus autem respónsum non dedit ei. Dicit ergo ei Pilátus: **S.** Mihi non lóqueris? nescis quia potestátem há-

C. When Pilate, therefore, had heard this saying, he feared the more. And he entered into the hall again; and he said to Jesus: **S.** Whence art thou? **C.** But Jesus gave him no answer. Pilate therefore saith to him: **S.** Speakest thou not to me? Knowest thou not

beo crucifígere te, et potestátem hábeo dimíttere te? **C.** Respóndit Iesus: ✠ Non habéres potestátem advérsum me ullam, nisi tibi datum esset désuper. Proptérea, qui me trádidit tibi, maius peccátum habet. **C.** Et exínde quærébat Pilátus dimíttere eum. Iudǽi autem clamábant dicéntes:

that I have power to crucify the, and I have power to release thee? **C.** Jesus answered: ✠ Thou shouldst not have any power against me, unless it were given thee from above. Therefore, he that hath delivered me to thee hath a greater sin. **C.** And from henceforth Pilate sought to release him. But the Jews cried out, saying:

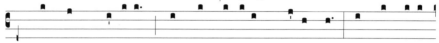

S. Si hunc dimíttis, non es amícus Cǽsa- ris. Omnis enim,
S. If thou release this Man, thou art not Caesar's friend. For whosoever

qui se regem fa-cit, contradí-cit Cǽsa-ri.
maketh himself a king speaketh against Caesar.

C. Pilátus autem cum audísset hos sermónes, addúxit foras Iesum, et sedit pro tribunáli, in loco qui dícitur Lithóstrotos, hebráice autem Gábbatha. Erat autem Parascéve Paschæ, hora quasi sexta, et dicit Iudǽis: **S.** Ecce Rex vester. **C.** Illi autem clamábant:

C. Now when Pilate had heard these words, he brought Jesus forth and sat down in the judgment seat, in the place that is called Lithostrotos, and in Hebrew Gabbatha. And it was Paraseve of the Pasch, about the sixth hour; and he saith to the Jews: **S.** Behold your King. **C.** But they cried out:

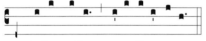

S. Tolle, tolle, cruci-fíge e-um.

S. Away with him. Away with him: Crucify him.

C. Dicit eis Pilátus: **S.** Regem vestrum crucifigam? **C.** Respondérunt pontífices:

C. Pilate saith to them: **S.** Shall I crucify your King? **C.** The chief priests answered:

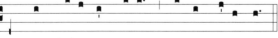

S. Non habémus regem, ni- si Cǽsa- rem.

S. We have no king but Caesar.

C. Tunc ergo trádidit eis illum ut crucifigerétur.

C. Then, therefore, he delivered him to them to be crucified.

At Calvary

Suscepérunt autem Iesum, et eduxérunt. Et báiulans sibi crucem, exívit in eum, qui dícitur Calváriæ lo-

And they took Jesus and led him forth. And bearing his cross, He went forth to that place which is called Cal-

cum, hebráice autem Gólgotha: ubi crucifixérunt eum, et cum eo álios duos, hinc et hinc, médium autem Iesum.

Scripsit autem et títulum Pilátus: et pósuit super crucem. Erat autem scriptum: Iesus Nazarénus, Rex Iudæórum. Hunc ergo títulum multi Iudæórum legérunt, quia prope civitátem erat locus, ubi crucifíxus est Iesus. Et erat scriptum hebráice, græce, et latíne. Dicébant ergo Piláto pontífices Iudæórum:

And Pilate wrote a title also: and he put it upon the cross. And the writing was: Jesus of Nazareth, the King of the Jews. This title therefore many of the Jews did read: because the place where Jesus was crucified was nigh to the city. And it was written in Hebrew, Greek, and in Latin. Then the chief priests of the Jews said to Pilate:

vary but in Hebrew Golgotha.; where they crucified him, and with him two others, one on each side and Jesus in the midst.

S. No-li scríbe-re, Rex Iudæ-órum, sed qui-a ipse di-xit: Rex sum
S. Write not: The King of the Jews; but that he said: I am the King

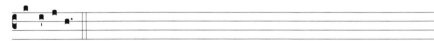

Iudæ-órum.
of the Jews.

C. Respóndit Pilátus: **S.** Quod scripsi, scripsi. **C.** Mílites ergo cum crucifixíssent eum, accepérunt vestiménta eius (et fecérunt quátuor partes: unicuíque míliti partem), et túnicam. Erat autem túnica inconsútilis, désuper contéxta per totum. Dixérunt ergo ad ínvicem:

C. Pilate answered: **S.** What I have written, I have written. **C.** The soldiers therefore, when they had crucified him, took his garments and they made four parts, to every soldier a part and also his coat. Now the coat was without seam, woven from the top throughout. They said then one to another:

S. Non scindámus e-am, sed sorti-ámur de illa cu-ius sit.
S. Let us not cut it, but let us cast lots for it, whose it shall be.

C. Ut Scriptúra implerétur, dicens: Partíti sunt vestiménta mea sibi: et in vestem meam misérunt sortem. Et mílites quidem hæc fecérunt. Stabant autem iuxta crucem Iesu, mater eius, et soror matris eius María Cléophæ, et María Magdalé-

C. That the Scripture might be fulfilled which saith: *They have parted my garments among them, and upon my vesture they have cast lots.* And the soldiers indeed did these things. Now there stood by the cross of Jesus, his mother, and his mother's sister, Mary of

ne. Cum vidísset ergo Iesus matrem, et discípulum stantem quem diligébat, dicit matri suæ: ✠ Múlier, ecce fílius tuus. **C.** Deínde dicit discípulo: ✠ Ecce mater tua. **C.** Et ex illa hora accépit eam discípulus in sua.

Póstea sciens Iesus quia ómnia consummáta sunt, ut consummarétur Scriptúra, dixit: ✠ Sítio. **C.** Vas ergo erat pósitum acéto plenum. Illi autem spóngiam plenam acéto, hyssópo circumponéntes, obtulérunt ori eius. Cum ergo accepísset Iesus acétum, dixit: ✠ Consummátum est. **C.** Et inclináto cápite trádidit spíritum.

Cleophas, and Mary Magdalen. When Jesus therefore had seen his mother, and the disciple standing whom he loved, he saith to his mother: ✠ Woman, behold thy son. **C.** After that, he saith to the disciple: ✠ Behold thy mother. **C.** And from that hour, the disciple took her to his own.

Afterwards, Jesus, knowing that all things were now accomplished, that the Scripture might be fulfilled, said: ✠ I thirst. **C.** Now there was a vessel set there, full of vinegar. And they, putting a sponge full of vinegar about hyssop, put it to his mouth. Jesus therefore, when he had taken the vinegar, said: ✠ It is consummated. **C.** And bowing his head, he gave up the ghost.

(Here a pause is made, and all kneel).

Iudæi ergo (quóniam Parascéve erat) ut non remanérent in cruce córpora sábbato (erat enim magnus dies ille sábbati) rogavérunt Pilátum, ut frangeréntur eórum crura, et tolleréntur. Venérunt ergo mílites: et primi quidem fregérunt crura, et altérius, qui crucifíxus est cum eo. Ad Iesum autem cum veníssent, ut vidérunt eum iam mórtuum, non fregérunt eius crura, sed unus mílitum láncea latus eius apéruit, et contínuo exívit sanguis, et aqua. Et qui vidit, testimónium perhíbuit: et verum est testimónium eius. Et ille scit, quia vera dicit: ut et vos credátis. Facta sunt enim hæc, ut Scriptúra implerétur: Os non comminuétis ex eo. Et íterum ália Scriptúra dicit: Vidébunt in quem transfixérunt.

Then the Jews because it was the Parasceve, that the bodies might not remain upon the cross on the Sabbath day for that was a great Sabbath day, besought Pilate that their legs might be broken and that they might be taken away. The soldiers therefore came, and they broke the legs of the first, and of the other that was crucified with him. But after they were come to Jesus, when they saw that he was already dead, they did not break his legs. But one of the soldiers with a spear opened his side, and immediately there came out blood and water. And he that saw it hath given testimony: and his testimony is true. And he knoweth that he saith true: that you also may believe. For these things were done that the Scripture might be fulfilled: *You shall not break a bone of him.* And again another Scripture saith: *They shall look on him whom they pierced.*

The burial

Post hæc autem rogávit Pilátum Ioseph ab Arimathǽa (eo quod esset discípulus Iesu, occúltus autem propter metum Iudæórum) ut tólleret corpus Iesu. Et permísit Pilátus. Venit ergo, et tulit corpus Iesu. Venit autem et Nicodémus, qui vénerat ad Iesum nocte primum, ferens mixtúram myrrhæ, et áloës, quasi libras centum. Accepérunt ergo corpus Iesu, et ligavérunt illud línteis cum aromátibus, sicut mos est Iudǽis sepelíre. Erat autem in loco, ubi crucifíxus est, hortus: et in horto monuméntum novum, in quo nondum quisquam pósitus erat. Ibi ergo propter Parascéven Iudæórum, quia iuxta erat monuméntum, posuérunt Iesum.

And after these things, Joseph of Arimathea because he was a disciple of Jesus, but secretly for fear of the Jews besought Pilate that he might take away the body of Jesus. And Pilate gave leave. He came therefore and took away the body of Jesus. And Nicodemus also came he who at the first came to Jesus by night, bringing a mixture of myrrh and aloes, about a hundred pound weight. They took therefore the body of Jesus and bound it in linen cloths, with the spices, as the manner of the Jews is to bury. Now there was in the place where he was crucified, a garden: and in the garden a new sepulcher, wherein no man yet had been laid. There, therefore, because of the Parasceve of the Jews, they laid Jesus, because the sepulcher was nigh at hand.

PART II: SOLEMN COLLECTS

The celebrant puts on a black cope, the sacred ministers put on their black vestments, and the book is placed on the altar. At Flectámus génua, *all kneel until* Leváte.

For the Church

ORÉMUS, dilectíssimi nobis, pro Ecclésia sancta Dei: ut eam Deus et Dóminus noster pacificáre, adunáre, et custodíre dignétur toto orbe terrárum: subíciens ei principátus et potestátes: detque nobis quiétam et tranquíllam vitam degéntibus, glorificáre Deum, Patrem omnipoténtem.

Let us pray, dearly beloved, for the holy Church of God: that our Lord and God may deign to give it peace, keep it in unity, and guard it throughout the world, subjecting principalities and powers to it: and may grant unto us that, leading a peaceful and quiet life, we may glorify God, the Father almighty.

Orémus.

Flectámus génua.

Leváte.

Omnípotens sempitérne Deus, qui glóriam tuam ómnibus in Christo géntibus revelásti: custódi ópera misericórdiæ tuæ; ut Ecclésia tua, toto orbe diffúsa, stábili fide in confessióne tui nóminis persevéret. Per eúndem Dóminum.

℞. Amen.

Let us pray.

Let us kneel.

Arise.

Almighty and everlasting God, who in Christ hast revealed thy glory to all nations: guard the works of thy mercy; that thy Church, spread over the whole world, may with steadfast faith persevere in the confession of thy name: Through the same Lord.

For the Pope

ORÉMUS et pro beatíssimo Papa nostro *N.*; ut Deus et Dóminus noster, qui elégit eum in órdine episcopátus, salvum atque incólumem custódiat Ecclésiæ suæ sanctæ, ad regéndum pópulum sanctum Dei.

Orémus.

Flectámus génua.

Leváte.

Omnípotens sempitérne Deus, cuius iudício univérsa fundántur: réspice propítius ad preces nostras, et eléctum nobis Antístitem tua pietáte consérva; ut christiána plebs, quæ te gubernátur auctóre, sub tanto pontífice, credulitátis suæ méritis augeátur. Per Dóminum nostrum Iesum Christum, Fílium tuum: Qui tecum.

℞. Amen.

Let us pray also for our most blessed Pope *N.*, that our God and Lord, who chose him for the order of bishop, may keep him in health and safety for the Lord's holy Church, to govern the holy people of God.

Let us pray.

Let us kneel.

Arise.

Almighty and everlasting God, by whose judgment all things have been established: favorably regard our supplications, and in thy loving-kindness, preserve unto us our chosen bishop; so that the Christian people, who by thine authority are governed by so great a pontiff, may be continually enriched by the growing merits of their faith. Through our Lord.

For the Clergy and the Faithful

ORÉMUS et pro ómnibus epíscopis, presbýteris, diacónibus, subdiacónibus, acólythis, exorcístis, lectóribus, ostiáriis,

Let us pray also for all bishops, priests, deacons, subdeacons, acolytes, exorcists, lectors, porters, confessors, virgins and widows: and for all God's holy people.

confessóribus, virgínibus, víduis: et pro omni pópulo sancto Dei.

Orémus.

Flectámus génua.

Leváte.

Omnípotens sempitérne Deus, cuius Spíritu totum corpus Ecclésiæ sanctificátur et régitur: exáudi nos pro univérsis ordínibus supplicántes; ut grátiæ tuæ múnere, ab ómnibus tibi grádibus fidéliter serviátur. Per Dóminum nostrum...in unitáte eiúsdem.

℟. Amen.

Let us pray.

Let us kneel.

Arise.

Almighty and everlasting God, whose Spirit sanctifies and rules the whole body of the Church: graciously hear our pleas for all its orders; that by thy gift of grace, those of all types may serve thee faithfully. Through our Lord...in the unity of the same.

For Rulers

Orémus et pro ómnibus res públicas moderántibus, eorúmque ministériis et potestátibus: ut Deus et Dóminus noster mentes et corda eórum secúndum voluntátem suam dírigat ad nostram perpétuam pacem.

Orémus.

Flectámus génua.

Leváte.

Omnípotens sempitérne Deus, in cuius manu sunt ómnium potestátes et ómnium iura populórum: réspice benígnus ad eos, qui nos in potestáte regunt; ut ubíque terrárum, déxtera tua protegénte, et religiónis intégritas, et pátriæ secúritas indesinénter consístat. Per Dóminum nostrum Iesum Christum.

℟. Amen.

Let us pray also for all who govern the state, and their ministers and officials: that our God and Lord may direct their minds and hearts to seek perpetual peace for us, according to his will.

Let us pray.

Let us kneel.

Arise.

Almighty and everlasting God, in whose hand lies all the powers and the rights of peoples: look favorably on those who govern with power over us; that, by the protection of thy right hand, throughout all lands both the integrity of religion and the security of homelands may remain continually secure. Through our Lord Jesus Christ, thy Son.

For Catechumens

Orémus et pro catechúmenis nostris: ut Deus et Dóminus noster adapériat aures præcordiórum ipsórum ianuámque misericórdiæ; ut, per lavácrum regeneratiónis accépta remissióne ómnium peccatórum, et ipsi inveniántur in Christo Iesu, Dómino nostro.

Let us pray also for our catechumens: that our Lord and God may open the ears of their hearts for his mercy to enter in; that by the laver of regeneration they may receive forgiveness for all their sins, and that they may be found members of Jesus Christ, our Lord.

Orémus.
Flectámus génua.
Leváte.

Let us pray.
Let us kneel.
Arise.

Omnípotens sempitérne Deus, qui Ecclésiam tuam nova semper prole fecúndas: auge fidem et intelléctum catechúmenis nostris; ut, renáti fonte baptísmatis, adoptiónis tuæ fíliis aggregéntur. Per Dóminum nostrum.

℟. Amen.

Almighty and everlasting God, who causest thy Church to be ever fruitful with new offspring: increase the faith and understanding of our catechumens; that, reborn by the baptismal font, they may be numbered among thine adopted children. Through our Lord.

For the Needs of the Faithful

Orémus, dilectíssimi nobis, Deum Patrem omnipoténtem, ut cunctis mundum purget erróribus: morbos áuferat: famem depéllat: apériat cárceres: víncula dissólvat: peregrinántibus réditum: infirmántibus sanitátem: navigántibus portum salútis indúlgeat.

Let us pray, most dearly beloved, to God, the Father almighty, that he may cleanse the world of all errors: drive away maladies, hinder famines, open prison gates, break the chains of captives; grant to travelers a safe return, health to the sick, and a safe harbor to those at sea.

Orémus.
Flectámus génua.
Leváte.

Let us pray.
Let us kneel.
Arise.

Omnípotens sempitérne Deus, mæstórum consolátio, laborántium fortitúdo: pervéniant ad te preces de quacúmque tribulatióne clamántium; ut omnes sibi in necessitátibus suis misericórdiam tuam gáudeant

Almighty and everlasting God, comfort of the sorrowful, support of the weary: may the prayers of all who in their trouble cry out, come before thee; that all may rejoice that in their hour of need, thy mercy was at hand. Through our

affuísse. Per Dóminum.

℟. Amen.

For the Unity of the Church

Orémus et pro hæréticis et schismáticis: ut Deus et Dóminus noster éruat eos ab erróribus univérsis; et ad sanctam matrem Ecclésiam cathólicam atque apostólicam revocáre dignétur.

Orémus.
Flectámus génua.
Leváte.

Omnípotens sempitérne Deus, qui salvas omnes, et néminem vis períre: réspice ad ánimas diabólica fraude decéptas; ut, omni hærética pravitáte depósita, errántium corda resipíscant, et ad veritátis tuæ rédeant unitátem. Per Dñum.

℟. Amen.

Let us pray also for heretics and schismatics: that our Lord and God would free them of their errors; and deign to call them back to their mother, the holy, Catholic, and apostolic Church.

Let us pray.
Let us kneel.
Arise.

Almighty and everlasting God, who savest all, and willest not that any man perish: look down in pity upon the souls led astray and deceived by the devil; that, putting aside all depraved heresy, the hearts of those in error may be revived, and return to the unity of thy truth. Through our Lord.

For the Conversion of Jews

Orémus et pro Iudǽis: ut Deus et Dóminus noster illúminet corda eórum, ut agnóscant Iesum Christum salvatórem ómnium hóminum.

Orémus.
Flectámus génua.
Leváte.

Omnípotens sempitérne Deus, qui vis ut omnes hómines salvi fiant et ad agnitiónem veritátis véniant, concéde propítius, ut plenitúdine géntium in Ecclésiam tuam intránte omnis Israël salvus fiat. Per Dóminum. ℟. Amen.

Let us pray also for the Jews: that our Lord and God may illuminate their hearts, that they may acknowledge Jesus Christ as the Savior of all men.

Let us pray.
Let us kneel.
Arise.

Almighty and eternal God, who willest that all men be saved and come to recognize the truth, graciously grant, that as the fullness of peoples enters thy Church, all Israel may be saved. Through our Lord.

Lord Jesus Christ.

For the Conversion of Unbelievers

O RÉMUS et pro pagánis: ut Deus omnípotens áuferat iniquitátem a córdibus eó-rum; ut, relíctis idólis suis, conver-tántur ad Deum vivum et verum, et únicum Fílium eius Iesum Christum, Deum et Dóminum nostrum.

Orémus.

Flectámus génua.

Leváte.

O mnípotens sempitérne Deus, qui non mortem peccatórum, sed vitam semper inquíris: súscipe propí-tius oratiónem nostram, et líbera eos ab idolórum cultúra; et ággrega Ec-clésiæ tuæ sanctæ, ad laudem et gló-riam nóminis tui. Per Dóminum no-strum Iesum Christum, Fílium tuum: Qui tecum vivit et regnat in unitá-te Spíritus Sancti Deus, per ómnia sǽcula sæculórum.

℟. Amen.

Let us pray also for pagans: that almighty God would drive iniquity from their hearts; that, forsaking their idols, they may turn to the living and true God, and to his only Son, Jesus Christ, our Lord and God.

Let us pray.

Let us kneel.

Arise.

Almighty and everlasting God, who al-ways seekest the life, not the death, of sinners: mercifully receive our prayer, and free them from the cult of idols; and gather them into thy holy Church, to the praise and glory of thy name. Through our Lord Jesus Christ, thy Son: Who lives and reigns with thee in the unity of the Holy Spirit, one God, forever and ever.

PART III: THE ADORATION OF THE HOLY CROSS

After the solemn collects, the sacred ministers remove their black vestments in the sanctuary. Then the deacon (or the celebrant) goes with the acolytes to the sacristy. He returns in procession with a large Cross, veiled in violet, flanked by acolytes with lighted candles.

The celebrant receives the Cross in the sanctuary and goes to the Epistle side near the altar, below the steps. He unveils the top of the Cross, then intones the antiphon Ecce lignum crucis *by himself, and continues it together with the sacred ministers. The choir and the congregation sing the* ℟. Veníte adorémus. *After this, all kneel and adore the Cross for a short time.*

Antiphon at the Unveiling of the Cross

Cce lí- gnum Cru- cis, in quo sa- lus mun-di
pe-pén- dit

Behold the wood of the Cross, on which has hung the world's salvation.

All standing, answer:

℟. Ve- ní- te, ad- o- ré- mus. *Kneel.*

O come, let us adore him.

The Cross is shown a second and third time—at the corner of the altar, then in the center—with the antiphon and response sung a tone higher each time.

The Reproaches

The choir, divided into two, sings the following chants for as long as the adoration of the Cross continues.[1] The singing always ends with the doxology from the hymn Pange, língua...certáminis, *p. 164*

I

Two cantors, from the middle of the choir:

℣. Mi 6: 3-4

Opu-le me-us, quid fe- ci ti-bi? Aut in quo
contristá-vi te? Respón-de mi-hi. ℣. Qui- a e-dú- xi te

---

[1]Adoration of the Cross at the altar (celebrant, sacred ministers, clergy, and servers) consists of removing the shoes and making a simple genuflection three times before kissing the Cross. When the Cross is moved to the entrance of the sanctuary, the men then the women process up, genuflect once, and kiss the Cross.

de ter-ra　　Ægýpti: pa- rá-　　sti Crucem　Salva-tó- ri

tu- o.

O my people, what is it I have done unto thee? Or how have I grieved thee? Answer me. ℣. It is because I brought thee out of Egyptian lands: thou hast made ready a cross for thy Savior.

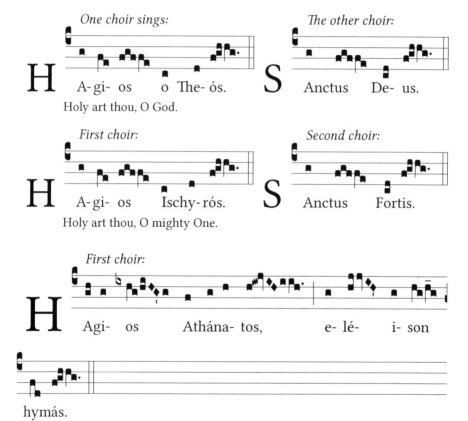

One choir sings:

H A- gi- os　　o The- ós.
Holy art thou, O God.

The other choir:

S Anctus　De- us.

First choir:

H A- gi- os　　Ischy- rós.
Holy art thou, O mighty One.

Second choir:

S Anctus　Fortis.

First choir:

H Agi- os　　Athána- tos,　　e- lé- i- son

hymás.

Second choir:

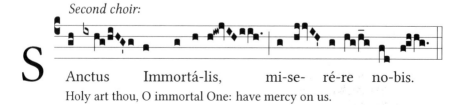

S Anctus　Immortá-lis,　mi-se- ré-re　no-bis.
Holy art thou, O immortal One: have mercy on us.

Two cantors of the second choir:

Qui- a e-dú- xi te per de-sér- tum quadra-gínta annis, et manna ci-bá-vi te, et intro-dú-xi in ter- ram sa-tis óptimam: pa-rá- sti Crucem Salva-tó- ri tu- o.

It is because for forty years I led thee through the wilderness, fed thee with manna, and brought thee into a land of plenty: thou hast made ready a cross for thy Savior.

The two choirs respond, in turn, Hágios o Theós, *etc.,* Sanctus Deus, *etc., as above.*

Two cantors of the first choir:

Quid ultra dé-bu- i fá-ce-re ti-bi, et non fe-ci? E- go qui-dem plan-tá-vi te ví-ne- am me- am spe-ci- o- sís-simam: et tu facta es mi-hi ni-mis amá- ra: a-cé-to namque si-tim me- am po-tá-sti: et lánce-a perfo-rásti la-tus Salva-tó- ri tu- o.

Hágios o Theós, etc.

What more ought I have done for thee, and did not do? Indeed, I planted thee to be the most beautiful of my vineyards: yet thou hast turned exceeding bitter to me: for, I was athirst and thou didst give me vinegar to drink: and with a lance didst pierce thy Savior's side.

II

The following Reproaches are sung in turn by sets of two cantors from each choir. After each verse, the two choirs together reply Pópule meus, *as below.*

Two cantors of the second choir:

E-go propter te flagellá-vi Ægýptum cum primogé-ni-tis su- is: et tu me flagellá-tum tra-di-dísti.

I scourged Egypt for thy sake, with her first-born sons: and thou didst scourge me and hand me over.

Both choirs repeat:

Opu-le me- us, quid fe- ci ti-bi? Aut in quo contristá-vi te? Respón-de mi-hi.

O my people, what is it I have done unto thee? Or how have I grieved thee? Answer me.

Two cantors of the first choir:

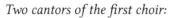

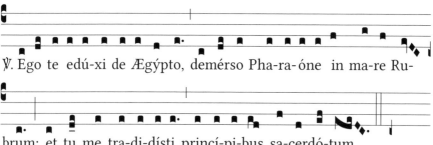

℣. Ego te edú-xi de Ægýpto, demérso Pha-ra-óne in ma-re Rubrum: et tu me tra-di-dísti princí-pi-bus sa-cerdó-tum.

Both choirs: Pópule meus.

I led thee out of Egypt, and drowned Pharaoh in the Red Sea: and thou hast handed me over to the chief priests.

Two cantors of the second choir:

℣. Ego ante te apé-ru- i ma- re: et tu ape-ru- ísti lánce- a la-tus me-um. Pópule meus.

I opened the sea before thee: and thou hast opened my side with a lance.

Two cantors of the first choir:

℣. Ego ante te præ-í-vi in co-lúmna nu- bis: et tu me du-xí- sti ad prætó-ri- um Pi-lá-ti. Pópule meus.

I went before thee in a pillar of cloud: and thou hast led me into the judgment hall of Pilate.

Two cantors of the second choir:

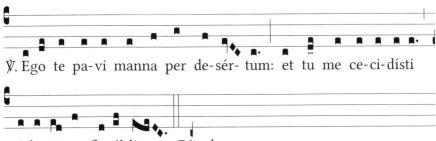

℣. Ego te pa-vi manna per de-sér- tum: et tu me ce-ci-dísti á-la-pis et flagél-lis. Pópule meus.

I fed thee with manna in the wilderness: and thou hast rained blows and scourges on me.

Two cantors of the first choir:

℣. Ego te po-tá-vi   aqua sa-lú-tis de pe- tra: et tu me po-tásti

fel-le   et a-cé-to.   Pópule meus.

I gave thee for drink saving water from the rock: and thou hast given me for drink gall and vinegar.

Two cantors of the second choir:

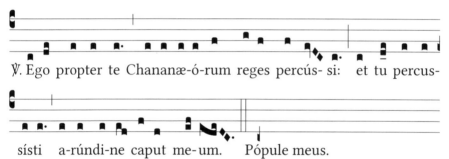

℣. Ego propter te Chananæ-ó-rum reges percús- si: et tu percus-

sísti   a-rúndi-ne caput me-um.   Pópule meus.

I struck down the kings of Canaan for thy sake: and thou hast struck my head with a reed.

Two cantors of the first choir:

℣. Ego de-di ti-bi sceptrum regá- le: et tu de-dísti cá-pi-ti me-

o spí-ne- am co-rónam.   Pópule meus.

I gave to thee a royal scepter: and thou didst give my head a crown of thorns.

Two cantors of the second choir:

℣. Ego te exaltá-vi magna virtú- te: et tu me suspendísti in

pa-tí-bu-lo Cru-cis. Pópule meus.

I raised thee up with great strength: and thou hast hanged me on the gibbet of the cross.

III

Both choirs then sing:

℣. cf. Ps 66

Ant. IV.

Crucem tu-am * ado-rámus, Dó-mi-ne: et sanctam re-

surrecti- ónem tu-am laudámus et glo-ri- fi-cámus: ecce e-nim

propter lignum ve- nit gáudi- um in u-ni-vérso mundo.

Ps. De- us mi-se-re- á-tur nostri, et be-ne-dí-cat no-bis: * illú-

mi-net vultum su-um super nos, et mi-se-re- á-tur nostri.

Repeat Ant. Crucem tuam.

Thy Cross, O Lord, we adore: and thy holy resurrection we laud and magnify: for behold, by the wood [of the Cross], joy has come into all the world *Ps.* May God have mercy on us and bless us: may he cause the light of his countenance to shine upon us, and have mercy on us.

IV

And then the ℣. Crux fidélis[2] *is sung with the hymn* Pange lingua...certámi-nis, *as below. After the first stanza of the hymn, the* ℣. Crux fidélis *is re-peated as far as* * Dulce lignum; *after the second stanza,* Dulce lignum *is repeated.*

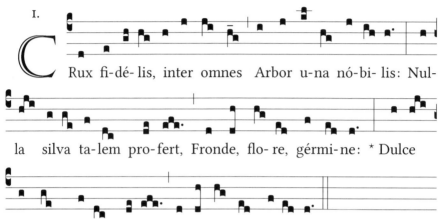

Rux fi-dé- lis, inter omnes Arbor u-na nó-bi- lis: Nul-la silva ta-lem pro-fert, Fronde, flo- re, gérmi-ne: * Dulce lignum, dulces clavos, Dulce pondus sústi-net.

Faithful Cross! above all other, One and only noble Tree! None in foliage, none in blossom, None in fruit thy peer may be; Sweetest Wood and sweetest Iron! Sweetest Weight is hung on thee.

Hymn

Ange, lingua, glo-ri- ó- si Præ-li- um certámi-nis, Et su- per Cru-cis trophæ-um Dic tri- úmphum nó-bi- lem: Quá-li- ter Red-émptor orbis Immo-lá- tus ví-ce-rit.

Repeat Crux fidélis *as far as* * Dulce lignum.

Sing, my tongue, the glorious battle Sing the last, the dread affray; O'er the Cross, the victor's trophy, Sound the high triumphal lay: Tell how Christ, the world's Redeemer, As a victim won the day.

---

[2]The text here is the restored version from the 1908 Vatican Edition Gradual. For the hymn with the revised verses as in the Roman Breviary and the Roman Missal, *Pange, lingua...láuream,* see the Appendix, p. 275.

2. De pa-réntis pro-toplá-sti Fraude Factor cóndo-lens, Quando

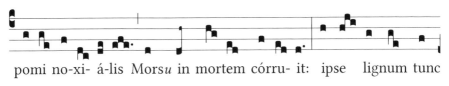

pomi no-xi- á-lis Mors*u* in mortem córru- it: ipse   lignum tunc

no-tá-vit, Damna lign*i* ut sólve-ret. * Dulce lignum.

God, His Maker, sorely grieving That the first-made Adam fell, When he ate the fruit of sorrow, Whose reward was death and hell, Noted then this Wood, the ruin Of the ancient wood to quell.

3. Hoc opus nostræ sa-lú- tis   Ordo de-po-pósce-rat: Multi- fór-

mis pro-di-tó-ris   Ars ut ar-tem fál-le-ret: Et me- dé-lam ferret

inde,   Hostis unde læ-se-rat. Crux fidélis.

For the work of our salvation Needs would have his order so, And the multiform deceiver's Art by art would overthrow, And from thence would bring the med'cine Whence the insult of the foe.

4. Quando ve-nit ergo sa-cri Ple-ni-tú-do témpo-ris, Missus   est

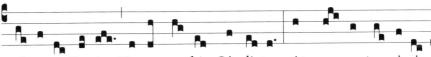

ab arce Patris Na-tus, or-bis Cóndi-tor: Atque   ventre virgi-

ná-li   Ca-ro fa-ctus pró-di- it. * Dulce lignum.

Wherefore, when the sacred fullness Of the appointed time was come, This world's Maker left his Father, Sent the heav'nly mansion from, And proceeded, God Incarnate, Of the Virgin's holy womb.

5. Va-git infans inter arcta Cóndi-tus præ-sé-pi- a: Membra

pannis invo-lú-ta   Virgo Ma- ter ál-li-gat: Et ma- nus pe-

désque et cru-ra Stricta cingit fásci- a. Crux fidélis.

Weeps the Infant in the manger That in Bethlehem's stable stands; And his limbs the Virgin Mother Doth compose in swaddling bands, Meetly thus in linen folding Of her God the feet and hands.

6. Lustris sex qui iam per-á-ctis, Tempus implens córpo-ris:

Se vo- lénte na-tus ad hoc, Passi- ó- ni dé-di-tus, Agnus   in

Cru-cis le-vá-tur   Immo-lándus stí-pi-te. * Dulce lignum.

Thirty years among us dwelling, His appointed time fulfilled, Born for this, He meets his Passion, For this that he freely willed: On the Cross the Lamb is lifted, Where his life-blood shall be spilled.

7. Hic a-cé-tum, fel, a-rúndo, Spu-ta, cla-vi, lánce- a: Mi-te cor-

pus perfo-rá-tur, Sanguis, unda pró-flu- it: Terra, pontus, astra,

mundus, Quo la-vántur flúmi-ne! Crux fidélis.

He endured the nails, the spitting, Vinegar, and spear, and reed; From that holy Body broken Blood and water forth proceed: Earth, and stars, and sky, and ocean, By that flood from stain are free.

8. Flecte ramos, arbor al-ta, Tensa la-xa vísce-ra: Et ri- gor len-

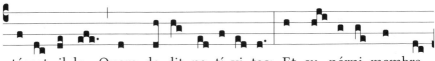

téscat il- le, Quem de-dit na-tí-vi-tas: Et su- pérni membra

Re-gis Mi-ti tendas stí-pi-te. * Dulce lignum.

Bend thy boughs, O Tree of glory! Thy relaxing sinews bend; For awhile the ancient rigor, That thy birth bestowed, suspend; And the King of heavenly beauty On thy bosom gently tend!

9. So-la digna tu fu- í-sti Ferre sæcli pré-ti- um, Atque portum

præpa-rá-re Nauta mundo náufra-go: Quem sa- cer cru- or per-

únxit, Fusus Agni córpo-re. Crux fidélis.

Thou alone wast counted worthy This world's ransom to uphold; For a ship-wrecked race preparing Harbor, like the Ark of old; With the sacred Blood anointed From the smitten lamb that rolled.

¶ *The doxology is never omitted:*

10. Gló-ri- a et honor De- o   Usquequáque Al-tís-simo: Una

Pa-tri, Fi- li- óque,   Incly-to Pa-rá-cli-to: Cu- i   laus est et pot-

éstas Per æ-térna sǽ-cu-la.   A-men. * Dulce lignum.

Praise and honor to the Father, Praise and honor to the Son, Praise and honor to the Spirit, Ever Three, and ever One, One in Might and One in Glory, While eternal ages run.

PART IV: HOLY COMMUNION

After all have adored the Cross, it is placed at the center of the altar, together with the acolytes' lighted candles. The sacred ministers remove their black stoles and put on violet Mass vestments.

The deacon (or if there is no deacon, the celebrant himself) goes to the altar of repose with the acolytes. All wait in silence until they return. As they come back to sanctuary with the Blessed Sacrament, all kneel and the choir sings the following antiphons:

1 Ant.

I.

12th *c.*

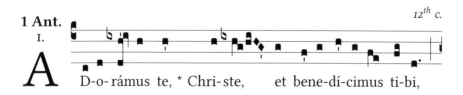

A

D-o- rámus te, * Chri- ste,   et bene-dí-cimus ti-bi,

qui- a per Crucem tu-am redemí-sti mundum.

We adore thee, O Christ, and we bless thee: for by thy Cross, thou hast redeemed the world.

11th c.

2 Ant.
VIII.

P ER lignum * servi fa- cti su- mus, et per sanctam Cru-

cem li-be-rá- ti su- mus: fructus ár-bo-ris se-dú-xit nos, Fí-li- us

De- i red-   émit nos.

Through the wood [of a tree] were we enslaved, and through the holy Cross have we been set free: the fruit of the tree deceived us, the Son of God hast redeemed us.

11th c.

3 Ant.
VII.

S Alvá-tor mundi, salva nos: * qui per Crucem et Sán-

gui-nem rede-místi nos, auxi-li- á-re no-bis, te depre-cámur,

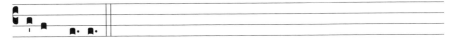

De- us noster.

Save us, Savior of the world: thou who by thy Cross and Blood, didst redeem us, help us, we pray thee, our God.

The celebrant, with hands joined:

Orémus. Præcéptis salutáribus móniti, et divína institutióne formáti, audémus dícere:	Let us pray. Instructed by thy saving precepts, and following thy divine institution, we presume to say:

Together, all present continue with him:

Pater noster, qui es in cælis:
Sanctificétur nomen tuum.
Advéniat regnum tuum.
Fiat volúntas tua, sicut in cælo, et in terra.
Panem nostrum cotidiánum da nobis hódie:
Et dimítte nobis débita nostra,
sicut et nos dimíttimus debitóribus nostris.
Et ne nos indúcas in tentatiónem;
sed líbera nos a malo. | Amen.

Then the celebrant, with hands extended, continues alone:

Líbera nos, quǽsumus, Dómine, ab ómnibus malis, prætéritis, præséntibus et futúris: et intercedénte beáta et gloriósa semper Vírgine Dei Genetríce María, cum beátis Apóstolis tuis Petro et Paulo, atque Andréa, et ómnibus Sanctis, da propítius pacem in diébus nostris: ut, ope misericórdiæ tuæ adiúti, et a peccáto simus semper líberi et ab omni perturbatióne secúri. Per eúndem Dóminum nostrum Iesum Christum, Fílium tuum: Qui tecum vivit et regnat in unitáte Spíritus Sancti Deus, per ómnia sǽcula sæculórum.
℟. Amen.

Deliver us, we beseech thee, O Lord, from all evils, past, present, and to come; and by the intercession of the blessed and glorious Mary, ever Virgin, Mother of God, together with thy holy Apostles, Peter and Paul, and Andrew and of all the saints, mercifully grant peace in our days, that through the assistance of thy mercy we may be always free from sin, and secure from all disturbance. Through the same our Lord Jesus Christ, thy Son: Who lives and reigns with thee in the unity of the Holy Spirit, one God, forever and ever.

Then the celebrant adds, in a low voice:

Percéptio Córporis tui, Dómine Iesu Christe, quod ego indígnus súmere præsúmo, non mihi provéniat in iudícium et condemnatiónem: sed pro tua pietáte prosit mihi ad tutaméntum mentis et córporis, et ad medélam percipiéndam: Qui vivis et regnas cum Deo Patre, in unitáte Spíritus Sancti, Deus, per ómnia sǽcula sæculórum. Amen.

Let not the partaking of thy Body, O Lord Jesus Christ, which I, all unworthy, presume to receive, turn to my judgment and condemnation; but through thy goodness, may it be to me a safeguard and remedy, both of soul and body: Who live and reign with God the Father, in the unity of the Holy Spirit, one God, forever and ever. Amen.

He uncovers the ciborium, genuflects, takes one of the hosts holding it over the ciborium, bows and striking his breast says three times:

Dómine, non sum dignus, ut intres sub tectum meum: sed tantum dic verbo, et sanábitur ánima mea.	Lord, I am not worthy that thou shouldst enter under my roof; say but the word, and my soul shall be healed.

He then signs himself with the Blessed Sacrament, and adds in a low voice:

Corpus Dómini nostri Iesu Christi custódiat ánimam meam in vitam ætérnam. Amen.	The Body of our Lord Jesus Christ preserve my soul unto life everlasting. Amen.

He then receives Holy Communion.

The deacon, together with all present, say the Confíteor *in the usual way:*

Confíteor Deo omnipoténti, beátæ Maríæ semper Vírgini, beáto Michaéli Archángelo, beáto Ioánni Baptístæ, sanctis Apóstolis Petro et Paulo, ómnibus Sanctis, et tibi pater: quia peccávi nimis cogitatióne, verbo et ópere: mea culpa, mea culpa, mea máxima culpa. Ideo precor beátam Maríam semper Vírginem, beátum Michaélem Archángelum, beátum Ioánnem Baptístam, sanctos Apóstolos Petrum et Paulum, omnes Sanctos, et te pater, oráre pro me ad Dóminum Deum nostrum.	I confess to almighty God, to blessed Mary ever Virgin, to blessed Michael the Archangel, to blessed John the Baptist, to the holy Apostles Peter and Paul, to all the saints, and to thee, father, that I have sinned exceedingly in thought, word and deed: through my fault, through my fault, through my most grievous fault. Therefore I beseech blessed Mary, ever Virgin, blessed Michael the Archangel, blessed John the Baptist, the holy Apostles Peter and Paul, all the saints, and thee, father, to pray for me to the Lord our God.

The celebrant genuflects, turns towards the people and says the absolution:

Misereátur vestri omnípotens Deus, et, dimíssis peccátis vestris, perdúcat vos ad vitam ætérnam.	May the almighty God have mercy upon you, forgive you your sins, and bring you to life everlasting.

℞. Amen.

Indulgéntiam, absolutiónem ✠ et remissiónem peccatórum vestrórum tríbuat vobis omnípotens et miséricors Dóminus.	May the almighty and merciful Lord grant you pardon, absolution, and remission of your sins.

℞. Amen.

The celebrant turns towards the altar, genuflects, and takes the ciborium; he turns towards the people in the usual way in the middle of the altar and says:

Ecce Agnus Dei, ecce qui tollit peccáta mundi.

Behold, the Lamb of God, behold him who taketh away the sins of the world.

And then he adds, three times: Dómine, non sum dignus, *as above.*

And then Holy Communion is distributed, as on Holy Thursday. During this, Psalm 21 *may be sung, as below, or any of the responsories from Matins of Good Friday, p.* 270

Psalm 21

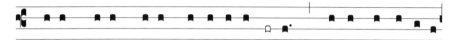

1. De- us, De- us me- us, réspi-ce in me: † qua-re me de-*re-li-*

quí- sti?* longe a sa-lú-te me-a verba de-lictó-rum me-ó- rum.

O God my God, look upon me: why hast thou forsaken me? Far from my salvation are the words of my sins.

2. Deus meus, clamábo per diem, et *non exáu*dies: * et nocte, et non ad insipiéntiam **mi**hi.

O my God, I shall cry by day, and thou wilt not hear: and by night, and it shall not be reputed as folly in me.

3. Tu autem in *sancto* **há**bitas: * laus Israël.

But thou dwellest in the holy place, the praise of Israel.

4. In te speravérunt *patres* **no**-stri: * speravérunt, et liberásti **e**os.

In thee have our fathers hoped: they have hoped, and thou hast delivered them.

5. Ad te clamavérunt, et *sal-vi* **fa**cti sunt: * in te speravérunt, et non sunt confúsi.

They cried to thee, and they were saved: they trusted in thee, and were not confounded.

6. Ego autem sum vermis, *et non* **ho**mo: * oppróbrium hóminum, et abiéctio **ple**bis.

But I am a worm, and no man: the reproach of men, and the outcast of the people.

7. Omnes vidéntes me *derisé-*
runt me: * locúti sunt lábiis, et
movérunt **ca**put.

All they that saw me have laughed
me to scorn: they have spoken with
the lips, and wagged the head.

8. Sperávit in Dómino, erí*pi-*
at **e**um: * salvum fáciat eum,
quóniam vult **e**um.

He hoped in the Lord, let him deliver
him: let him save him, seeing he
delighteth in him.

9. Quóniam tu es, qui extraxísti
me de **ven**tre: * spes mea ab
ubéribus matris **me**æ.

For thou art he that hast drawn me
out of the womb: my hope from the
breasts of my mother.

10. In te proiéctus sum ex
útero: † de ventre matris
meæ Deus *meus* **es** tu, * ne
discésseris **a** me:

I was cast upon thee from the womb:
from my mother's womb thou art my
God, depart not from me.

11. Quóniam tribulátio *próxi-*
ma est: * quóniam non est qui
ádiuvet.

For tribulation is very near: for there
is none to help me.

12. Circumdedérunt me *vítu-*
li **mul**ti: * tauri pingues
obse**dé**runt me.

Many calves have surrounded me: fat
bulls have besieged me.

13. Aperuérunt super *me os* **su**-
um: * sicut leo rápiens et
rúgiens.

They have opened their mouths
against me, as a lion ravening and
roaring.

14. Sicut a*qua ef***fú**sus sum: * et
dispérsa sunt ómnia ossa **me**a.

I am poured out like water; and all
my bones are scattered.

15. Factum est cor meum tamquam ce*ra liqué*scens: * in
médio ventris **me**i.

My heart is become like wax melting
in the midst of my bowels.

16. Aruit tamquam testa virtus
mea, † et lingua mea adhǽsit
fáu*cibus* **me**is: * et in púlverem
mortis dedu**xí**sti me.

My strength is dried up like a
potsherd, and my tongue hath
cleaved to my jaws: and thou hast
brought me down into the dust of
death.

17. Quóniam circumdedérunt me
canes **mul**ti: * concílium
malignántium ob**sé**dit me.

For many dogs have encompassed me:
the council of the malignant hath
besieged me.

18. Fodérunt manus meas et *pedes* **me**os: * dinumeravérunt ómnia ossa **me**a. | They have dug my hands and feet. They have numbered all my bones.

19. Ipsi vero consideravérunt et inspexérunt me: † divisérunt sibi vesti*ménta* **me**a, * et super vestem meam misérunt **sor**tem. | And they have looked and stared upon me: they parted my garments amongst them; and upon my vesture they cast lots.

20. Tu autem, Dómine, ne elongáveris auxílium *tuum* **a** me: * ad defensiónem meam **cón**spice. | But thou, O Lord, remove not thy help to a distance from me; look towards my defense.

21. Erue a frámea, Deus, *ánimam* **me**am: * et de manu canis únicam **me**am. | Deliver, O God, my soul from the sword: my only one from the hand of the dog.

22. Salva me ex o*re* leó-nis: * et a córnibus unicórnium humilitátem **me**am. | Save me from the lion's mouth; and my lowness from the horns of the unicorns.

23. Narrábo nomen tuum frá*tri-bus* **me**is: * in médio Ecclésiæ lau**dá**bo te. | I will declare thy name to my brethren: in the midst of the church will I praise thee.

24. Qui timétis Dóminum, lau*dá-te* **e**um: * univérsum semen Iacob, glorificáte **e**um. | Ye that fear the Lord, praise him: all ye the seed of Jacob, glorify him.

25. Tímeat eum omne *semen* **Is**raël: * quóniam non sprevit, neque despéxit deprecatiónem **páu**peris: | Let all the seed of Israel fear him: because he hath not slighted nor despised the supplication of the poor man.

26. Nec avértit fáciem *su-am* **a** me: * et cum clamárem ad eum, exau**dí**vit me. | Neither hath he turned away his face from me: and when I cried to him he heard me.

27. Apud te laus mea in ecclé*si-a* **ma**gna: * vota mea reddam in conspéctu timéntium **e**um. | With thee is my praise in a great church: I will pay my vows in the sight of them that fear him.

28. Edent páuperes, et saturabúntur: † et laudábunt Dóminum qui re*quírunt* **e**um: * vi-
vent corda eórum in sǽculum
sǽculi.

The poor shall eat and shall be filled:
and they shall praise the Lord that
seek him: their hearts shall live for
ever and ever.

29. Reminiscéntur et convertén-
tur ad **Dó**minum * univérsi
fines **ter**ræ:

All the ends of the earth shall
remember, and shall be converted to
the Lord.

30. Et adorábunt in con*spé*-
ctu **e**ius * univérsæ famíliæ
Géntium.

And all the kindreds of the Gentiles
shall adore in his sight.

31. Quóniam Dómi*ni est* **re**-
gnum: * et ipse dominábitur
Géntium.

For the kingdom is the Lord's; and
he shall have dominion over the
nations.

32. Manducavérunt et adora-
vérunt omnes *pingues* **ter**-
ræ: * in conspéctu eius cadent omnes qui descéndunt in
terram.

All the fat ones of the earth have
eaten and have adored: all they that
go down to the earth shall fall before
him.

33. Et ánima mea *illi* **vi**-
vet: * et semen meum sérviet
ipsi.

And to him my soul shall live: and
my seed shall serve him.

34. Annuntiábitur Dómino generátio ventúra: † et annuntiábunt cæli iustítiam eius pópulo *qui na*scé*tur, * quem fecit
Dóminus.

There shall be declared to the Lord a
generation to come: and the heavens
shall show forth his justice to a
people that shall be born, which the
Lord hath made.

After the Communion, the vessels are purified in the usual way. The ciborium is placed in the tabernacle.

The book is placed in the center of the altar, and the celebrant and sacred ministers go to it and the following Collects are sung:

Orémus.

Super pópulum tuum quǽsumus, Dómine, qui passiónem et mortem Fílii tui devóta mente recóluit, benedíctio copiósa descéndat, indulgéntia véniat, consolátio tribuátur, fides sancta succréscat, redémptio sempitérna firmétur. Per eúndem Christum Dóminum nostrum.

℟. Amen.

Let us pray.

May abundant blessing descend, we beseech thee O Lord, upon thy people, who have devoutly recalled to mind the passion and death of thy Son; may they receive indulgent pardon, be given consolation and an increase in holy faith, and may their eternal redemption be made secure. Through the same Christ our Lord.

Orémus.

Omnípotens et miséricors Deus, qui Christi tui beáta passióne et morte nos reparásti: consérva in nobis óperam misericórdiæ tuæ; ut huius mystérii participatióne, perpétua devotióne vivámus. Per eúndem Christum Dóminum nostrum.

℟. Amen.

Let us pray.

Almighty and merciful God, who hast renewed us by the blessed passion and death of thy Christ: maintain in us the work of thy mercy; that by sharing in this mystery, we may live in continual and devoted fidelity. Through the same Christ our Lord.

Orémus.

Reminíscere miseratiónum tuárum, Dómine, et fámulos tuos ætérna protectióne sanctífica, pro quibus Christus, Fílius tuus, per suum cruórem instítuit paschále mystérium. Per eúndem Christum Dóminum nostrum.

℟. Amen.

Let us pray.

Be mindful of thy mercies, O Lord, and by thy eternal protection sanctify thy servants, for whom Christ, thy Son, instituted the paschal mystery through his blood. Through the same Christ our Lord.

The celebrant and sacred ministers go down from the altar, genuflect, and return to the sacristy with the acolytes and other servers.

Vespers is omitted, and Compline is recited in choir as on Holy Thursday, p. 125, without chant or lighted candles. Later, the Blessed Sacrament is brought privately from the altar to a place of reservation, and the altar is stripped—leaving only the Cross and candles.

HOLY SATURDAY

THE EASTER VIGIL

The altar is prepared with cloths and candlesticks. All of the candles and sanctuary lights are extinguished. The fire is lit from a flint and kindled at the church door, or on the porch, or even inside the church.

BLESSING OF THE NEW FIRE

The celebrant, wearing a violet cope, and the sacred ministers, in violet dalmatic and tunicle, process to the place of the fire with the cross, holy water, an empty thurible, and incense (including large grains for the candle). The celebrant blesses the new fire:

℣. Dóminus vobíscum.

℟. Et cum spíritu tuo.

Orémus.

DEUS, qui per Fílium tuum, angulárem scílicet lápidem, claritátis tuæ ignem fidélibus contulísti: prodúctum e sílice, nostris profutúrum úsibus, novum hunc ignem sanctí✠fica: et concéde nobis, ita per hæc festa paschália cæléstibus desidériis inflammári; ut ad perpétuæ claritátis, puris méntibus, valeámus festa pertíngere. Per eúndem Christum Dóminum nostrum.

℟. Amen.

The Lord be with you.

And with thy spirit.

Let us pray.

O God, who through thy Son, the corner-stone, hast bestowed upon the faithful thy burning brightness: sanctify this new fire, struck forth from a stone, for our benefit: and grant that we may be enkindled with the desire of heaven by these Easter festivals; so that we may prevail, pure in heart, to reach the festival of perpetual brightness. Through the same Christ our Lord.

In silence, the celebrant sprinkles the new fire with holy water. The thurible is filled with coals from the fire. The celebrant then imposes incense, blesses it, and incenses the new fire.

BLESSING OF THE PASCHAL CANDLE

The celebrant uses a stylus to cut a cross in the wax, saying:

1) Christus heri et hódie.	Christ yesterday and today.

(vertical line)

2) Princípium et Finis.	Beginning and End.

(horizontal line)

3) Alpha	Alpha

(above the vertical line: A)

4) et Omega;	and Omega;

(below the vertical line: Ω)

5) Ipsíus sunt témpora	His are the times

(first digit of current year in upper left angle)

6) et sǽcula.	and the ages

(second digit of current year in upper right angle)

7) Ipsi glória et impérium	To him be glory and dominion

(third digit of current year in lower left angle)

8) per univérsa æternitátis sǽcula. Amen.	through all ages of eternity. Amen.

(fourth digit of current year in lower right angle)

$$\begin{array}{c} \overset{3}{\underset{1}{\text{A}}} \\ {}^{5}\,2\;\Big|\;0\,{}^{6} \\ \rule{2cm}{0.4pt} \\ {}_{7}\,1\;\Big|\;7\,{}_{8} \\ \underset{4}{\Omega} \end{array}$$

The deacon presents the grains of incense to the celebrant. They are sprinkled with holy water and incensed. He then fixes them into the candle, saying:

$$\begin{array}{c} 1 \\ 4 \quad 2 \quad 5 \\ 3 \end{array}$$

1) Per sua sancta vúlnera	By his wounds, holy
2) gloriósa	and glorious,
3) custódiat	may he guard
4) et consérvet nos	and keep us,
5) Christus Dóminus. Amen.	Christ the Lord. Amen.

Then, the deacon, lights a small taper at the new fire, which the celebrant then uses to light the paschal candle, saying:

Lumen Christi glorióse resurgéntis	May the light of Christ, in glory rising,
Díssipet ténebras cordis et mentis.	Dispel darkness from hearts and minds.

The paschal candle is now blessed:

℣. Dóminus vobíscum.

The Lord be with you.

℟. Et cum spíritu tuo.

And with thy spirit.

Orémus.

Let us pray.

Véniat, quǽsumus, omnípotens Deus, super hunc incénsum céreum larga tuæ bene✠dictiónis infúsio: et hunc noctúrnum splendórem invisíbilis regenerátor inténde; ut non solum sacrifícium, quod hac nocte litátum est, arcána lúminis tui admixtióne refúlgeat; sed in quocúmque loco ex huius sanctificatiónis mystério áliquid fúerit deportátum, expúlsa diabólicæ fraudis nequítia, virtus tuæ maiestátis assístat. Per Christum Dóminum nostrum.

Upon this lighted candle, we beseech thee, almighty God, may there come an abundant outpouring of thy blessing: and do thou, who dost renew while unseen, kindle this nocturnal splendor; that not only the sacrifice, offered this night, may shine with the hidden mingling of thy light, but further, that into whatsoever place is brought anything from the mystery of this sanctification, the devil's cunning may be driven out, and the power of thy majesty take its place. Through Jesus Christ our Lord.

℟. Amen.

PROCESSION OF THE PASCHAL CANDLE

The deacon, wearing a white dalmatic, carries the lighted paschal candle, and leads the procession into the church. When he enters, he sings:

Light of Christ.

Lumen   Chri- sti.

All kneel and answer:

Thanks be to God.

De- o   grá- ti- as.

All rise, and the celebrant lights his own candle from the paschal candle. The deacon leads the procession to the middle of the church, and sings on a higher note:

Lumen Christi.

Again, all kneel, and answer:

Deo grátias.

All rise, and the candles of the clergy are now lit. The deacon now goes in front of the altar and sings for the third time, on an even higher note:

Lumen Christi.

Again, all kneel, and answer:

Deo grátias.

All rise, and now the candles of the faithful and all of the lights of the church are lit—excepting the altar candles. The deacon places the candle on its stand in the center of the sanctuary, takes the book, and receives the blessing from the celebrant.

Iube, Domne, benedícere.

Dóminus sit in corde tuo et in lábiis tuis: ut digne et competénter annúnties suum paschále præcónium: In nómine Patris, et Fílii, ✚ et Spíritus Sancti. Amen.

Pray, sir, a blessing.

The Lord be in thy heart and on thy lips, that thou mayest worthily, and in a becoming manner, announce his Easter Proclamation: In the name of the Father, and the Son, and the Holy Spirit. Amen.

The deacon places the book on the lectern and incenses it, then he incenses the paschal candle while walking around it.

EASTER PROCLAMATION (EXSULTET)

All stand and hold their lighted candles. The deacon faces the paschal candle and sings the Præconium Paschale:

EXSÚLTET iam Angélica turba cælórum: exsúltent divína mystéria: et pro tanti Regis victória, tuba ínsonet salutáris.

Gáudeat et tellus tantis irradiáta fulgóribus: et ætérni Regis splendóre illustráta, totíus orbis se séntiat amisísse calíginem.

Lætétur et mater Ecclésia, tanti lúminis adornáta fulgóribus: et magnis populórum vócibus hæc aula resúltet.

Let the angelic choirs of heaven now exult: exult in the divine mysteries: and for the victory of so great a King, let the trumpet of salvation sound.

Let the earth be glad, made radiant by such splendor: and ablaze with the brightness of the eternal King, let the whole world see its darkness scattered.

Let our mother the Church also rejoice, adorned with the flash of so much light: and let this temple resound with the great voice of the people.

Quaprópter astántes vos, fratres caríssimi, ad tam miram huius sancti lúminis claritátem, una mecum, quæso, Dei omnipoténtis misericórdiam invocáte. Ut qui me non meis méritis intra Levitárum númerum dignátus est aggregáre: lúminis sui claritátem infúndens, Cérei huius laudem implére perfíciat. Per Dóminum nostrum Iesum Christum, Fílium suum: qui cum eo vivit et regnat in unitáte Spíritus Sancti Deus...

Wherefore I stand before you, most beloved brethren, who are here present in the wondrous brightness of this holy light, invoke with me, I ask you, the mercy of God almighty. That he who has deigned, for no merits of mine, to number me among the Levites, may pour forth the brightness of his light upon me, that I may perfectly praise this candle. Through our Lord Jesus Christ, his Son, who lives and reigns with him in the unity of the Holy Spirit, one God forever and ever.

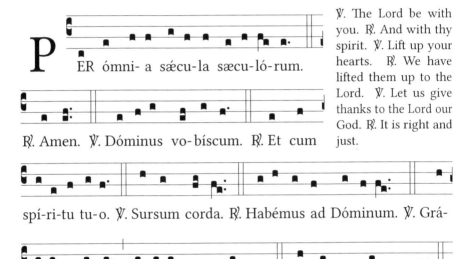

℣. The Lord be with you. ℟. And with thy spirit. ℣. Lift up your hearts. ℟. We have lifted them up to the Lord. ℣. Let us give thanks to the Lord our God. ℟. It is right and just.

PER ómni- a sǽcu-la sæcu-ló-rum. ℟. Amen. ℣. Dóminus vo-bíscum. ℟. Et cum spí-ri-tu tu-o. ℣. Sursum corda. ℟. Habémus ad Dóminum. ℣. Grá-ti- as agámus Dómino De-o nostro. ℟. Dignum et iustum est.

Vere dignum et iustum est, invisíbilem Deum Patrem omnipoténtem Filiúmque eius unigénitum, Dóminum nostrum Iesum Christum, toto cordis ac mentis afféctu et vocis ministério personáre. Qui pro nobis ætérno Patri Adæ débitum solvit: et véteris piáculi cautiónem pio cruóre detérsit.

It is truly meet and just, with our entire heart and the affection of our mind, and with the ministry of our voices, to acclaim the invisible God, the Father almighty, and his only-begotten Son, our Lord Jesus Christ. Who for our sake paid the debt of Adam to the eternal Father: and shedding his own precious blood, canceled the guilt of ancient sinfulness.

Hæc sunt enim festa paschália, in quibus verus ille Agnus occíditur, cuius sánguine postes fidélium consecrántur.

Hæc nox est, in qua primum patres nostros, fílios Israël edúctos de Ægýpto, Mare Rubrum sicco vestígio transíre fecísti.

Hæc ígitur nox est, quæ peccatórum ténebras colúmnæ illuminatióne purgávit.

Hæc nox est, quæ hódie per univérsum mundum in Christo credéntes, a vítiis sæculi et calígine peccatórum segregátos, reddit grátiæ, sóciat sanctitáti.

Hæc nox est, in qua, destrúctis vínculis mortis, Christus ab ínferis victor ascéndit. Nihil enim nobis nasci prófuit, nisi rédimi profuísset.

O mira circa nos tuæ pietátis dignátio!

O inæstimábilis diléctio caritátis: ut servum redímeres, Fílium tradidísti!

O certe necessárium Adæ peccátum, quod Christi morte delétum est!

O felix culpa, quæ talem ac tantum méruit habére Redemptórem!

O vere beáta nox, quæ sola méruit scire tempus et horam, in qua Christus ab ínferis resurréxit! Hæc nox est, de qua scriptum est: Et nox sicut dies illuminábitur: Et nox illuminátio mea in delíciis meis.

These are the Passover rites, in which that true Lamb is slain, with whose blood the doorposts of the faithful are consecrated.

This is the night, in which thou didst cause our forefathers, the children of Israel to pass through the Red Sea dryshod, leading them out of Egypt.

This therefore is the night, which by the light of the pillar, dissipated the darkness of sinners.

This is the night, in which even today, throughout the world, those who believe in Christ are separated from worldly vices and the darkness of sin, to be restored to grace and united in sanctity.

This is the night, in which, destroying the chains of death, Christ arose victorious from the grave. For it would have profited us nothing to have been born, unless to also be redeemed.

O wondrous condescension of thy care towards us!

O inestimable affection of love: that thou mightest redeem a slave, thou didst deliver up thy Son!

O truly necessary sin of Adam, which was destroyed by the death of Christ!

O happy fault, that merited so great and so excellent a Redeemer!

O truly blessed night, which alone deserved to know the time and hour, in which Christ rose again from hell! This is the night, of which it is written: And the night shall be as clear as the day; and the night is my light in my delights.

Huius ígitur sanctificátio noctis fugat scélera, culpas lavat: et reddit innocéntiam lapsis et mæstis lætítiam. Fugat ódia, concórdiam parat et curvat impéria.

In huius ígitur noctis grátia, súscipe, sancte Pater, incénsi huius sacrifícium vespertínum: quod tibi in hac Cérei oblatióne solémni, per ministrórum manus de opéribus apum, sacrosáncta reddit Ecclésia.

Sed iam colúmnæ huius præcónia nóvimus, quam in honórem Dei rútilans ignis accéndit. Qui licet sit divísus in partes, mutuáti tamen lúminis detriménta non novit. Alitur enim liquántibus ceris, quas in substántiam pretiósæ huius lámpadis apis mater edúxit.

O vere beáta nox, quæ exspoliávit Ægýptios, ditávit Hebrǽos! Nox, in qua terrénis cæléstia, humánis divína iungúntur.

Orámus ergo te, Dómine: ut Céreus iste in honórem tui nóminis consecrátus, ad noctis huius calíginem destruéndam, indefíciens persevéret. Et in odórem suavitátis accéptus, supérnis lumináribus misceátur. Flammas eius lúcifer matutínus invéniat. Ille, inquam, lúcifer, qui nescit occásum. Ille, qui regréssus ab ínferis, humáno géneri serénus illúxit.

Precámur ergo te, Dómine: ut nos fámulos tuos, omnémque clerum, et devotíssimum pópulum: una cum beatíssimo Papa nostro *N.*, et Antísti-

Therefore the hallowing of this night puts to flight all wickedness, cleanses sins: and restores innocence to the fallen and gladness to the sorrowful. It drives out hatreds, fosters concord, and brings down the mighty.

Wherefore, on this night of grace, receive, O holy Father, the evening sacrifice of this incense: which holy Church solemnly offers to thee in this candle, through the hands of thy servants, from the work of bees.

But now we know the praises of this pillar, which the shining fire enkindles for God's honor. Which, although divided into parts, yet never dims from its light being shared. For it is fed by the melting wax, which is drawn out by mother bees, to be the substance of this precious torch.

O truly blessed night, which plundered the Egyptians, and enriched the Hebrews! A night, in which are joined the heavenly to the earthly, and the divine to the human.

We beseech thee, therefore, O Lord: that this candle, hallowed to honor of thy name, may continue to burn to dissipate the darkness of this night. Receive it as an odor of sweetness, and let it mix with the heavenly lights. Let the morning star still find its flame. That morning star, I mean, which knows no setting. He, who returning from the grave, serenely shone forth upon mankind.

We beseech thee therefore, O Lord: that thou wouldst grant peaceful times during these paschal joys, and vouchsafe to rule, govern, and keep with thy

te nostro *N.*, quiéte témporum concéssa, in his paschálibus gáudiis, assídua protectióne régere, gubernáre et conserváre dignéris.

Réspice étiam ad eos, qui nos in potestáte regunt, et, ineffábili pietátis et misericórdiæ tuæ múnere, dírige cogitatiónes eórum ad iustítiam et pacem, ut de terréna operositáte ad cæléstem pátriam pervéniant cum omni pópulo tuo. Per eúndem Dóminum nostrum Iesum Christum, Fílium tuum: Qui tecum vivit et regnat in unitáte Spíritus Sancti Deus...

constant protection us thy servants, and all the clergy, and the devout people: together with our most holy Father, Pope *N.* and our Bishop *N.*

Have regard also for those who reign over us, and, grant them thine ineffable kindness and mercy, direct their thoughts in justice and peace, that from their earthy toil, they may come to their heavenly reward with all thy people. Per eúndem Dóminum nostrum Iesum Christum, Fílium tuum: Qui tecum vivit et regnat in unitáte Spíritus Sancti Deus, per ómnia sǽcula sæculórum.

Per ómni- a sæcu- la sæcu- ló- rum. ℟. Amen.

The clergy and congregation extinguish their candles.

THE LESSONS

The lessons are sung—without title or conclusion—from the center of the sanctuary, facing north towards the paschal candle, that is, with the altar to the right and the nave of the church to the left.

The celebrant, sacred ministers, and all others sit for the lessons.

First Lesson
Gn 1: 1-31; 2: 1-2.

In princípio creávit Deus cælum et terram. Terra autem erat inánis et vácua, et ténebræ erant super fáciem abýssi: et Spíritus Dei ferebátur super aquas.

Dixítque Deus: « Fiat lux ». Et facta est lux. Et vidit Deus lucem quod esset bona: et divísit lucem a ténebris. Appellavítque lucem Diem, et ténebras Noctem: factúmque est véspere et mane, dies unus.

In the beginning God created heaven and earth. And the earth was void and empty, and darkness was upon the face of the deep: and the Spirit of God moved over the waters.

And God said: Be light made. And light was made. And God saw the light that it was good: and he divided the light from the darkness. And he called the light Day, and the darkness Night: and there was evening and morning, one day.

Dixit quoque Deus: « Fiat firmaméntum in médio aquárum: et dívidat aquas ab aquis ». Et fecit Deus firmaméntum, divisítque aquas quæ erant sub firmaménto, ab his quæ erant super firmaméntum. Et factum est ita. Vocavítque Deus firmaméntum Cælum: et factum est véspere et mane, dies secúndus.

Dixit vero Deus: « Congregéntur aquæ, quæ sub cælo sunt, in locum unum: et appáreat árida ». Et factum est ita. Et vocávit Deus áridam, Terram: congregationésque aquárum appellávit Mária. Et vidit Deus quod esset bonum.

Et ait: « Gérminet terra herbam viréntem, et faciéntem semen, et lignum pomíferum fáciens fructum iuxta genus suum, cuius semen in semetípso sit super terram ». Et factum est ita. Et prótulit terra herbam viréntem, et faciéntem semen iuxta genus suum, lignúmque fáciens fructum, et habens unumquódque seméntem secúndum spéciem suam. Et vidit Deus quod esset bonum. Et factum est véspere et mane, dies tértius.

Dixit autem Deus: « Fiant luminária in firmaménto cæli, et dívidant diem ac noctem, et sint in signa et témpora, et dies et annos: ut lúceant in firmaménto cæli, et illúminent terram ». Et factum est ita. Fecítque Deus duo luminária magna: lumináre maius, ut præésset diéi, et lumináre minus, ut præésset nocti: et stellas. Et pósuit eas in firmaménto cæ-

And God said: Let there be a firmament made amidst the waters: and let it divide the waters from the waters. And God made a firmament, and divided the waters that were under the firmament from those that were above the firmament. And it was so. And God called the firmament Heaven: and the evening and morning were the second day.

God also said: Let the waters that are under the heaven be gathered together into one place; and let the dry land appear. And it was so done. And God called the dry land Earth: and the gathering together of the waters he called Seas. And God saw that it was good.

And he said: Let the earth bring forth his green herb, and such as may seed, and the fruit tree yielding fruit after its kind, which may have seed in itself upon the earth. And it was so done. And the earth brought forth the green herb, and such as yieldeth seed according to its kind, and the tree that beareth fruit, having seed, each one according to its kind. And God saw that it was good. And the evening and morning were the third day.

And God said: Let there be lights made in the firmament of heaven to divide the day and the night, and let them be for signs, and for seasons, and for days and years: to shine in the firmament of heaven, and to give light upon the earth. And it was so done. And God made two great lights: a greater light to rule the day; and a lesser light to rule the night: and the stars. And he set them in

li, ut lucérent super terram, et præés-
sent diéi ac nocti, et divíderent lucem
ac ténebras. Et vidit Deus quod esset bonum. Et factum est véspere et
mane, dies quartus.

Dixit étiam Deus: « Prodúcant
aquæ réptile ánimæ vivéntis, et vo-
látile super terram sub firmaménto
cæli ». Creavítque Deus cete grán-
dia, et omnem ánimam vivéntem atque motábilem, quam prodúxerant
aquæ in spécies suas, et omne vo-
látile secúndum genus suum. Et vidit Deus quod esset bonum. Benedixítque eis, dicens: « Créscite, et
multiplicámini, et repléte aquas maris: avésque multiplicéntur super terram ». Et factum est véspere et mane,
dies quintus.

Dixit quoque Deus: « Prodú-
cat terra ánimam vivéntem in géne-
re suo: iuménta, et reptília, et bé-
stias terræ secúndum spécies suas ».
Factúmque est ita. Et fecit Deus bé-
stias terræ iuxta spécies suas, et iuménta, et omne réptile terræ in géne-
re suo. Et vidit Deus quod esset bonum, et ait: « Faciámus hóminem ad
imáginem et similitúdinem nostram:
et præsit píscibus maris, et volatílibus cæli, et béstiis, universǽque terræ, omníque réptili quod movétur in
terra ».

Et creávit Deus hóminem ad
imáginem suam: ad imáginem Dei
creávit illum, másculum et féminam

the firmament of heaven, to shine upon
the earth, and to rule the day and the
night, and to divide the earth, and to
rule the day and the night, and to divide the light and the darkness. And God
saw that it was good. And the evening
and morning were the fourth day.

God also said: Let the waters bring
forth the creeping creature having life,
and the fowl that may fly over the earth
under the firmament of heaven. And
God created the great whales, and every living and moving creature which
the waters brought forth, according to
their kinds, and every winged fowl according to its kind. And God saw that it
was good. And he blessed them, saying:
Increase and multiply, and fill the waters of the sea: and let the birds be multiplied upon the earth. And the evening
and the morning were the fifth day.

And God said: Let the earth bring
forth the living creature in its kind, cattle, and creeping things, and beasts of
the earth according to their kinds. And
it was so done. And God made the beasts
of the earth according to their kinds, and
cattle, and every thing that creepeth on
the earth after its kind. And God saw
that it was good. And he said: Let us
make man to our own image and likeness: and let him have dominion over
the fishes of the sea, and the fowls of the
air, and the beasts, and the whole earth,
and every creeping creature that moveth
upon the earth.

And God created man to his own
image: to the image of God he created
him, male and female he created them.

creávit eos. Benedixítque illis Deus, et ait: « Créscite et multiplicámini, et repléte terram, et subícite eam, et dominámini píscibus maris, et volatílibus cæli, et univérsis animántibus, quæ movéntur super terram ». Dixítque Deus: « Ecce dedi vobis omnem herbam afferéntem semen super terram, et univérsa ligna quæ habent in semetípsis seméntem géneris sui, ut sint vobis in escam: et cunctis animántibus terræ, omníque vólucri cæli, et univérsis, quæ movéntur in terra, et in quibus est ánima vivens, ut hábeant ad vescéndum ». Et factum est ita. Vidítque Deus cuncta quæ fécerat: et erant valde bona. Et factum est véspere et mane, dies sextus.

Igitur perfécti sunt cæli et terra, et omnis ornátus eórum. Complevítque Deus die séptimo opus suum, quod fécerat: et requiévit die séptimo ab univérso ópere quod patrárat.

And God blessed them, saying: Increase and multiply, and fill the earth, and subdue it, and rule over the fishes of the sea, and the fowls of the air, and all living creatures that move upon the earth. And God said: Behold, I have given you every herb-bearing seed upon the earth, and all trees that have in themselves seed of their own kind, to be your meat: and to all the beasts of the earth, and to every fowl of the air, and to all that move upon the earth, and wherein there is life, that they may have to feed upon. And it was so done. And God saw all the things that he had made, and they were very good. And the evening and morning were the sixth day.

So the heavens and the earth were finished, and all the furniture of them. And on the seventh day God ended his work which he had made: and he rested on the seventh day from all his work which he had done.

All rise for the prayer.

Prayer

The celebrant: Orémus.
The deacon: Flectámus génua.

Let us pray.
Let us kneel.

All kneel for little while.

The deacon: Leváte.
The celebrant:

Arise.

Deus, qui mirabíliter creásti hóminem, et mirabílius redemísti: da nobis, quǽsumus, contra oblectaménta peccáti, mentis ratióne persístere; ut mereámur ad ætérna gáudia perveníre. Per Dóminum.

O God, who so wondrously created man, and yet more wondrously redeemed him: grant us, we pray, to withstand in our minds all allurements of sin; that we may merit to attain eternal joys. Through our Lord Jesus Christ.

Second Lesson
Ex 14: 24-31; 15: 1.

In diébus illis: Factum est in vigília matutína, et ecce respíciens Dóminus super castra Ægyptiórum per colúmnam ignis et nubis, interfécit exércitum eórum: et subvértit rotas cúrruum, ferebantúrque in profúndum. Dixérunt ergo Ægýptii: « Fugiámus Israélem: Dóminus enim pugnat pro eis contra nos ».

Et ait Dóminus ad Móysen: « Exténde manum tuam super mare, ut revertántur aquæ ad Ægýptios super currus et équites eórum ». Cumque extendísset Móyses manum contra mare, revérsum est primo dilúculo ad priórem locum: fugientibúsque Ægýptiis occurrérunt aquæ, et invólvit eos Dóminus in médiis flúctibus. Reversǽque sunt aquæ, et operuérunt currus et équites cuncti exércitus Pharaónis, qui sequéntes ingréssi fúerant mare: nec unus quidem supérfuit ex eis. Fílii autem Israël perrexérunt per médium sicci maris, et aquæ eis erant quasi pro muro a dextris et a sinístris: liberavítque Dóminus in die illa Israël de manu Ægyptiórum. Et vidérunt Ægýptios mórtuos super littus maris, et manum magnam, quam exercúerat Dóminus contra eos: timuítque pópulus Dóminum, et credidérunt Dómino, et Móysi servo eius. Tunc cécinit Móyses, et fílii Israël carmen hoc Dómino, et dixérunt:

In those days: The morning watch was come, and behold the Lord, looking upon the Egyptian army through the pillar of fire and of the cloud, slew their host: and overthrew the wheels of the chariots, and they were carried into the deep. And the Egyptians said: Let us flee from Israel: for the Lord fighteth for them against us.

And the Lord said to Moses: Stretch forth thy hand over the sea, that the waters may come again upon the Egyptians, upon their chariots and horsemen. And when Moses had stretched forth his hand towards the sea, it returned at the first break of day to the former place: and as the Egyptians were fleeing away the waters came upon them, and the Lord shut them up in the middle of the waves. And the waters returned, and covered the chariots and the horsemen of all the army of Pharao, who had come into the sea after them: neither did there so much as one of them remain. But the children of Israel marched through the midst of the sea upon dry land, and the waters were to them as a wall on the right hand and on the left: and the Lord delivered Israel on that day out of the hand of the Egyptians. And they saw the Egyptians dead upon the sea shore, and the mighty hand that the Lord had used against them: and the people feared the Lord, and they believed the Lord, and Moses his servant. Then Moses and the children of Israel sung this canticle to the Lord, and said:

Canticle
VIII.

Anté- mus * Dó-mi-no: glo-ri-ó-se e- nim hono-ri-fi- cá- tus est: equum et ascen- só- rem pro-ié-cit in ma- re: adiú-tor et pro-téctor factus est mi-hi in sa- lú- tem. ℣. Hic De-us me-us, et hono-rábo e- um: De-us patris me- i, et exal- tá- bo e- um. ℣. Dó- mi-nus cónte-rens bel- la: Dó- mi-nus * no-men est il- li.

Let us sing to the Lord: for he is gloriously honored: the horse and the rider he hath thrown into the sea: he has become my helper and protector unto salvation. ℣. He is my God, and I will honor him: the God of my father, and I will extol him. ℣. He is the Lord that destroys wars: the Lord is his name.

Prayer

Orémus.	Let us pray.
Flectámus génua.	Let us kneel.
Leváte.	Arise.

Deus, cuius antíqua mirácula étiam nostris sǽculis coruscáre sentímus: dum quod uni pópulo, a persecutióne Ægyptíaca liberándo, déxteræ tuæ poténtia contulísti, id in salútem géntium per aquam regeneratiónis operáris: præsta; ut in Abrahæ fílios, et in Israëlíticam dignitátem, totíus mundi tránseat plenitúdo. Per Dóminum.

O God, whose ancient wonders shine forth in undimmed splendor even in our day: for what thou didst once, by the strength of thy right arm, to free a single people from Egyptian slavery, now thou dost, by the water of new birth, for the salvation of the Gentiles: grant that the whole world may be numbered with Abraham's children and share the dignity of Israel. Through our Lord.

Third Lesson

Is 4: 2-6.

In die illa erit germen Dómini in magnificéntia, et glória, et fructus terræ sublímis, et exultátio his, qui salváti fúerint de Israël. Et erit: Omnis qui relíctus fúerit in Sion, et resíduus in Ierúsalem, sanctus vocábitur, omnis qui scriptus est in vita in Ierúsalem. Si ablúerit Dóminus sordes filiárum Sion, et sánguinem Ierúsalem láverit de médio eius, in spíritu iudícii, et spíritu ardóris. Et creábit Dóminus super omnem locum montis Sion, et ubi invocátus est, nubem per diem, et fumum, et splendórem ignis flammántis in nocte: super omnem enim glóriam protéctio. Et tabernáculum erit in umbráculum diéi ab æstu, et in securitátem, et absconsiónem a túrbine, et a plúvia.

In that day the bud of the Lord shall be in magnificence and glory, and the fruit of the earth shall be high, and a great joy to them that shall have escaped of Israel. And it shall come to pass, that every one that shall be left in Sion, and that shall remain in Jerusalem, shall be called holy, every one that is written in life in Jerusalem. If the Lord shall wash away the filth of the daughters of Sion, and shall wash away the blood of Jerusalem out of the midst thereof, by the spirit of judgment and by the spirit of burning. And the Lord will create upon every place of Mount Sion, and where he is called upon, a cloud by day, and a smoke and the brightness of a flaming fire in the night: for over all the glory shall be a protection. And there shall be a tabernacle for a shade in the daytime from the heat, and for a security and covert from the whirlwind, and from rain.

Is 5: 1-2, 7

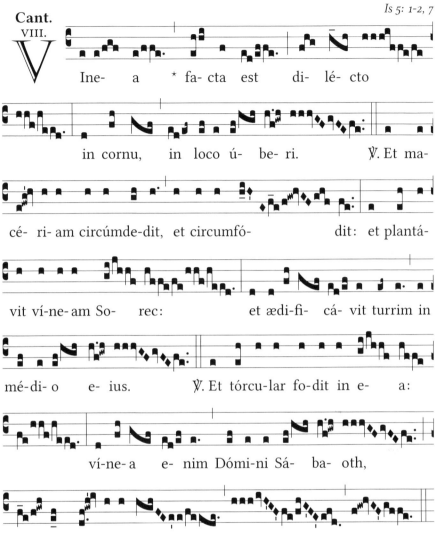

Cant. VIII.

Vinea * facta est dilécto in cornu, in loco úberi. ℣. Et matériam circúmdedit, et circumfódit: et plantávit víneam Sorec: et ædificávit turrim in médio eius. ℣. Et tórcular fodit in ea: vínea enim Dómini Sábaoth, domus * Isra-ël est.

My beloved had a vineyard on a hill, in a fruitful place. ℣. And he enclosed it with a fence, and made a ditch round it: and planted it with the vine of Sorec: and built a tower in the midst thereof. ℣. And he made a winepress in it: for the vineyard of the Lord of hosts is the house of Israel.

Prayer

Orémus.	Let us pray.
Flectámus génua.	Let us kneel.
Leváte.	Arise.

Deus, qui in ómnibus Ecclésiæ tuæ fíliis sanctórum prophetárum voce manifestásti, in omni lo-

O God, who by the mouth of the holy prophets hast made known to all the children of thy Church, that, in every place

co dominatiónis tuæ, satórem te bo-
nórum séminum, et electórum pál-
mitum esse cultórem: tríbue pópulis tuis, qui et vineárum apud te nómine censéntur, et ségetum; ut, spi-
nárum et tribulórum squalóre rese-
cáto, digna efficiántur fruge fecúndi.
Per Dóminum.

where thy majesty is adored, thou art
the sower of good seed and the vine-
dresser that cultivatest choice branches:
grant to thy people, who are to thee as
vines and wheatfields, that all thorns and
briers may be rooted out, that they may
bring forth good and plenteous fruit.
Through our Lord.

Fourth Lesson

Dt 31: 22-30.

In diébus illis: Scripsit Móyses cán-
ticum et dócuit fílios Israël. Præ-
cepítque Dóminus Iósue fílio Nun et
ait: « Confortáre, et esto robústus:
tu enim introdúces fílios Israël in
terram, quam pollícitus sum, et ego
ero tecum ». Postquam ergo scripsit
Móyses verba legis huius in volúmi-
ne, atque complévit: præcépit Leví-
tis, qui portábant arcam fœderis Dómini dicens: « Tóllite librum istum,
et pónite eum in látere arcæ fœderis
Dómini Dei vestri: ut sit ibi contra te
in testimónium. Ego enim scio con-
tentiónem tuam, et cervícem tuam
duríssimam. Adhuc vivénte me, et in-
grediénte vobíscum, semper conten-
tióse egístis contra Dóminum: quanto magis cum mórtuus fúero? Con-
gregáte ad me omnes maióres na-
tu per tribus vestras, atque doctó-
res, et loquar audiéntibus eis sermónes istos, et invocábo contra eos cælum et terram. Novi enim quod post
mortem meam iníque agétis, et decli-
nábitis cito de via, quam præcépi vobis: et occúrrent vobis mala in ex-

In those days: Moses wrote the canticle, and taught it to the children of Israel. And the Lord commanded Josue the
son of Nun, and said: Take courage, and
be valiant: for thou shalt bring the children of Israel into the land which I have
promised, and I will be with thee. Therefore after Moses wrote the words of this
law in a volume, and finished it: he commanded the Levites, who carried the ark
of the covenant of the Lord, saying: Take
this book, and put it in the side of the
ark of the covenant of the Lord your
God: that it may be there for a testimony against thee. For I know thy obsti-
nacy and thy most stiff neck. While I am
yet living, and going in with you, you
have always been rebellious against the
Lord: how much more when I shall be
dead? Gather unto me all the ancients
of your tribes, and your doctors, and I
will speak these words in their hearing,
and will call heaven and earth to witness against them. For I know that after my death, you will do wickedly and
will quickly turn aside from the way that
I have commanded you: and evils shall

trémo témpore, quando fecéritis malum in conspéctu Dómini, ut irritétis eum per ópera mánuum vestrárum ». Locútus est ergo Móyses, audiénte univérso cœtu Israël, verba cárminis huius, et ad finem usque complévit.

come upon you in the latter times, when you shall do evil in the sight of the Lord, to provoke him by the works of your hands. Moses therefore spoke in the hearing of the whole assembly of Israel the words of this canticle, and finished it even to the end.

Dt 32: 1-4

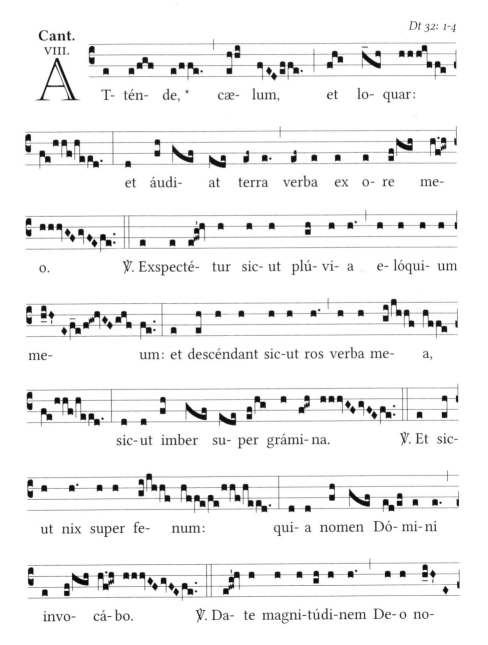

Cant. VIII.

AT-tén- de, * cæ- lum, et lo- quar:

et áudi- at terra verba ex o- re me- o.

℣. Exspecté- tur sic-ut plú-vi-a e-lóqui-um me- um: et descéndant sic-ut ros verba me- a,

sic-ut imber su-per grámi-na. ℣. Et sic-ut nix super fe- num: qui-a nomen Dó-mi-ni invo-cá-bo. ℣. Da-te magni-túdi-nem De-o no-

stro: De-us, ve-ra ópe-ra e- ius, et o-

mnes vi- æ e-ius iudí- ci- a. ℣. De- us fi-dé-lis,

in quo non est in-íqui- tas: iu- stus et sanctus *

Dóminus.

Attend, O heaven, and I will speak: and let the earth hear the words that come out of my mouth. ℣. Let my speech be expected like the rain: and let my words fall like the dew: like the shower upon the grass. ℣. And like the snow upon the dry herb: because I will invoke the name of the Lord. ℣. Confess the greatness of our Lord: the works of God are perfect, and all his ways are justice. ℣. God is faithful, in whom there is no iniquity: the Lord is just and holy.

Prayer

Orémus.

Flectámus génua.

Leváte.

Deus, celsitúdo humílium et fortitúdo rectórum, qui per sanctum Móysen púerum tuum, ita erudíre pópulum tuum sacri cárminis tui decantatióne voluísti, ut illa legis iterátio fíeret étiam nostra diréctio: éxcita in omnem iustificatárum géntium plenitúdinem poténtiam tuam, et da lætítiam, mitigándo terrórem; ut, ómnium peccátis tua remissióne delétis, quod denuntiátum est in ultiónem, tránseat in salútem. Per Dóminum nostrum.

Let us pray.

Let us kneel.

Arise.

O God, the exaltation of the lowly and strength of the just, who, through thy holy servant Moses, wast pleased to teach thy people by the chanting of thy sacred canticle; so that this repetition of the law should also be our guidance: show forth thy power to the multitude of peoples justified by thee, and by allaying their terror, grant them joy: that, all sins being blotted out by thy forgiveness, the threatened vengeance may give way to salvation. Through our Lord Jesus Christ, thy Son, who lives and reigns.

THE FIRST PART OF THE LITANY

At the end of the prayer, all kneel.

The Litany is sung by two cantors, kneeling in the middle of the sanctuary. Meanwhile, everything is prepared for the blessing of baptismal water.

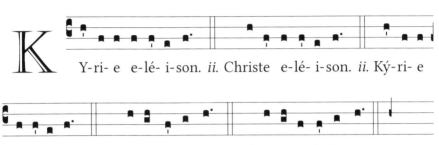

Y-ri- e e-lé- i-son. *ii.* Christe e-lé- i-son. *ii.* Ký-ri- e
e-lé- i-son. *ii.* Christe, audi nos. *ii.* Christe, exáudi nos. *ii.*
     Christ, hear us.   Christ, graciously hear us.

Pa- ter de cæ- lis **De**- us,   mi-se-*ré-re* **no**-bis.

God, the Father of heaven,	have mercy on us.
Fili, Redémptor mundi **De**us,	God the Son, Redeemer of the world,
mise*rére* **no**bis.	have mercy.
Spíritus Sancte, **De**us, mise*rére.*	God the Holy Ghost, have mercy.
Sancta Trínitas, unus **De**us,	Holy Trinity, one God, have mercy.
mise*rére.*	

Sancta Ma-**rí**- a,   o-*ra pro* **no**-bis.

Holy Mary,	pray for us.
Sancta Dei **Gé**nitrix, *ora pro* **no**bis.	Holy Mother of God, pray.
Sancta Virgo **vír**ginum, o*ra.*	Holy Virgin of virgins, pray.
Sancte **Mí**chaël, o*ra.*	Saint Michael, pray.
Sancte **Gá**briel, o*ra.*	Saint Gabriel, pray.
Sancte **Rá**phaël, o*ra.*	Saint Raphael, pray.

Omnes sancti Ange-li et arch-**án**ge-li, o-rá-*te pro* **no**-bis.

All holy Angels and Archangels,		pray for us.	
Omnes sancti beatórum Spirí-tuum **ór**dines, orá*te pro* **no**bis.		All holy orders of blessed Spirits,	pray for us.
Sancte Ioánnes Ba**ptí**sta, o*ra*.		Saint John the Baptist,	pray.
Sancte **Io**seph, o*ra*.		Saint Joseph,	pray.
Omnes sancte Patriárchæ et Pro**phé**tæ, orá*te*.		All holy Patriarchs and Prophets,	pray.

Sancte **Pe**- tre,   o-*ra pro* **no**-bis.

Saint Peter,		pray for us.	
Sancte **Pau**le, o*ra*.		Saint Paul,	pray.
Sancte Andr**é**a, o*ra*.		Saint Andrew,	pray.
Sancte Io**án**nes, o*ra*.		Saint John,	pray.
Omnes sancti Apóstoli et Evange**lí**stæ, orá*te*.		All holy Apostles and Evangelists,	pray.
Omnes sancti discípuli **Dó**mini, orá*te*.		All holy Disciples of the Lord,	pray.
Sancte **Sté**phane, o*ra*.		Saint Stephen,	pray.
Sancte Laur**én**ti, o*ra*.		Saint Lawrence,	pray.
Sancte Vin**cén**ti, o*ra*.		Saint Vincent,	pray.
Omnes sancti **Már**tyres, orá*te*.		All holy Martyrs,	pray.
Sancte Silv**és**ter, o*ra*.		Saint Silvester,	pray.
Sancte Greg**ó**ri, o*ra*.		Saint Gregory,	pray.
Sancte Augus**tí**ne, o*ra*.		Saint Augustine,	pray.
Omnes sancti Pontífices et Confess**ó**res, orá*te*.		All holy Bishops and Confessors,	pray.
Omnes sancti Doct**ó**res, orá*te*.		All holy Doctors,	pray.
Sancte Ant**ó**ni, o*ra*.		Saint Anthony,	pray.
Sancte Bene**dí**cte, o*ra*.		Saint Benedict,	pray.
Sancte Do**mí**nice, o*ra*.		Saint Dominic,	pray.
Sancte Fran**cí**sce, o*ra*.		Saint Francis,	pray.
Omnes sancti Sacerdótes et Le**ví**tæ, orá*te*.		All holy Priests and Levites,	pray.

Omnes sancti Mónachi et Eremítæ,	o*ra*te.	All holy Monks and Hermits,	pray.
Sancta María Magda**lé**na,	o*ra*.	Saint Mary Magdalene,	pray.
Sancta **A**gnes,	o*ra*.	Saint Agnes,	pray.
Sancta Cæcília,	o*ra*.	Saint Cecilia,	pray.
Sancta **A**gatha,	o*ra*.	Saint Agatha,	pray.
Sancta Ana**stá**sia,	o*ra*.	Saint Anastasia,	pray.
Omnes sanctæ Vírgines et **Ví**duæ,	o*ra*te.	All holy Virgins and Widows,	pray.
Omnes Sancti et Sanctæ **De**i,	intercé*di*te *pro* **no**bis.	All holy men and women, Saints of God,	intercede for us

All rise, and the cantors return to their places.

If the church has a baptismal font, baptismal water is blessed, as below. Otherwise, the Renewal of Baptismal Promises is done immediately, p. 200

THE BLESSING OF BAPTISMAL WATER

℣. Dóminus vobíscum.

℟. Et cum spíritu tuo.

      Orémus.

The Lord be with you.

And with thy spirit.

      Let us pray.

Omnípotens sempitérne Deus, adésto magnæ pietátis tuæ mystériis, adésto sacraméntis: et ad recreándos novos pópulos, quos tibi fons baptísmatis párturit, spíritum adoptiónis emítte; ut, quod nostræ humilitátis geréndum est ministério, virtútis tuæ impleátur efféctu. Per Dóminum nostrum Iesum Christum, Fílium tuum: Qui tecum vivit et regnat in unitáte Spíritus Sancti Deus...

Almighty and everlasting God, be present by these mysteries of thy great kindness, be present in the sacraments: and to recreate the new peoples, born to thee by the baptismal font, send forth the spirit of adoption; that what is to be done by our humble service, may be accomplished and fulfilled by thy power. Through our Lord Jesus Christ, thy Son: Who lives and reigns with thee in the unity of the Holy Spirit, one God, forever and ever.

P ER ómni- a sǽcu-la sǽcu-ló-rum.

℟. Amen. ℣. Dóminus vo-bíscum. ℟. Et cum

℣. The Lord be with you. ℟. And with thy spirit. ℣. Lift up your hearts. ℟. We have lifted them up to the Lord. ℣. Let us give thanks to the Lord our God. ℟. It is right and just.

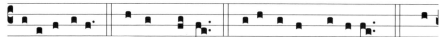

spí-ri-tu tu-o. ℣. Sursum corda. ℟. Habémus ad Dóminum. ℣. Grá-

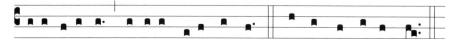

ti- as agámus Dómino De-o nostro. ℟. Dignum et iustum est.

Vere dignum et iustum est, æquum et salutáre, nos tibi semper et ubíque grátias ágere: Dómine sancte, Pater omnípotens, ætérne Deus: Qui invisíbili poténtia sacramentórum tuórum mirabíliter operáris efféctum: Et licet nos tantis mystériis exsequéndis simus indígni: Tu tamen grátiæ tuæ dona non déserens, etiam ad nostras preces aures tuæ pietátis inclínas. Deus, cuius Spíritus super aquas inter ipsa mundi primórdia ferebátur: ut iam tunc virtútem sanctificatiónis aquárum natúra concíperet. Deus, qui, nocéntis mundi crímina per aquas ábluens, regeneratiónis spéciem in ipsa dilúvii effusióne signásti: ut, uníus eiusdémque eleménti mystério, et finis esset vítiis et orígo virtútibus. Réspice, Dómine, in fáciem Ecclésiæ tuæ, et multíplica in ea regeneratiónes tuas, qui grátiæ tuæ affluéntis ímpetu lætíficas civitátem tuam: fontémque baptísmatis áperis toto orbe terrárum géntibus innovándis: ut, tuæ maiestátis império, sumat Unigéniti tui grátiam de Spíritu Sancto.

It is truly meet and just, right and salutary, that we should always, and in all places, give thanks to thee: O holy Lord, Father almighty, eternal God: who by thine power unseen, dost wondrously produce the effect of thy sacraments: and though we are unworthy to perform such great mysteries: thou dost not abandon the gifts of thy grace, and thou dost in pity decline thy ears, even to our prayers. O God, whose Spirit in the very beginning of the world moved over the waters, that even then the substance of water might take to itself sanctifying power. O God, who by water didst wash away the crimes of the guilty world, and by the outpouring of the deluge didst prefigure regeneration: that the mystery of one and the same element might bring an end to vice and a beginning of virtue. Look down, O Lord, on the face of thy Church, and multiply in her thy regenerations, who by the streams of thine abundant grace, fillest thy city with joy: and openest the font of Baptism all over the world for the renewal of the nations: that by the command of thy majesty, she may receive the grace of thine only Son from the Holy Spirit.

He divides the waters with his hand in the form of a cross.

Qui hanc aquam, regenerándis homínibus præparátam, arcána sui núminis admixtióne fecúndet: ut, sanctificatióne concépta, ab immaculáto divíni fontis útero, in novam renáta creatúram, progénies cæléstis emérgat: Et quos aut sexus in córpore aut ætas discérnit in témpore, omnes in unam páriat grátia mater infántiam. Procul ergo hinc, iubénte te, Dómine, omnis spíritus immúndus abscédat: procul tota nequítia diabólicæ fraudis absístat. Nihil hic loci hábeat contráriæ virtútis admíxtio: non insidiándo circúmvolet: non laténdo subrépat: non inficiéndo corrúmpat.

May he, by the hidden virtue of his divinity, render fruitful this water prepared for the regeneration of men: that from the immaculate womb of this divine font, conceived by sanctification, a heavenly offspring may emerge, reborn a new creature: and may grace, their mother, bring forth all, however different in sex or age, alike in spiritual infancy. By thy bidding, O Lord, therefore, may all unclean spirits, depart from hence: may all malice of diabolical deceit be entirely banished. Here let no admixture of the enemy's power prevail: let him not go about to lay snares: may he not creep in by stealth: may he not corrupt with his poison.

He touches his hand to the water.

Sit hæc sancta et ínnocens creatúra líbera ab omni impugnatóris incúrsu, et totíus nequítiæ purgáta discéssu. Sit fons vivus, aqua regénerans, unda puríficans: ut omnes hoc lavácro salutífero diluéndi, operánte in eis Spíritu Sancto, perféctæ purgatiónis indulgéntiam consequántur.

May this holy and innocent creature be free from all the assaults of the adversary, and purified by the destruction of all wickedness. May it be a living fountain, a regenerating water, a purifying stream: that all those that are to be washed in this saving bath may obtain, by the operation of the Holy Spirit, the grace of a perfect cleansing.

He makes the sign of the cross three times over the water.

Unde bene✝díco te, creatúra aquæ, per Deum vivum, per Deum verum, per Deum sanctum: per Deum, qui te in princípio verbo separávit ab árida: cuius Spíritus super te ferebátur.

Therefore, I bless thee, O creature of water, by the living God, by the true God, by the holy God: by that God who in the beginning, separated thee by a word from the dry land: whose Spirit moved over thee.

He divides the water and sprinkles some toward the four corners of the world.

Qui te de paradísi fonte manáre fecit, et in quátuor flumínibus totam terram rigáre præcépit. Qui te in

He who made thee flow from the fountain of paradise, and commanded thee to water the whole earth with thy

desérto amáram, suavitáte índita, fecit esse potábilem, et sitiénti pópulo de petra prodúxit. Bene✠díco te et
per Iesum Christum, Fílium eius únicum, Dóminum nostrum: qui te in
Cana Galilǽæ signo admirábili sua
poténtia convértit in vinum. Qui pédibus super te ambulávit: et a Ioánne in Iordáne in te baptizátus est. Qui
te una cum sánguine de látere suo
prodúxit: et discípulis suis iussit, ut
credéntes baptizaréntur in te, dicens:
« Ite, docéte omnes gentes, baptizán-
tes eos in nómine Patris, et Fílii, et
Spíritus Sancti ».

four rivers. Who, when thou wast bitter in the desert, made thee sweet, and
fit to drink, and produced thee out of a
rock for the people thirsting. I bless thee
also by Jesus Christ, his only Son, our
Lord: who in Cana of Galilee changed
thee into wine, by a wondrous sign of his
power. Who with his feet walked upon
thee: and was baptized in thee by John
in the Jordan. Who gave thee forth from
his side together with blood: and commanded his disciples, that those that believe should be baptized in thee, saying:
"Go, teach all nations, baptizing them in
the name of the Father, and of the Son,
and of the Holy Spirit."

He continues in a low tone:

Hæc nobis præcépta servánti-
bus, tu, Deus omnípotens, clemens
adésto: tu benígnus aspíra.

Do thou, almighty God, in thy
clemency assist us who observe this
commandment: do thou benignly inspire us.

Three times, he breathes over the water in the form of a cross.

Tu has símplices aquas tuo ore
benedícito: ut præter naturálem e-
mundatiónem, quam lavándis possunt adhibére corpóribus, sint étiam
purificándis méntibus efficáces.

Do thou with thy mouth bless these
pure waters: that besides their natural
power to cleanse the body, they may
also prove efficacious for the purifying
of souls.

The candle is dipped into the water three times, successively deeper, each time singing in the preface tone:

Descéndat in hanc plenitúdinem
fontis virtus Spíritus Sancti.

May the power of the Holy Spirit
descend into the fullness of this font.

With the candle held in the water, he breathes over it three times in the form of the Greek letter Ψ, saying:

Totámque huius aquæ substántiam regenerándi fecúndet efféctu.

And render the whole substance of
this water fruitful for regeneration.

He takes the candle out of the water.

Hic ómnium peccatórum máculæ deleántur: hic natúra ad imáginem tuam cóndita, et ad honórem sua reformáta princípii, cunctis vetustátis squalóribus emundétur: ut omnis homo, sacraméntum hoc regeneratiónis ingréssus, in veræ innocéntiæ novam infántiam renascátur.

Here may the stains of all sins be washed out: here may the nature that was created in thine image, and reformed to the honor of its author, be cleansed from all the filth of the old man: that all who receive the sacrament of regeneration, may be reborn into a new infancy of true innocence.

The conclusion is recited not sung:

Per Dóminum nostrum Iesum Christum, Fílium tuum: Qui ventúrus est iudicáre vivos et mórtuos, et sæculum per ignem.

℟. Amen.

Through our Lord Jesus Christ, thy Son: who shall come to judge the living and the dead, and the world, by fire.

Some of the water is taken out and reserved for sprinkling. Then, oil of catechumens is poured into the water in the form of a cross.

Sanctificétur ✚, et fecundétur fons iste óleo salútis renascéntibus ex eo, in vitam ætérnam.

℟. Amen.

May this font be sanctified and made fruitful by the oil of salvation, for those who are born anew therein, unto life everlasting.

Holy chrism is poured into the water.

Infúsio chrísmatis Dómini nostri Iesu Christi, et Spíritus Sancti Parácliti, fiat in nómine sanctæ Trinitátis.

℟. Amen.

May the infusion of the chrism of our Lord Jesus Christ, and of the Holy Spirit the Comforter, be made in the name of the Holy Trinity.

He pours the oil of catechumens and holy chrism together into the water, and breathes thee times over the water in the from of a cross.

Commíxtio chrísmatis sanctificatiónis, et ólei unctiónis, et aquæ baptísmatis, páriter fiat in nómine Patris, et Fí✚lii, et Spíritus Sancti. ℟. Amen.

May this commingling of the chrism of sanctification, the oil of unction, and the water of baptism, be made in the name of the Father, and of the Son, and of the Holy Spirit.

He then mixes the oil with the water.

¶ *At this point the sacrament of Baptism may be administered in the usual way, p. 290. Otherwise, the procession to the font is begun.*

Procession to the Font

The blessed baptismal water is brought to the baptismal font in procession.
The paschal candle remains in the sanctuary. During the procession, the canticle
is sung:

Cant. VIII.

Ps 41: 2-4

SIc-ut cer- vus   * de-sí- de-rat   ad fontes aquá-

rum: i- ta   de- sí-de-rat ánima me-a   ad te,

De- us.   ℣. Si-tí- vit ánima me-   a   ad De-

um vi-   vum: quando vé-ni- am, et appa- ré-

bo   ante fá- ci- em De- i me- i?

℣. Fu- é- runt mi-hi lácrimæ me-   æ

panes di- e ac no- cte,   dum dí-ci- tur mi-hi per

síngu-los di- es: U- bi   est * De- us tu-us?

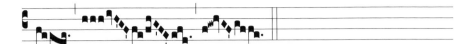

As the hart panteth after the fountains of water: so my soul panteth after thee, O God. ℣. My soul hath thirsted after the strong living God: when shall I come and appear before the face of my God? ℣. My tears have been my bread day and night, whilst it is said to me daily: Where is thy God?

The blessed water is poured into the font.

℣. Dóminus vobíscum.	The Lord be with you.
℟. Et cum spíritu tuo.	And with thy spirit.
Orémus.	Let us pray.

Omnípotens sempitérne Deus, réspice propítius ad devotiónem pópuli renascéntis, qui, sicut cervus, aquárum tuárum éxpetit fontem: et concéde propítius; ut fídei ipsíus sitis, baptísmatis mystério, ánimam corpúsque sanctíficet. Per Dóminum nostrum Iesum Christum, Fílium tuum.

O almighty and everlasting God, look with favor upon the devotion of the people to be reborn, who, as a hart longing to slake its thirst, desire to the fount of thy waters; vouchsafe that their thirst for faith, by the mystery of baptism, may avail to sanctify them in soul and in body. Through our Lord Jesus Christ.

He incenses the font, then all return to the sanctuary in silence.

If the baptistery is separate from the church, the water may be blessed at the font. In which case, the procession leaves, with the lighted paschal candle, during the Litany, after the invocation Sancta Trínitas, unus Deus. *The two cantors at the center and the congregation remain in the church, and continue the Litany, repeating from* Sancta María *if necessary. Separately, the canticle* Sicut cervus *is sung by the clergy and choir in the procession to the baptistery, and before the blessing begins, the prayer* Omnípotens sempitérne Deus, réspice *is said, as above. The blessing itself takes place as above, p. 193. After the blessing (and any baptisms), all return in silence.*

RENEWAL OF BAPTISMAL PROMISES

The celebrant changes into a white stole and cope. All stand, holding re-lighted candles.

Hac sacratíssima nocte, fratres caríssimi, sancta Mater Ecclésia, récolens Dómini nostri Iesu Christi mortem ei sepultúram, eum redamándo vígilat; et, célebrans eiúsdem gloriósam resurrectiónem, lætabúnda gaudet.

Quóniam vero, ut docet Apóstolus, consepúlti sumus cum Christo per baptísmum in mortem, quómodo Christus resurréxit a mórtuis, ita et nos in novitáte vitæ opórtet ambuláre; sciéntes, véterem hóminem nostrum simul cum Christo crucifíxum esse, ut ultra non serviámus peccáto. Existimémus ergo nos mórtuos quidem esse peccáto, vivéntes autem Deo in Christo Iesu Dómino nostro.

Quaprópter, fratres caríssimi, quadragesimáli exercitatióne absolúta, sancti baptísmatis promissiónes renovémus, quibus olim sátanæ et opéribus eius, sicut et mundo, qui inimícus est Dei, abrenuntiávimus, et Deo in sancta Ecclésia cathólica fidéliter servíre promísimus.

Itaque:
Celebrant: Abrenuntiátis Sátanæ?
All: Abrenuntiámus.
Celebrant: Et ómnibus opéribus eius?
All: Abrenuntiámus.
Celebrant: Et ómnibus pompis eius?
All: Abrenuntiámus.
Celebrant: Créditis in Deum, Patrem omnipoténtem, Creatórem cæli et

On this most sacred night, dearly beloved brethren, Holy Mother Church, recalling the death and burial of our Lord Jesus Christ, returneth his love by keeping vigil; and aboundeth with joy at celebrating his glorious Resurrection.

But because, as the Apostle teaches, we are baptized into his death and buried together with Christ: and as Christ rose again from the dead, so we too must walk in newness of life; knowing that our old man hath been crucified together with Christ so that we shall no longer be in servitude to sin. Let us therefore look upon ourselves therefore as dead indeed to sin but living to God in Christ Jesus our Lord.

Therefore, dearly beloved brethren, the Lenten observance now completed, let us renew the promises of baptism by which formerly we renounced Satan and his works, and the world likewise, the enemy of God; and by which we promised to serve God faithfully in the Holy Catholic Church.

Therefore:
Celebrant: Do you renounce Satan?
All: We do renounce him.
Celebrant: And all his works?

All: We do renounce them.
Celebrant: And all his pomps?
All: We do renounce them.
Celebrant: Do you believe in God the Father almighty, Creator of

terræ?

All: Crédimus.

Celebrant: Créditis in Iesum Christum, Fílium eius únicum, Dóminum nostrum, natum et passum?

All: Crédimus.

Celebrant: Créditis et in Spíritum Sanctum, sanctam Ecclésiam cathólicam, Sanctórum communiónem, remissiónem peccatórum, carnis resurrectiónem, et vitam ætérnam?

All: Crédimus.

Celebrant: Nunc autem una simul Deum precémur, sicut Dóminus noster Iesus Christus oráre nos dócuit:

All: Pater noster, qui es in cælis: Sanctificétur nomen tuum: Advéniat regnum tuum: Fiat volúntas tua, sicut in cælo, et in terra. Panem nostrum cotidiánum da nobis hódie: Et dimítte nobis débita nostra, sicut et nos dimíttimus debitóribus nostris. Et ne nos indúcas in tentatiónem. Sed líbera nos a malo.

Celebrant: Et Deus omnípotens, Pater Dómini nostri Iesu Christi, qui nos regenerávit ex aqua et Spíritu Sancto, quique nobis dedit remissiónem peccatórum, ipse nos custódiat grátia sua in eódem Christo Iesu Dómino nostro in vitam ætérnam.

All: Amen.

heaven and earth?

All: We do believe.

Celebrant: Do you believe in Jesus Christ, his only Son, our Lord, who was born into this world and who suffered for us?

All: We do believe.

Celebrant: Do you also believe in the Holy Spirit, the holy Catholic Church, the communion of Saints, the forgiveness of sins, the resurrection of the body, and life everlasting?

All: We do believe.

Celebrant: And now let us pray together as one, just as our Lord Jesus Christ taught us to pray:

All: Our Father, who art in heaven: Hallowed be thy name: Thy kingdom come: Thy will be done on earth as it is in heaven: Give us this day our daily bread: And forgive us our trespasses, as we forgive them that trespass against us. And lead us not into temptation. But deliver us from evil.

Celebrant: And may God almighty, the Father of our Lord Jesus Christ, who hath regenerated us by water and the Holy Spirit, and who hath given us remission of sins, may he by his grace keep us in the same Christ Jesus our Lord to life everlasting.

All: Amen.

The celebrant then sprinkles the people with the newly blessed holy water, after which all extinguish and lay down their candles, and kneel.

THE SECOND PART OF THE LITANY

The cantors begin the second part of the Litany. Meanwhile, the celebrant and sacred ministers return to the sacristy to put on white Mass vestments, the paschal candle is moved from the center to the Gospel side, and the altar is prepared for Mass.

Propí-*ti- us* **e**-sto,   parce no-bis, Dómi-ne.
Be merciful,   spare us, O Lord.
Propí-*ti- us* **e**-sto,   exáu-di nos, Dómi-ne.
Be merciful,   graciously hear us, O Lord.

Ab *omni* **ma-** lo,   lí-be-ra nos, Dómi-ne.
From all evil,   deliver us, O Lord.

Ab o*mni peccá*to,	líbera.	From all sin,	deliver.
A mo*rte perpé*tua,	líbera.	From everlasting death,	deliver.
Per mystérium sanctæ incarnati*ónis* **tu**æ,	líbera.	Through the mystery of thy holy incarnation,	deliver.
Per ad*véntum* **tu**um,	líbera.	Through thine Advent,	deliver.
Per nativi*tátem* **tu**am,	líbera.	Through thy Nativity,	deliver.
Per baptísmum et sanctum ieiú*nium* **tu**um,	líbera.	Through thy Baptism and holy fasting, deliver.	
Per crucem et passi*ónem* **tu**am,	líbera.	Through thy Cross and Passion, deliver.	
Per mortem et sepult*úram* **tu**am,	líbera.	Through thy Death and Burial, deliver.	
Per sanctam resurrecti*ónem* **tu**am,	líbera.	Through thy holy Resurrection, deliver.	
Per admirábilem ascensi*ónem* **tu**am,	líbera.	Through thy wonderful Ascension, deliver.	
Per advéntum Spíritus San*cti* Pa*rá*cliti,	líbera.	Through the coming of the Holy Spirit, the Paraclete, deliver.	
In di*e iu*dícii,	líbera.	In the day of judgment, deliver.	

Pec*ca*-**tó**- res,
We sinners,

te rogámus, audi nos.
ask thee hear us.

Ut no*bis* **par**cas,
    te rogámus, audi nos.

That thou wouldst spare us,
    We ask thee, hear us.

Ut Ecclésiam tuam sanctam ' rége-re et conserváre *dign**é*ris,   te.

That thou wouldst vouchsafe to govern and preserve thy holy Church, we ask thee.

Ut domnum apostólicum et omnes ecclesiásticos órdines ' in sancta religióne conserváre *dign**é*ris, te.

That thou wouldst vouchsafe to preserve our Pope, and all orders of the Church, in holy religion, we ask thee.

Ut inimícos sanctæ Ecclésiæ ' humiliáre *dign**é*ris,   te.

That thou wouldst vouchsafe to humble the enemies of holy Church, we ask thee.

Ut régibus et princípibus christiánis ' pacem et veram concórdiam donáre *dign**é*ris,   te.

That thou wouldst vouchsafe to give peace and true concord to Christian kings and princes,   we ask thee.

Ut nosmetípsos in tuo sancto servítio ' confortáre et conserváre *dign**é*ris,   te.

That thou wouldst vouchsafe to confirm and preserve us in thy holy service, we ask thee.

Ut ómnibus benefactóribus nostris ' sempitérna bona *retrí*buas,   te.

That thou wouldst render eternal blessings to all our benefactors, we ask thee.

Ut fructus terræ ' dare et conserváre *dign**é*ris,   te.

That thou wouldst vouchsafe to give and preserve the fruits of the earth, we ask thee.

Ut ómnibus fidélibus defúnctis ' réquiem ætérnam donáre *dign**é*ris, te.

That thou wouldst vouchsafe to grant eternal rest to all the faithful departed,   we ask thee.

Ut nos exaudíre *dign**é*ris,   te.

That thou wouldst vouchsafe to hear us, we ask thee.

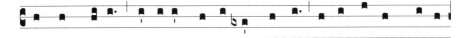

Agnus De- i, qui tollis peccá- ta mundi, parce no- bis, Dómi-
Lamb of God, who takest away the sins of the world, spare us, O Lord.

ne.   Agnus De- i, qui tollis peccá- ta mundi,   exáudi nos Dó-

Lamb of God, who takest away the sins of the world, graciously hear us, O Lord.

mi-ne.   Agnus De- i, qui tollis peccá- ta mundi, mi-se-ré-re no-

Lamb of God, who takest away the sins of the world, have mercy on us.

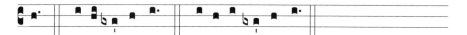

bis. Christe, audi nos. Christe, ex-áudi nos.

Christ, hear us.   Christ, graciously hear us.

THE SOLEMN VIGIL MASS OF EASTER

At the end of the Litany, all stand, and the cantors intone Kýrie, eléison.

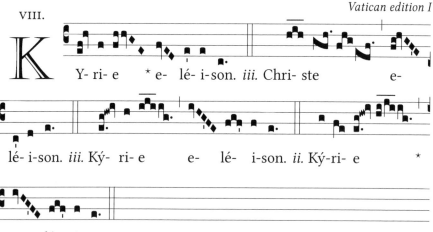

During this, the celebrant and the sacred ministers ascend and incense the altar, omitting the usual prayers at the foot of the altar.

The celebrant intones the Glória in excélsis, *and during the singing the bells are rung and images are unveiled.*

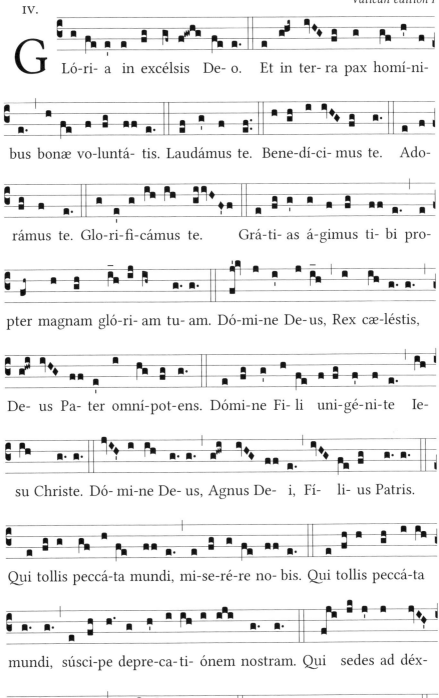

IV.

G Ló-ri- a in excélsis De- o. Et in ter- ra pax homí-ni-

bus bonæ vo-luntá- tis. Laudámus te. Bene-dí-ci- mus te. Ado-

rámus te. Glo-ri-fi-cámus te.   Grá-ti- as á-gimus ti- bi pro-

pter magnam gló-ri- am tu- am. Dó-mi-ne De-us, Rex cæ-léstis,

De- us Pa- ter omní-pot-ens. Dómi-ne Fi- li uni-gé-ni-te Ie-

su Christe. Dó- mi-ne De- us, Agnus De- i, Fí- li- us Patris.

Qui tollis peccá-ta mundi, mi-se-ré-re no- bis. Qui tollis peccá-ta

mundi, súsci-pe depre-ca-ti- ónem nostram. Qui   sedes ad déx-

te-ram Patris, mi-se-ré-re no- bis. Quóni- am tu so-lus sanctus.

Tu so-lus Dó- minus. Tu so-lus Altíssimus, Ie- su Christe. Cum

Sancto Spí- ri-tu, in gló-ri- a De- i Pa-tris. A- men.

Collect

℣. Dóminus vobíscum.

℟. Et cum spíritu tuo.

Orémus.

Deus, qui hanc sacratíssimam noctem glória domínicæ Resurrectiónis illústras: consérva in nova famíliæ tuæ progénie adoptiónis spíritum, quem dedísti; ut, córpore et mente renováti, puram tibi exhíbeant servitútem. Per eúndem Dóminum.

The Lord be with you.

And with thy spirit.

Let us pray.

O God, who ennoblest this most sacred night with the glory of the Lord's Resurrection: preserve the spirit of adoption which thou hast given to the new progeny of thy household; that being renewed in body and mind, they may render thee undiluted service. Through the same Lord.

Léctio Epístolæ beáti Pauli Apóstoli ad Colossénses
Col 3: 1-4.

Fratres: si consurrexístis cum Christo, quæ sursum sunt quǽrite, ubi Christus est in déxtera Dei sedens: quæ sursum sunt sápite, non quæ super terram. Mórtui enim estis, et vita vestra est abscóndita cum Christo in Deo. Cum Christus apparúerit, vita vestra: tunc et vos apparébitis cum ipso in glória.

Brethren: if you be risen with Christ, seek the things that are above, where Christ is sitting at the right hand of God: mind the things that are above, not the things that are upon the earth. For you are dead, and your life is hid with Christ in God. When Christ should appear, who is your life, then you also shall appear with him in glory.

After the epistle, all stand, and the celebrant intones:

VIII.

AL-le- lú- ia.

He sings this three times, each time starting on a higher pitch. The choir repeats it each time.

After the third Allelúia, *the choir continues: -.8*

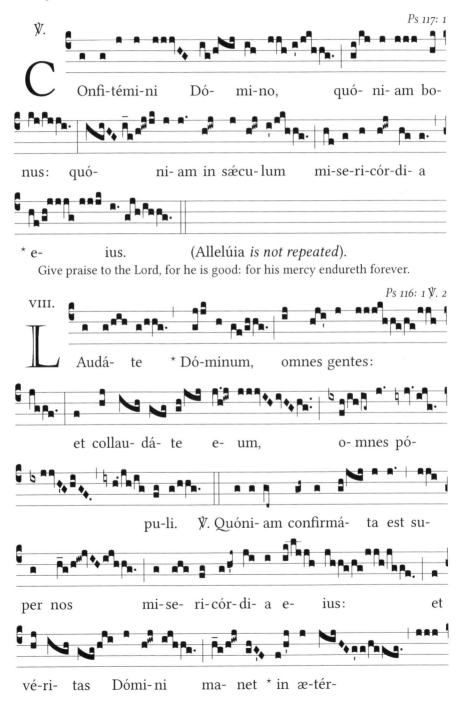

Ps 117: 1

℣.

COnfi-témi-ni Dó- mi-no, quó- ni- am bo-

nus: quó- ni- am in sǽcu- lum mi-se-ri-cór-di- a

* e- ius. (Allelúia *is not repeated*).

Give praise to the Lord, for he is good: for his mercy endureth forever.

Ps 116: 1 ℣. 2

VIII.

LAudá- te * Dó-minum, omnes gentes:

et collau- dá- te e- um, o- mnes pó-

pu-li. ℣. Quóni- am confirmá- ta est su-

per nos mi-se- ri-cór-di- a e- ius: et

vé-ri- tas Dómi- ni ma- net * in æ-tér-

num.

O praise the Lord, all ye nations: and praise him all ye people. ℣. For his mercy is confirmed upon us: and the truth of the Lord remaineth forever.

Candles are not carried at the Gospel, but the rest is as usual.

✝ Sequéntia sancti Evangélii secúndum Matthǽum
Mt 28: 1-7.

Véspere autem sábbati, quæ lucéscit in prima sábbati, venit María Magdaléne, et áltera María vidére sepúlcrum. Et ecce terræmótus factus est magnus. Angelus enim Dómini descéndit de cælo: et accédens revólvit lápidem, et sedébat super eum: erat autem aspéctus eius sicut fulgur: et vestiméntum eius sicut nix. Præ timóre autem eius extérriti sunt custódes, et facti sunt velut mórtui. Respóndens autem Angelus, dixit muliéribus: « Nolíte timére vos: scio enim, quod Iesum, qui crucifíxus est, quǽritis: non est hic: surréxit enim, sicut dixit. Veníte, et vidéte locum, ubi pósitus erat Dóminus. Et cito eúntes dícite discípulis eius, quia surréxit et ecce præcédit vos in Galilǽam: ibi eum vidébitis. Ecce prædíxi vobis ».

And in the end of the Sabbath, when it began to dawn toward the first day of the week, came Mary Magdalen and the other Mary to see the sepulcher. And behold there was a great earthquake. For an Angel of the Lord descended from heaven, and coming, rolled back the stone and sat upon it: and his countenance was as lightening and his raiment as snow. And for fear of him the guards were struck with terror and became as dead men. And the Angel answering, said to the women: Fear not you: for I know that you seek Jesus who was crucified: He is not here: for he is risen, as he said. Come and see the place where the Lord was laid. And going quickly, tell ye his disciples that he is risen: and behold he will go before you into Galilee: there you shall see him. Lo, I have foretold it to you.

The Credo *and the Offertory antiphon are omitted.*

Secret

Súscipe, quǽsumus, Dómine, preces pópuli tui, cum oblatiónibus hostiárum: ut paschálibus initiáta mystériis, ad æternitátis nobis medélam, te operánte, profíciant. Per Dóminum nostrum.

Accept, we beseech thee, O Lord, the prayers of thy people, with these sacrificial offerings: that what has begun in the paschal mysteries, may by thine arrangement, avail unto us health eternal. Through our Lord.

Preface of Easter: Te quidem, Dómine, omni témpore, sed in hac potíssimum noctem, *p.* 14.

Vatican edition I

IV.

Sanctus, * Sanctus, Sanctus Dóminus De-us Sába- oth. Ple-ni sunt cæ- li et terra gló- ri-a tu- a. Ho-sánna in ex-cél-sis. Be-ne-díctus qui ve-nit in nó- mi-ne Dómi-ni.

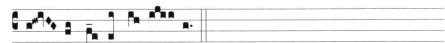

Ho- sánna in excél- sis.

In the Canon, the Communicántes *begins:*

Communicántes, et noctem sacra-tíssimam celebrántes Resurrec-tiónis Dómini nostri Iesu Christi se-cúndum carnem: sed et memóriam venerántes, in primis gloriósæ sem-per Vírginis Maríæ, Genetrícis eiús-dem Dei et Dómini nostri Iesu Chri-sti: † (*p.* 15)

In communion with, and celebrating the most sacred night of the resurrection of our Lord Jesus Christ according to the flesh, and also honoring in the first place the memory of the glorious ever Virgin Mary, Mother of our Lord and God Jesus Christ: †

And also, the Hanc ígitur *begins:*

Hanc ígitur oblatiónem servitú-tis nostræ, sed et cunctæ famí-liæ tuæ, quam tibi offérimus pro his quoque, quos regeneráre dignátus es ex aqua et Spíritu Sancto, tríbuens eis remissiónem ómnium peccató-rum, quǽsumus, Dómine, ut placátus accípias: ¶ (*p.* 16)

We therefore, beseech thee, O Lord, to be appeased and accept this oblation of our service, as also of thy whole family: offering it up to thee on behalf of these also whom thou hast been pleased to bring to a new birth by water and the Holy Spirit, giving them remission of all their sins: ¶

The Agnus Dei, *the prayer* Dómine Iesu Christe, qui dixísti, *and the kiss of peace are omitted.*

After Holy Communion, Lauds is sung in choir, as below.

LAUDS OF EASTER SUNDAY

Ant.
VI.

L-le-lú-ia, * alle-lú-ia, alle-lú-ia.

Psalm 150

1. Laudá- te Dóminum in san*ctis* e- ius: * laudá-te e- um in fir-

mamén-to vir*tú-tis* e-ius. *Flex:* bene-sonánti-bus: †

Praise ye the Lord in his holy places: praise ye him in the firmament of his power.

2. Laudáte eum in virtúti*bus* e-ius: * laudáte eum secúndum multitúdinem magnitú*dinis* eius.

Praise ye him for his mighty acts: praise ye him according to the multitude of his greatness.

3. Laudáte eum in so*no* tu-bæ: * laudáte eum in psaltério, *et* cíthara.

Praise him with sound of trumpet: praise him with psaltery and harp.

4. Laudáte eum in týmpano, *et* choro: * laudáte eum in chor*dis*, *et* órgano.

Praise him with timbrel and choir: praise him with strings and organs.

5. Laudáte eum in cýmbalis benesonántibus: † laudáte eum in cýmbalis iubila*tió*nis: * omnis spíritus *laudet* Dóminum.

Praise him on high sounding cymbals: praise him on cymbals of joy: let every spirit praise the Lord.

6. Glória Patri *et* **Fí**lio, * et Spirí*tui* **San**cto.

7. Sicut erat in princípio, et nunc, *et* **sem**per, * et in sǽcula sæcu*lórum.* Amen.

Ant.

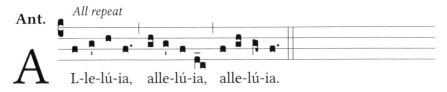

L-le-lú-ia, alle-lú-ia, alle-lú-ia.

There is no Chapter, Hymn, or ℣. The celebrant intones the antiphon Et valde mane *at once.*

Antiphon at the Benedictus

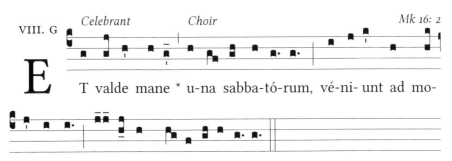

numéntum, or-to iam so-le, alle-lú-ia.

And very early in the morning, the first day of the week, they come to the sepulcher, the sun being now risen.

The altar is incensed during the canticle Benedíctus:

Canticle of Zachary
Lk 1:68-79.

1. Be-ne-díctus Dómi-nus, De-us Isra-ël: * qui-a vi-si-tá-vit, et

fe-cit redempti-ónem ple-bis su-æ:

Blessed be the Lord God of Israel: because he hath visited and wrought the redemption of his people:

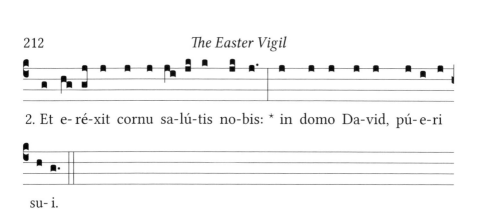

2. Et e-ré-xit cornu sa-lú-tis no-bis: * in domo Da-vid, pú-e-ri

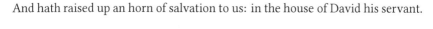

su- i.

And hath raised up an horn of salvation to us: in the house of David his servant.

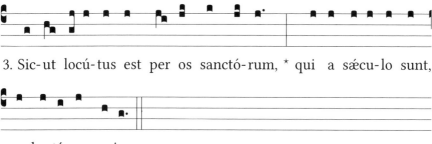

3. Sic-ut locú-tus est per os sanctó-rum, * qui a sǽcu-lo sunt,

prophe-tá-rum e-ius:

As he spoke by the mouth of his holy prophets, who are from the beginning:

4. Sa-lú-tem ex in-i-mí-cis nostris, * et de manu ómni- um, qui

odé-runt nos.

Salvation from our enemies, and from the hand of all that hate us.

5. Ad fa-ci- éndam mi-se-ri-córdi- am cum pá-tri-bus nostris: *

et memo-rá-ri testaménti su- i sancti.

To perform mercy to our fathers: and to remember his holy testament.

6. Iusiu-randum, quod iu-rá-vit ad Abraham patrem nostrum, *

da-tú-rum se no-bis:

The oath, which he swore to Abraham our father, that he would grant to us:

7. Ut si-ne timó-re, de manu in-imi-có-rum nostró-rum li-be-rá-

ti, * servi- ámus il-li.

That being delivered from the hand of our enemies, we may serve him without fear.

8. In sancti-tá-te, et iustí-ti- a co-ram ipso, * ómni-bus di- ébus

nostris.

In holiness and justice before him, all our days.

9. Et tu, pu- er, prophé-ta Altís-si-mi vocábe-ris: * præ-í-bis e-nim

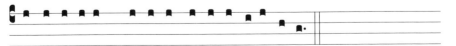

ante fá-ci- em Dómi-ni, pa-rá-re vi- as e-ius:

And thou, child, shalt be called the prophet of the Highest: for thou shalt go before the face of the Lord to prepare his ways:

10. Ad dandam sci- énti- am sa-lú-tis ple-bi e-ius: * in remissi- ó-

nem pecca-tó-rum e- ó-rum:

To give knowledge of salvation to his people: unto the remission of their sins:

11. Per vísce-ra mi-se-ri-córdi- æ De- i nostri: * in qui-bus vi-si-

tá-vit nos, ó-ri- ens ex alto:

Through the bowels of the mercy of our God: in which the Orient from on high hath visited us:

12. Il-luminá-re his, qui in ténebris, et in umbra mortis sedent: *

ad di-ri-géndos pedes nostros in vi- am pa-cis.

To enlighten them that sit in darkness, and in the shadow of death: to direct our feet into the way of peace.

13. Gló-ri- a Pa-tri, et Fí-li- o, * et Spi-rí-tu- i Sancto.

14. Sic-ut e-rat in princí-pi- o, et nunc, et semper, * et in sǽcu-la

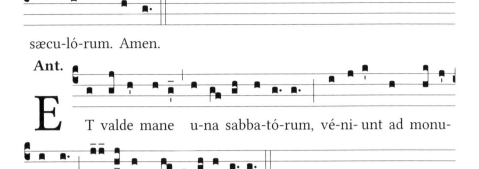

sæcu-ló-rum. Amen.

Ant.

ET valde mane u-na sabba-tó-rum, vé-ni-unt ad monu-

méntum, or-to iam so-le, alle-lú-ia.

Prayer (Postcommunion)

℣. Dóminus vobíscum.

℟. Et cum spíritu tuo.

Orémus.

Spíritum nobis, Dómine, tuæ caritátis infúnde: ut, quos sacraméntis Paschálibus satiásti tua fácias pietáte concórdes. Per Dóminum nostrum Iesum Christum, Fílium tuum: Qui tecum vivit et regnat in unitáte eiúsdem Spíritus Sancti Deus, per ómnia sǽcula sæculórum.

℟. Amen.

℣. Dóminus vobíscum.

℟. Et cum spíritu tuo.

The Lord be with you.

And with thy spirit.

Let us pray.

Impart to our souls, O Lord, the Spirit of thy love, that those whom thou hast fed with this paschal mystery may be united in harmony by thy merciful goodness. Through our Lord Jesus Christ, thy Son: Who lives and reigns with thee in the unity of the same Holy Spirit, one God, forever and ever.

The Lord be with you.

And with thy spirit.

The deacon:

VIII.

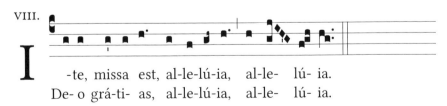

I-te, missa est, al-le-lú-ia, al-le- lú- ia.

De-o grá-ti- as, al-le-lú-ia, al-le- lú- ia.

Then follows the blessing as usual. The Last Gospel is omitted.

EASTER SUNDAY OF THE RESURRECTION

Sprinkling with Holy Water

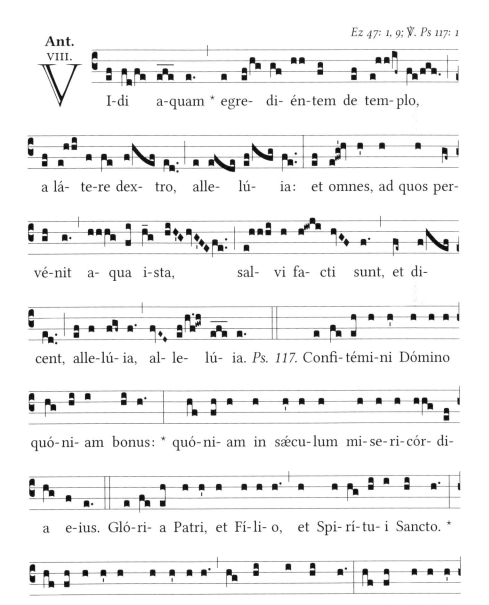

Ant. VIII.

Ez 47: 1, 9; ℣. Ps 117: 1

VIdi aquam * egre- di- én-tem de tem-plo,

a lá- te-re dex- tro, alle- lú- ia: et omnes, ad quos per-

vé-nit a- qua i-sta, sal- vi fa- cti sunt, et di-

cent, alle-lú- ia, al- le- lú- ia. *Ps. 117.* Confi- témi-ni Dómino

quó-ni- am bonus: * quó-ni- am in sæcu-lum mi-se-ri-cór- di-

a e-ius. Gló-ri- a Patri, et Fí-li- o, et Spi- rí-tu- i Sancto. *

Sic-ut e-rat in princí-pi- o, et nunc, et semper, et in sæcu-la

sæcu- ló-rum. Amen. *Repeat the Ant.* Vidi aquam.

I saw water gushing from the right side of the temple, alleluia: and all who received this water were healed and they shall say, alleluia, alleluia. *Ps.* Give praise to the Lord, for he is good: for his mercy endureth for ever.

℣. Osténde nobis, Dómine, misericór-diam tuam, allelúia.

Show us, O Lord, thy mercy, alleluia.

℟. Et salutáre tuum da nobis, allelúia.

And grant us thy salvation, alleluia.

℣. Dómine, exáudi oratiónem meam.

O Lord, hear my prayer.

℟. Et clamor meus ad te véniat.

And let my cry come unto thee.

℣. Dóminus vobíscum.

The Lord be with you.

℟. Et cum spíritu tuo.

And with thy spirit.

Orémus.

Let us pray.

Exáudi nos, Dómine, sancte Pater omnípotens, ætérne Deus: et míttere dignéris sanctum Angelum tuum de cælis: qui custódiat, fóveat, prótegat, vísitet, atque deféndat omnes habitántes in hoc habitáculo. Per Christum Dóminum nostrum.

Graciously hear us, O Lord, almighty Father, eternal God: and deign to send down from heaven thy holy angel: that he may guard, cherish, protect, visit, and defend all who dwell in this house. Through Christ our Lord.

℟. Amen.

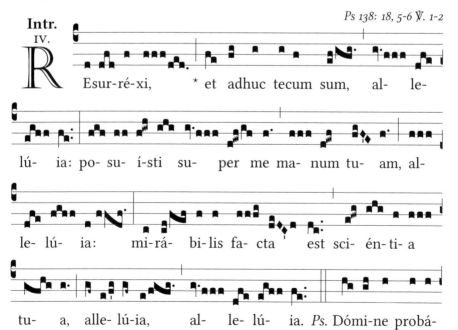

Intr. IV.   *Ps 138: 18, 5-6 ℣. 1-2*

R Esur-ré-xi, * et adhuc tecum sum, al- le-lú- ia: po- su- í-sti su- per me ma- num tu- am, al-le- lú- ia: mi-rá- bi-lis fa- cta est sci- én-ti- a tu- a, alle- lú-ia, al- le- lú- ia. *Ps.* Dómi-ne probá-

sti me, et cogno-vísti me: * tu cogno-vísti sessi- ónem me- am, et

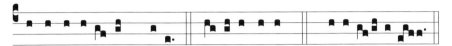

re-surrecti- ó-nem me- am. Gló-ri- a Patri. (*p.* 303) E u o u a e.

I arose, and am still with thee, alleluia: thou hast laid thy hand upon me, alleluia: thy knowledge is become wonderful, alleluia, alleluia. *Ps.* Lord, thou hast proved me, and known me: thou hast known my sitting down, and my rising up.

Kýrie, eléison, *p.* 204, *or:*

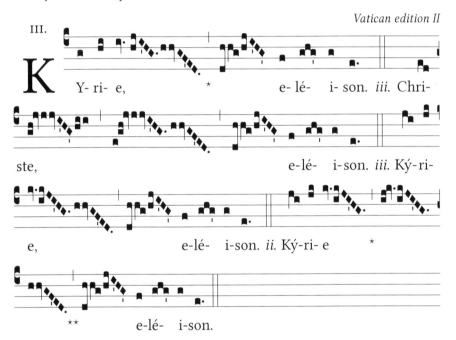

Glória in excélsis, *p.* 205, *or:*

Ado- rámus te. Glo-ri-fi-cá- mus te. Grá-ti- as á-gimus ti-bi

propter ma-gnam gló- ri- am tu- am. Dómi-ne De-us, Rex cæ-

léstis, De-us Pa-ter omnípot- ens. Dó- mi-ne Fi-li u-ni-gé-

ni-te Ie-su Christe. Dómi-ne De-us, Agnus De- i, Fí- li- us

Pa-tris. Qui tol- lis peccá-ta mundi, mi-se- ré-re no-bis.

Qui tol- lis peccá-ta mundi, súsci-pe depre-ca-ti- ó-nem no-

stram. Qui sedes ad déx-te-ram Pa- tris, mi-se- ré-re no-bis.

Quóni- am tu so- lus sanctus. Tu so-lus Dóminus. Tu so-lus Al-

tíssimus, Ie- su Chri- ste. Cum Sancto Spí- ri-tu, in gló-

ri- a De- i Pa- tris.　A-　　men.

Collect

Deus, qui hodiérna die per Uni-génitum tuum æternitátis no-bis áditum, devícta morte, reserásti: vota nostra, quæ præveniéndo aspí-ras, étiam adiuvándo proséquere. Per eúndem Dóminum.

O God, who on this day, through thine only-begotten Son, didst vanquish death and unseal for us the path to eternity: grant thine aid so that our desires, which thou hast anticipated and inspired, may also be pursued. Through the same Lord.

Léctio Epístolæ beáti Pauli Apóstoli ad Corínthios
1 Cor 5: 7-8.

Fratres: Expurgáte vetus fermén-tum, ut sitis nova conspérsio, si-cut estis ázymi. Etenim Pascha no-strum immolátus est Christus. Ita-que epulémur: non in ferménto véte-ri, neque in ferménto malítiæ et ne-quítiæ: sed in ázymis sinceritátis et veritátis.

Brethren: Purge out the old leaven, that you may be a new paste, as you are un-leavened: for Christ our Pasch is sacri-ficed. Therefore let us feast, not with the old leaven, not with the leaven of malice and wickedness, but with the unleavened bread of sincerity and truth.

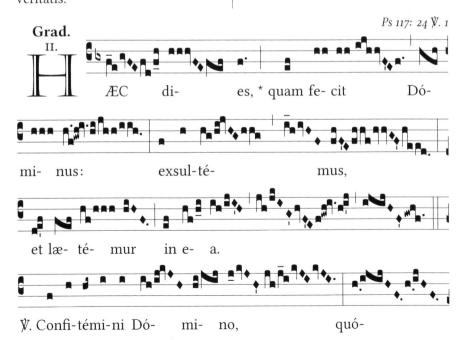

Ps 117: 24 ℣. 1

Grad.
II.

ÆC di-　　es, * quam fe- cit　　Dó-

mi- nus:　　exsul-té-　　　mus,

et læ- té- mur　in e-　a.

℣. Confi-témi-ni Dó-　mi- no,　　　quó-

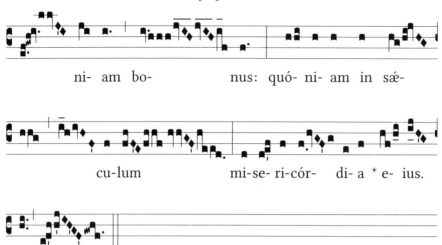

ni- am bo-   nus: quó- ni- am in sǽ-

cu-lum   mi-se- ri-cór-   di- a * e- ius.

This is the day which the Lord hath made: let us be glad and rejoice therein.
℣. Give praise to the Lord, for he is good: for his mercy endureth for ever.

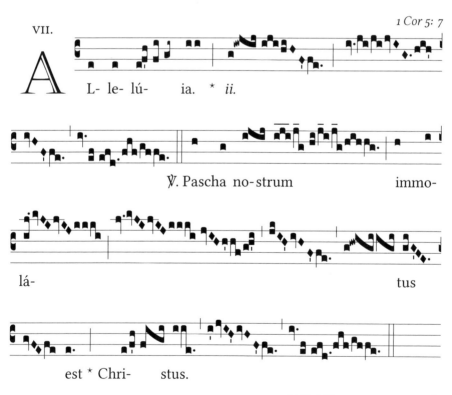

VII.

1 Cor 5: 7

AL- le- lú-   ia.   * *ii.*

℣. Pascha no-strum   immo-

lá-   tus

est * Chri-   stus.

(Allelúia *is not repeated*).

℣. Christ our Pasch is sacrificed.

The Sequence is now said:

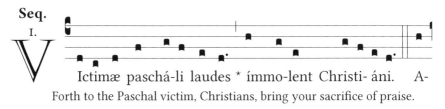

Ictimæ paschá-li laudes * ímmo-lent Christi- áni.   A-
Forth to the Paschal victim, Christians, bring your sacrifice of praise.

gnus redémit oves: Christus ínno-cens Patri re-conci-li- á-vit
The Lamb redeemed the sheep: And Christ, the sinless One, hath to the Father

pecca-tó-res. Mors et vi-ta du- éllo confli-xé-re mi-rándo: dux
sinners reconciled. Together, Death and Life in strange conflict strove: the Prince

vi-tæ mórtu-us, regnat vi-vus. Dic no-bis Ma-rí- a, quid vi-dí-
of Life, who died, now liveth and reigneth. What thou sawest, Mary, say, as thou

sti in vi- a? Sepúlcrum Christi vi-véntis, et gló-ri- am vi-di
wentest on the way? I saw the tomb wherein the Living One had lain; I saw his

re-surgéntis: Angé-li-cos testes, sudá-ri- um, et vestes. Surré-
glory as he rose again. Napkin and linen clothes, and Angels twain. Yea, Christ

xit Christus spes me- a: præcédet su-os in Ga-li-læ- am. Scimus
is risen, my hope and he: Will go before his own into Galilee.   We know

Christum surre-xísse   a mórtu- is ve-re: tu no-bis, victor Rex,
that Christ indeed has risen from the grave: thou King of Victory!

mi-se-ré-re.   A-men.   Alle-lú-ia.
Have mercy, Lord.

✠ Sequéntia sancti Evangélii secúndum Marcum

Mk 16: 1-7.

In illo témpore: María Magdaléne et María Iacóbi et Salóme emérunt arómata, ut veniéntes úngerent Iesum. Et valde mane una sabbatórum, véniunt ad monuméntum, orto iam sole. Et dicébant ad ínvicem: Quis revólvet nobis lápidem ab óstio monuménti? Et respiciéntes vidérunt revolútum lápidem. Erat quippe magnus valde. Et introëúntes in monuméntum vidérunt iúvenem sedéntem in dextris, coopértum stola cándida, et obstupuérunt. Qui dicit illis: Nolíte expavéscere: Iesum quǽritis Nazarénum, crucifíxum: surréxit, non est hic, ecce locus, ubi posuérunt eum. Sed ite, dícite discípulis eius et Petro, quia præcédit vos in Galilǽam: ibi eum vidébitis, sicut dixit vobis.

At that time: Mary Magdalen, and Mary the mother of James, and Salome, bought sweet spices that, coming, they might anoint Jesus. And very early in the morning, the first day of the week, they came to the sepulcher, the sun being now risen: and they said one to another: Who shall roll us back the stone from the door of the sepulcher? And looking, they saw the stone rolled back, for it was very great. And entering into the sepulcher, they saw a young man sitting on the right side, clothed with a white robe, and they were astonished. Who saith to them: Be not affrighted; you seek Jesus of Nazareth, who was crucified; he is risen, he is not here; behold the place where they laid him. But go, tell his disciples and Peter, that he goeth before you into Galilee; there you shall see him, as he told you.

The Credo *is said: I, p. 58, or:*

℣.

Credo in unum De- um, Patrem omnipot-éntem, factó-

rem cæ-li et terræ, vi-si-bí-li- um ó-mni- um, et invi- si-bí-

li- um. Et in unum Dóminum Ie-sum Christum, Fí-li- um De- i

uni-gé-ni-tum. Et ex Patre na- tum ante ómni- a sǽ- cu-la.

De-um de De-o, lumen de lúmi-ne, De-um ve-rum de De-o ve-

ro. Gé-ni-tum, non fa- ctum, consubstanti- á-lem Patri: per quem

ómni- a fa-cta sunt. Qui propter nos hómi-nes, et propter no-

stram sa- lú-tem descéndit de cæ-lis. Et incarná-tus est de Spí-

ri-tu Sancto ex Ma-rí- a Vírgi-ne: Et homo factus est. Cru- ci-

fí- xus ét-i- am pro no-bis: sub Pónti- o Pi-lá-to passus, et se-

púl- tus est. Et re-surré-xit térti- a di- e, secúndum Scriptú-ras.

Et ascéndit in cæ- lum: sedet ad déxte-ram Pa- tris. Et í-te-

rum ventú-rus est cum gló-ri- a, iudi-cá-re vi-vos et mórtu-os:

cu-ius regni non e-rit fi-nis. Et in Spí-ri-tum Sanctum, Dómi-

num, et vi-vi-fi-cántem: qui ex Patre Fi-li- óque pro-cé-dit. Qui

cum Patre et Fí-li- o simul ado-rá-tur, et conglo-ri-fi-cá-tur:

qui locú-tus est per Prophé-tas. Et unam sanctam cathó-li-cam et

apostó-li-cam Ecclé-si- am. Confí-te- or unum baptísma in re-

missi- ónem pecca-tó-rum. Et exspécto re-surrecti- ónem mortu-

ó-rum. Et vi-tam ventú-ri sǽ-cu-li. A-　　　　　men.

Offert.
IV.

Ps 75: 9-10

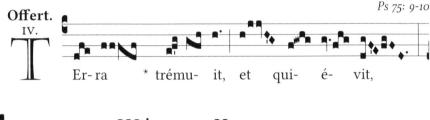

Er- ra　　* trému- it, et　qui- é- vit,

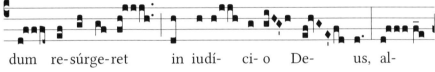

dum　re-súrge-ret　　in iudí- ci- o　De-　us, al-

le-　　　　lú-ia.

The earth trembled and was still, when God arose in judgment, alleluia.

Secret

Súscipe, quǽsumus, Dómine, preces pópuli tui, cum oblatiónibus hostiárum: ut paschálibus initiáta mystériis, ad æternitátis nobis medélam, te operánte, profíciant. Per Dóminum nostrum.

Accept, we beseech thee, O Lord, the prayers of thy people, with these sacrificial offerings: that what has begun in the paschal mysteries, may by thine arrangement, avail unto us health eternal. Through our Lord.

Preface of Easter: Te quidem, Dómine, omni témpore, sed in hac potíssimum die, *p.* 14.

Sanctus, *p. 209, or:*

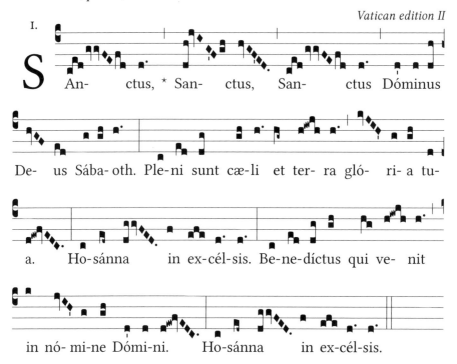

Vatican edition II

I.

SAn- ctus, * San- ctus, San- ctus Dóminus

De- us Sába- oth. Ple-ni sunt cæ-li et ter- ra gló- ri- a tu-

a. Ho-sánna in ex-cél-sis. Be-ne-díctus qui ve- nit

in nó- mi-ne Dómi-ni. Ho-sánna in ex-cél-sis.

In the Canon, through Easter Saturday, the Communicántes *begins:*

Communicántes, et diem sacratíssimum celebrántes Resurrectiónis Dómini nostri Iesu Christi secúndum carnem: sed et memóriam venerántes, in primis gloriósæ semper Vírginis Maríæ, Genetrícis eiúsdem Dei et Dómini nostri Iesu Christi: †
(p. 15)

In communion with, and celebrating the most sacred day of the resurrection of our Lord Jesus Christ according to the flesh, and also honoring in the first place the memory of the glorious ever Virgin Mary, Mother of our Lord and God Jesus Christ: †

And also, the Hanc ígitur *begins:*

Hanc ígitur oblatiónem servitútis nostræ, sed et cunctæ famíliæ tuæ, quam tibi offérimus pro his quoque, quos regeneráre dignátus es ex aqua et Spíritu Sancto, tríbuens eis remissiónem ómnium peccatórum, quǽsumus, Dómine, ut placátus accípias: ¶ *(p. 16)*

We therefore, beseech thee, O Lord, to be appeased and accept this oblation of our service, as also of thy whole family: offering it up to thee on behalf of these also whom thou hast been pleased to bring to a new birth by water and the Holy Spirit, giving them remission of all their sins: ¶

1 Cor 5: 7-8

Comm.
VI.

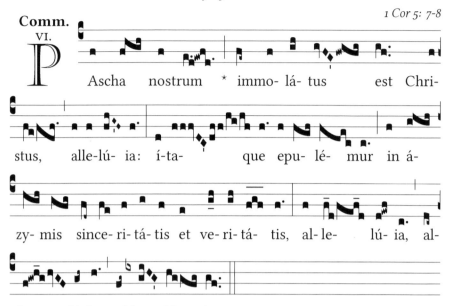

P Ascha   nostrum   * immo- lá- tus   est Chri-

stus,   alle-lú- ia: í-ta-   que epu- lé-   mur in á-

zy- mis   since- ri- tá- tis et ve- ri- tá- tis, al- le-   lú- ia,   al-

le-   lú-ia, al-le- lú-   ia.

Christ, our Pasch is sacrificed, alleluia: therefore let us feast with the unleavened
bread of sincerity and truth, alleluia, alleluia, alleluia.

Psalm 117
℣. *1-2, 5, 8, 10-11, 13-17, 21-26.*

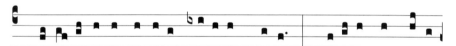

1. Confi-témi-ni Dómino quóni- am bonus: * quóni- am in sǽcu-

lum mi-se-ri-córdi- a e-ius. *Ant.*
Give praise to Lord, for he is good: for his mercy endureth for ever.

2. Di-cat nunc Isra- ël quóni- am bonus: * quóni- am in sǽcu-lum

mi-se-ri-córdi- a e-ius. *Ant.*
Let Israel now say that he is good: that his mercy endureth for ever.

3. De tri-bu-la-ti- óne invo-cá-vi Dóminum: * et exaudí-vit me

in la-ti-tú-di-ne Dóminus. *Ant.*

In my trouble I called upon the Lord: and the Lord heard me, and enlarged me.

4. Bonum est confí-de- re in Dómino, * quam confí-de-re in hó-

mi-ne. *Ant.*

It is good to confide in the Lord, rather than to have confidence in man.

5. Omnes gentes circu-ié-runt me: * et in nómi-ne Dómi-ni

qui- a ultus sum in e-os. *Ant.*

All nations compassed me about: and in the name of the Lord I have been revenged on them.

6. Circumdántes cir-cumdedé-runt me: * et in nómi-ne Dómi-ni

qui- a ultus sum in e-os. *Ant.*

Surrounding me they compassed me about: and in the name of the Lord I have been revenged on them.

7. Impúlsus evérsus sum ut cáde- rem: * et Dómi- nus suscé-

pit me.   *Ant.*

Being pushed I was overturned that I might fall: but the Lord supported me.

8. For-ti-túdo me-a, et laus me-a Dóminus: * et factus est mi-hi

in sa-lú-tem. *Ant.*

The Lord is my strength and my praise: and he is become my salvation.

9. Vox exsulta-ti- ónis, et sa-lú-tis: * in tabernácu-lis iustó-rum.

Ant.

The voice of rejoicing and of salvation is in the tabernacles of the just.

10. Déxte- ra Dómi-ni fe-cit virtú-tem: déxte-ra Dómi-ni exaltá-

vit me, déxte-ra Dómi-ni fe-cit virtú-tem. *Ant.*

The right hand of the Lord hath wrought strength: the right hand of the Lord hath exulted me, the right hand of the Lord hath wrought strength.

11. Non mó-ri- ar, sed vi-vam: * et narrábo ó-pe-ra Dómi-ni.

Ant.

I shall not die, but live: and shall declare the works of the Lord.

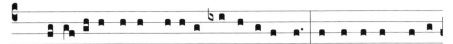

12. Confi-tébor ti-bi quóni- am exaudísti me: * et factus es mi-hi

in sa-lú-tem. *Ant.*

I will give glory to thee because thou hast heard me: and art become my salvation.

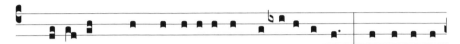

13. Lá-pi-dem, quem reprobavé-runt æ-di-fi-cántes: * hic factus est

in ca-put ángu-li. *Ant.*

The stone which the builders rejected: the same is become the head of the corner.

14. A Dómino fa-ctum est istud: * et est mi-rá-bi-le in ó-cu-lis

nostris. *Ant.*

This is the Lord's doing: and it is wonderful in our eyes.

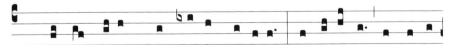

15. Hæc est di- es, quam fe-cit Dóminus: * exsultémus et læ-té-

mur in e- a. *Ant.*

This is the day which the Lord hath made: let us be glad and rejoice therein.

16. O Dómi-ne, salvum me fac, O Dómi-ne, bene prospe-rá-re: *

bene-díctus qui ve-nit in nómi-ne Dómi-ni.   *Ant.*

O Lord, save me: O Lord, give good success: blessed be he that cometh in the name Lord.

℣. Gló-ri- a Patri, et Fí-li- o,   et Spi- rí-tu- i Sancto. * Sic-ut e-rat

in princí-pi- o,   et nunc, et semper, et in sǽcu-la sæcu-ló-rum.

Amen.   *Ant.*

Postcommunion

Spíritum nobis, Dómine, tuæ caritátis infúnde: ut, quos sacraméntis paschálibus satiásti, tua fácias pietáte concórdes. Per Dóminum nostrum Iesum Christum, Fílium tuum:
Qui tecum vivit et regnat in unitáte eiúsdem Spíritus Sancti Deus, per
ómnia sǽcula sæculórum.
℟. Amen.

Pour forth upon us, O Lord, the spirit
of thy love: that, those who have been
fed with paschal sacraments, may by
thy loving-kindness, be one in heart.
Through our Lord Jesus Christ, thy Son:
Who lives and reigns with thee in the
unity of the same Holy Spirit, one God,
forever and ever.

VIII.

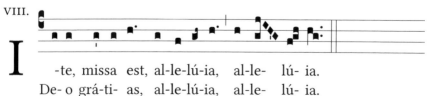

I-te, missa est, al-le-lú-ia,   al-le-   lú- ia.
De- o grá-ti- as, al-le-lú-ia, al-le-   lú- ia.

APPENDIX

PALM SUNDAY

Additional Chants for the Procession

8

¶ *Previously sung before the Gospel that precedes the procession with palms.*

Jn 11: 47-50, 53 • Vatican Gradual 143

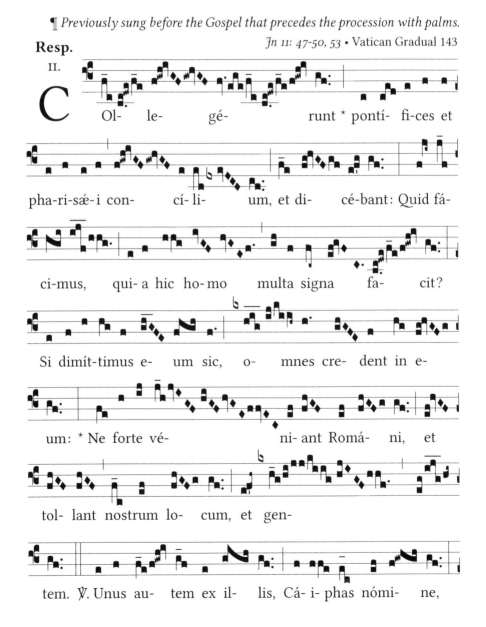

Resp.

II.

COl- le- gé- runt * pontí- fi-ces et pha-ri-sǽ-i con- cí- li- um, et di- cé-bant: Quid fá-ci-mus, qui- a hic ho-mo multa signa fa- cit? Si dimít-timus e- um sic, o- mnes cre- dent in e- um: * Ne forte vé- ni- ant Romá- ni, et tol- lant nostrum lo- cum, et gen- tem. ℣. Unus au- tem ex il- lis, Cá- i- phas nómi- ne,

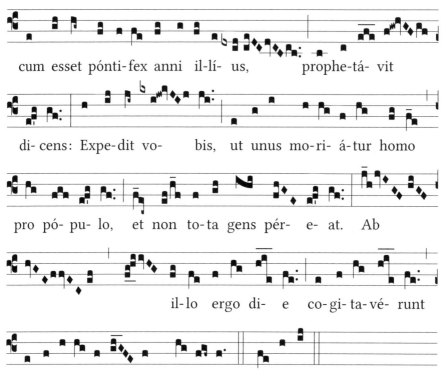

cum esset pónti-fex anni il-lí- us, prophe-tá- vit

di- cens: Expe-dit vo- bis, ut unus mo-ri- á-tur homo

pro pó- pu- lo, et non to-ta gens pér- e- at. Ab

il-lo ergo di- e co-gi- ta-vé- runt

interfí-ce-re e- um, di-céntes. * Ne forte.

The chief priests and the Pharisees gathered a council and said: What do we, for this man doth many miracles? If we let him alone so, all will believe in him: * And the Romans will come, and take away our place and nation. ℣. But one of them, called Caiphas, being the high priest that year, prophesied, saying: It is expedient for you that one man should die for the people, and that the whole nation perish not. From that day, therefore, they devised to put him to death, saying: * And the Romans will come, and take away our place and nation.

9

¶ *Previously sung before the Gospel that precedes the procession with palms.*

Mt 26: 39, 41 • Vatican Gradual 144

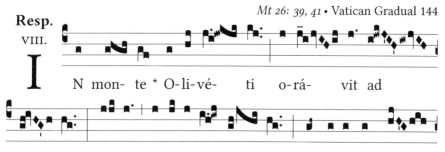

Resp.
VIII.

I N mon- te * O-li-vé- ti o-rá- vit ad

Pa- trem: Pa- ter, si fí- e-ri pot- est, tránse- at a me

ca- lix i- ste: * Spí- ri-tus qui- dem promptus est, ca-

ro autem in- fír- ma: fi- at vo-lún-tas tu- a.

℣. Vi-gi-lá-te, et o-rá- te, ut non intré-tis in ten-

ta-ti- ó- nem. * Spí- ri-tus.

℣. On mount Olivet he prayed to his Father: Father, if it may be, let this chalice pass from me: * The spirit is indeed willing, but the flesh weak: thy will be done. ℣. Watch and pray, that ye enter not into temptation. * The spirit is indeed etc.

10

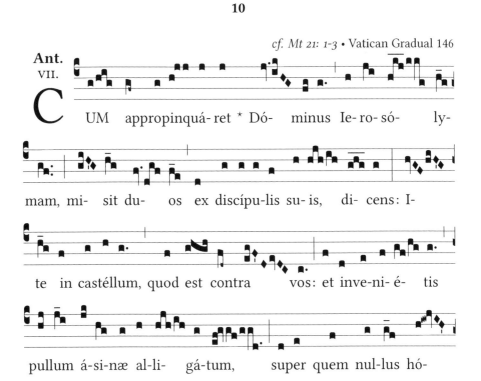

cf. Mt 21: 1-3 • Vatican Gradual 146

Ant.
VII.

C UM appropinquá- ret * Dó- minus Ie-ro-só- ly-

mam, mi- sit du- os ex discípu-lis su- is, di- cens: I-

te in castéllum, quod est contra vos: et inve-ni- é- tis

pullum á-si-næ al-li- gá-tum, super quem nul-lus hó-

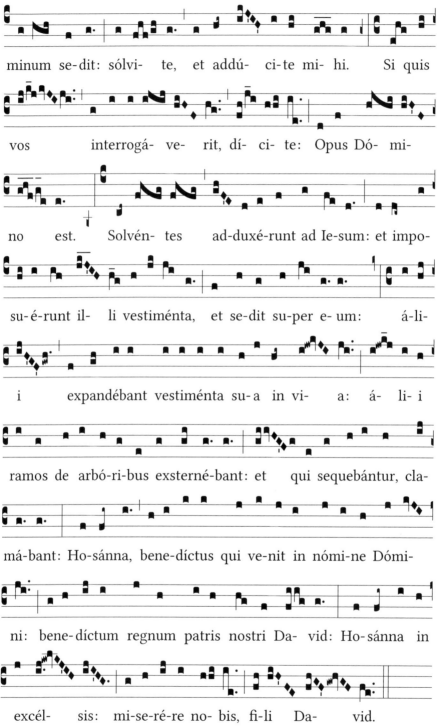

minum se-dit: sólvi- te, et addú- ci-te mi- hi. Si quis

vos interrogá- ve- rit, dí- ci- te: Opus Dó- mi-

no est. Solvén- tes ad-duxé-runt ad Ie-sum: et impo-

su-é-runt il- li vestiménta, et se-dit su-per e- um: á-li-

i expandébant vestiménta su-a in vi- a: á- li- i

ramos de arbó-ri-bus exsterné-bant: et qui sequebántur, cla-

má-bant: Ho-sánna, bene-díctus qui ve-nit in nómi-ne Dómi-

ni: bene-díctum regnum patris nostri Da- vid: Ho-sánna in

excél- sis: mi-se-ré-re no- bis, fi-li Da- vid.

When our Lord drew nigh to Jerusalem, he sent two of his disciples, saying: Go
ye into the village over against you: and you shall find an ass's colt tied, on which

no man hath sat: loose it, and bring it to me. If any man shall question you, say: The
Lord hath need of it. They loosed it and brought it to Jesus: and laid their garments
upon it, and he sat thereon: some spread their garments in the way: others strewed
branches from the trees: and those who followed cried out: Hosanna, blessed is
he that cometh in the name of the Lord: blessed be the reign of our father David:
Hosanna in the highest, O son of David, have mercy on us.

11

cf. Jn 12: 12-13 • Vatican Gradual 148

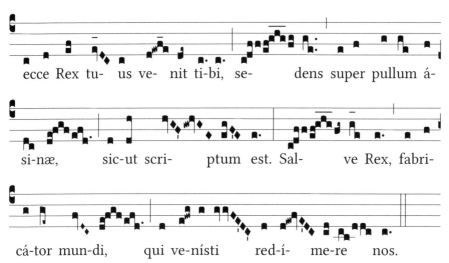

ecce Rex tu- us ve- nit ti-bi, se- dens super pullum á-si-næ, sic-ut scri- ptum est. Sal- ve Rex, fabri-cá-tor mun-di, qui ve-nísti red-í- me-re nos.

When the people heard that Jesus was coming to Jerusalem, they took palm branches: and went forth to meet him, and the children cried out, saying: This is he that is come for the salvation of the people. He is our salvation, and the redemption of Israel. How great is he whom the Thrones and Dominions go forth to meet! Fear not, O daughter of Sion; behold thy King cometh to thee sitting on an ass's colt, as it is written. Hail, O King, creator of the world, who art come to redeem us!

12

cf. Jn 12: 1, 12-13 • Vatican Gradual 149

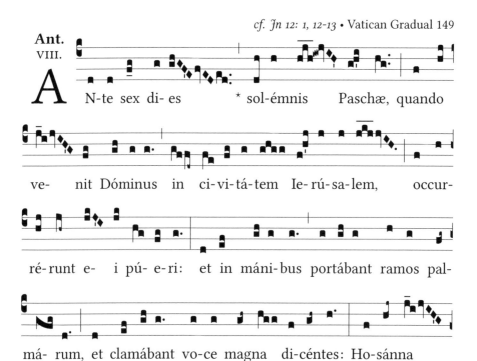

Ant.
VIII.

ANte sex di- es * sol-émnis Paschæ, quando ve- nit Dóminus in ci-vi-tá-tem Ie-rú-sa-lem, occur-ré-runt e- i pú- e-ri: et in máni-bus portábant ramos pal-má- rum, et clamábant vo-ce magna di-céntes: Ho-sánna

in excél-sis: bene-díctus qui ve-ní-sti in mul-

ti-tú- di-ne mi-se-ri-cór-di- æ: Ho-sánna

in excél-sis.

Six days before the solemn feast of the Passover, when our Lord came into the city of Jerusalem, the children met him: and in their hands they carried palm branches, and they cried out with a loud voice, saying: Hosanna in the highest: blessed art thou who art come in the multitude of thy mercy: Hosanna in the highest.

13

Ad libitum, a variation of antiphon 5, p. 36.

12th c. • Graduale Romanum 174

Ant.
VIII. G

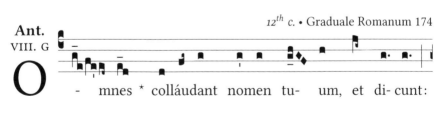

O - mnes * colláudant nomen tu- um, et di- cunt:

« Be- ne-díctus qui ve- nit in nó- mi-ne Dómi-ni. Ho- sánna

in ex-cél-sis ». *Ps.* Lauda, Ierúsalem. *p.* 36.

14

Hymn

10th c. • Liber Hymnarius 65

II.

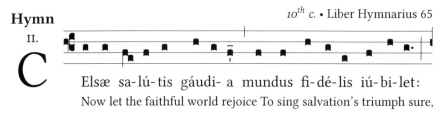

C Elsæ sa-lú-tis gáudi- a mundus fi-dé-lis iú-bi-let:
Now let the faithful world rejoice To sing salvation's triumph sure,

Ie-sus, redémptor ómni- um, mortis per-émit prínci-pem.
For Jesus Christ redeemed us all And overcame the prince of death.

2. Palmæ et olívæ súrculos
cœtus viándo déferens,
« Hosánna David fílio »
claris frequéntat vócibus.

The crowd on the road carrying up
alms and olive branches
repeat with loud voices:
"Hosanna to the Son of David."

3. Nos ergo summo príncipi
currámus omnes óbviam;
melos canéntes glóriæ,
palmas gerámus sóbrias.

Let us all therefore run
to meet the highest King,
singing sweet songs of glory,
soberly bearing palms.

4. Cursúsque nostros lúbricos
donis beátis súblevet,

May he with gifts of grace
  keep us from straying on dang'rous
    paths,

grates ut omni témpore
ipsi ferámus débitas.

that we may give him
due thanks at all times.

5. Deo Patri sit glória
eiúsque soli Fílio
cum Spíritu Paráclito,
in sempitérna sæcula. Amen.

Glory to God the Father
and to his only Son
with the Spirit Paraclete
for eternal ages.

15

Ancient hymn for Palm Sunday; Ambrosian melody.

I

Hymn

II.

Agnum sa-lú-tis gáudi- um Læ-té-tur omne sǽ-cu-

Let age to age with great delight Acclaim salvation's cheering sight,

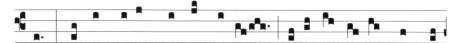

lum, Ie- sus redémptor ómni- um   Saná- vit orbem lángui-

Since Jesus our Redeemer hath Raised up the fainting world from death.

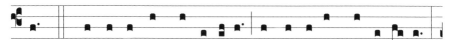

dum. 2. Sex ante Paschæ fé-ri- as, Advé-nit in Bethá-ni- am,

Six days before the Paschal feast Nigh Bethany His journey ceased,

Ubi pi- e post trídu- um   Re- susci- tá- vit Lá- za- rum.

Where He with love, now three days o'er Did Lazarus to life restore.

3. Nardi Ma- rí- a písti- ci Sumpsit libram mox ópti- mi.

There Mary took of spikenard dear The pound untainted, without peer,

Unxit be- á- tos Dómi- ni   Pedes, ri- gándo lácrymis.

Embalmed her Master's blessèd feet Bedewing them with teardrops sweet.

4. Post hæc iugá- lis á- sinæ, Ie- sus supérnus árbi- ter,

Then Jesus, highest Judge of all Upon a colt, an ass's foal,

Pullo sedebat, íncly- tam　　Pergé- bat Ie- ró- sol- ymam.
Was pleased to sit, and thusly passed To proud Jerusalem at last.

5. O quam stupénda pí- e- tas, Mi- ra De- i cleménti- a,
O marvelous that tender love, O meekness rare of God above,

Sessor a-sél-li fí- e-ri,　　Digná-tur auctor sæcu-li.
That He who made creation wide On ass's colt should deign to ride!

II

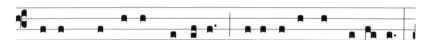

6. O-lim prophé-ta præsci- us Prædí-xit almo spí- ri- tu:
'Twas He the Seer's clear spirit eyed, And thrilling voice foretold,

« Exsúlta, » di-cens, « fí-li- a　　Si- on, sa- tis et iú-bi-la! »
When "Daughter," rise and shout he cried, "Shout, Sion, and behold!"

7. « Rex, ecce, tu- us húmi- lis, No- li timé- re, vé- ni- et,
"Thy King doth come, yon lowly One, Fear not, Behold the sign,

Pullo iugá- lis ré- si- dens,　　Ti- bi be- nígnus pá- ti- ens. »
On foal of ass He rideth on, Meek, patient and benign."

8. Ramos vi- réntes súmpse- rat, Palma re- cí- sos té- ne- ra,
From tender palm the gath'ring throng The new-cut branches bore along,

Turba pro-céssit óbvi- am, Re-gi per-énni plú-rima.
And crowding came into the way To meet the King of endless day.

III

9. Cœtus sequens et prævi- us Sanctóque plenus spí- ri-tu
Before, behind, in concourse run, And in the Spirit's might,

Clamábat: « In altíssi- mis Ho- sánna Da- vid fí- li- o. »
"Hosanna" cry, "to David's Son Hosanna in the height!"

10. Qui- dam so- lú- tis própri- is Vi- am tegébant vés- ti- bus,
Some strip them of their garments gay To deck the royal road,

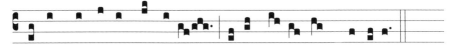

Plu-résque flo-res cándidum I-ter pa-rá-bant Dómino.
Some with bright flowers bestrew the way As less unmeet for God.

IV

11. Ad cu-ius omnis cí-vi-tas Commóta ingréssum trému-
At His approach with thrill intense The trembling city rang;

it, Hebræ-a pro-les áure- a Laudes fe- ré- bat dé- bi-tas.

But Judah's golden innocence His worthiest praises sang.

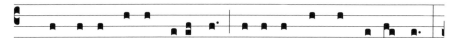

12. Nos ergo tanto Iúdi- ci Currámus omnes óbvi- am,

O let us thus run forth to greet Th' Almighty Judge and King,

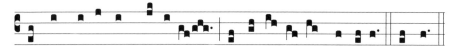

Palmas ge-réntes gló-ri-æ Mente ca-namus sóbri- a. Amen.

And bearing palms of glory meet With childlike spirit sing.

16

Hymn
I.

St. Bernard of Clairvaux († 1153) • Liber Hymnarius 124

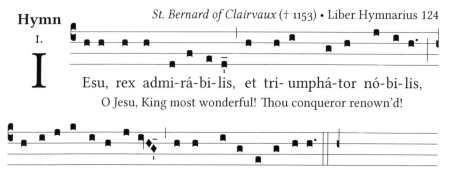

Esu, rex admi-rá-bi-lis, et tri- umphá-tor nó-bi-lis,

O Jesu, King most wonderful! Thou conqueror renown'd!

dulcédo in-effá-bi-lis, to-tus de-si-de-rá-bi-lis:

Thou sweetness most ineffable! In whom all joys are found!

2. Rex virtútum, rex glóriæ,
rex insígnis victóriæ,
Iesu, largítor grátiæ,
honor cæléstis cúriæ:

O King of glory! King of might!
From whom all graces come;
O beauty, honor, infinite,
Of our celestial home!

3. Te cæli chorus prædicat

et tuas laudes réplicat.
Iesus orbem lætíficat
et nos Deo pacíficat.

Hark! how the Heav'ns with praise
o'erflow;
O priceless gift of blood!
Jesus makes glad the world below,
And gains us peace with God.

4. Iesus in pace ímperat,
quæ omnem sensum súperat,
hanc semper mens desíderat
et illo frui próperat.

In peace he reigns—that peace divine,
For mortal sense too high;
That peace for which my soul doth pine,
To which it longs to fly.

5. Iam prosequámur láudibus
Iesum, hymnis et précibus,
ut nos donet cæléstibus
cum ipso frui sédibus.

To him praise, glory, without end,
And adoration be;
O Jesu, grant us to ascend,
And reign in Heav'n with thee!

6. Iesu, flos matris vírginis,
amor nostræ dulcédinis,
laus tibi sine términis,
regnum beatitúdinis. Amen.

O Jesu! spotless Virgin flower!
Our life and joy! to thee
Be praise, beatitude, and power,
Through all eternity.

17 — Christus vincit I (Laudes regiæ)

Petitions are sung by cantors, with the choir making responses.

cf. Cantuale Romano-Seraphicum 264

Hristus vincit, Christus regnat, Christus ímpe-rat!
All Repeat: Christus vincit.
Christ conquers, Christ reigns, Christ commands.

Exáudi, Christe. *ii.* Ecclé-si-æ sanctæ De- i sa-lus perpé-tu-a!

Redémptor mundi. ℟. Tu il-lam ádiuva! Sancta Ma-rí- a. ℟. Tu

il-lam ádiuva! Sancte Io-seph: ℟. Tu il-lam ádiuva!
All Repeat: Christus vincit.

Give ear, O Christ. For the holy Church of God, uniting the faithful beyond the limits of kingdoms, may there be everlasting health! Redeemer of the world. ℟. Grant her assistance. | Holy Mary. ℟. Grant her assistance. | Saint Joseph. ℟. Grant her assistance.

II

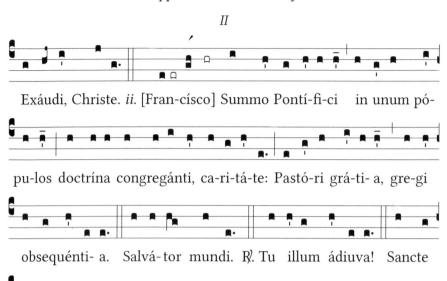

Exáudi, Christe. *ii.* [Fran-císco] Summo Pontí-fi-ci in unum pó-

pu-los doctrína congregánti, ca-ri-tá-te: Pastó-ri grá-ti- a, gre-gi

obsequénti- a. Salvá-tor mundi. ℟. Tu illum ádiuva! Sancte

Pe-tre. ℟. Tu illum ádiuva! Sancte Pau-le. ℟. Tu illum ádiuva!

All Repeat: Christus vincit.

Give ear, O Christ. For the Supreme Pontiff *N.*, who gathereth into one all peoples by his teaching, in charity: let there be dignity for the Shepherd, and obedience from the flock. O Savior of the world. ℟. Grant him assistance. | Saint Peter. ℟. Grant him assistance. | Saint Paul. ℟. Grant him assistance.

III

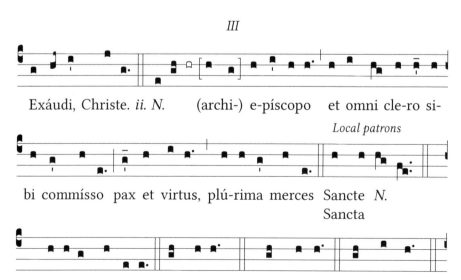

Exáudi, Christe. *ii. N.* (archi-) e-píscopo et omni cle-ro si-

Local patrons

bi commísso pax et virtus, plú-rima merces Sancte *N.*

Sancta

℟. Tu illum ádiuva! Rex regum. ℟. Rex noster. Spes nostra.

℟. Gló-ri- a nostra.

All Repeat: Christus vincit.

Give ear, O Christ. For *N.* our (Arch)bishop and for every cleric committed to him: let there be peace and strength, and a great bounty of good. Saint *N.* (local, diocesan patron) ℟. Grant him assistance. | King of kings. ℟. Our King. | Our hope. ℟. Our glory.

IV

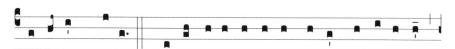

Exáudi, Christe. *ii.* Ma-gistrá-ti-bus et ómni-bus concí-vi-bus

no-bíscum o-ránti-bus: cordis ve-ra qui- es, vo-tó-rum efféctus.

Auxí-li- um christi- a-nó-rum. ℟. Tu illos ádiuva! Sancte Mícha-

el ℟. Tu illos ádiuva! *All Repeat:* Christus vincit.

Give ear, O Christ. To the magistrates and all fellow citizens praying with us: let the effect of their devotions be true rest for the heart. | Help of Christians. ℟. Grant him assistance. | Saint Michael. ℟. Grant him assistance.

Exáudi, Christe. *ii.* Ipsi so-li impé-ri- um, laus et iu-bi-lá-ti- o

per infi-ní-ta sæcu-la sæcu-ló-rum. ℟. Amen.

All Repeat: Christus vincit.

Give ear, O Christ. To him alone be empire, praise, and jubilation for endless ages of ages.

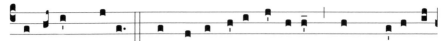

Exáudi, Christe. *ii.* Témpo-ra bóna vé-ni- ant, pax Christi vé-

ni- at redémptis sángui-ne Chrísti: Fe-lí-ci-ter! ℟. Fe-lí-ci-ter!

All

Fe-lí-ci-ter! Regnum Christi vé-ni- at! De- o grá-ti- as! A-men.

All

Christus vincit, Christus regnat, Christus ímpe-rat!

Give ear, O Christ. May they, redeemed by the blood of Christ, have prosperous times, let the Peace of Christ come: joyfully! ℟. Joyfully | Let the reign of Christ come! Thanks be to God! Amen.

18 — Christus vincit II

Aloys Kunc († 1895)
Chant Divers 251

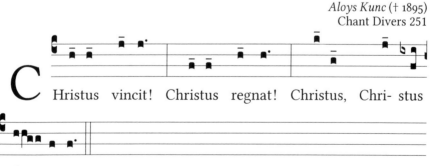

Hristus vincit! Christus regnat! Christus, Chri- stus

ím- pe-rat.

Christ conquers! Christ reigns! Christ, Christ commands.

1. *N.*   Summo Pontí-fi-ci   et uni-versá- li Papæ, vi-ta et

sa-lus perpé-tu- a. Christus.

For the Supreme Pontiff *N.*, the universal Pope: let there be perpetual life and salvation.

2. *N.,*   (archi-) e-pí-sco-po,   et omni cle-ro si-bi commisso,

pax, vi-ta   et sa-lus æ-térna. Christus.

For *N.* our (Arch)bishop and for every cleric committed to him: let there be eternal peace and life and salvation.

3. Témpo-ra bona vé-ni- ant, pax Christi vé-ni- at, Regnum Chri-

sti vé-ni- at. Christus.

May prosperous times come, may the peace of Christ come, may the reign of Christ come.

19 — **Christus vincit III**

Cantuale Romano-Seraphicum 266

VI. F

CHristus vincit, Christus regnat, Christus ímpe-rat!

Repeat: Christus vincit.

Christ conquers, Christ reigns, Christ commands.

Psalm 116

1. Laudá-te Dóminum, omnes Gentes: * laudá-te e-um, omnes pó-

pu-li: *Repeat:* Christus vincit.

O praise the Lord, all ye nations: praise him, all ye people.

2. Quóni- am confirmá-ta est super nos mi-se-ri-córdi- a e-ius: *

et vé-ri-tas Dómi-ni manet in æ-térnum. *Repeat:* Christus vincit.

For his mercy is confirmed upon us: and the truth of the Lord remaineth for ever.

3. Gló-ri- a Patri, et Fí-li- o, * et Spi-rí-tu- i Sancto.

Repeat: Christus vincit.

4. Sic-ut e-rat in princí-pi- o, et nunc, et semper, * et in sǽcu-la

sǽcu-ló-rum. Amen.   *Repeat:* Christus vincit.

Tract in a Psalm-tone

Liber Usualis 597

1. De- us, * De- us me- us, réspi-ce **in** me: * qua-re me de-re-*li-*

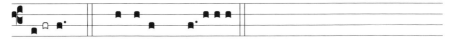

quí- sti? *Flex:* vi-débant me, † *The intonation is repeated at each verse.*

2. *Longe* a salúte **me**a * verba delictórum *me*órum.

3. *Deus* meus, clamábo per diem, nec ex**áu**dies: * et nocte, et non ad insipiénti*am* **mi**hi.

4. *Tu au*tem in sancto **há**bitas: * *laus* **Is**raël.

5. *In te* speravérunt patres **no**stri: * speravérunt, et liberá*sti* **e**os.

6. *Ad te* clamavérunt, et salvi **fa**cti sunt: * in te speravérunt, et non sunt *con***fú**si.

7. *Ego* autem sum vermis, et non **ho**mo: * oppróbrium hóminum, et abiéctio **ple**bis.

8. *Omnes* qui vidébant me, † aspernabántur me: * locúti sunt lábiis, et mové*runt* **ca**put.

9. *Sperá*vit in Dómino, erípiat **e**um: * salvum fáciat eum, quóniam *vult* **e**um.

10. *Ipsi* vero consideravérunt et conspexérunt me: † divisérunt sibi vestiménta **me**a, * et super vestem meam misé*runt* **sor**tem.

11. *Líbe*ra me de ore le**ó**nis: * et a córnibus unicornuórum humilitá*tem* **me**am.

12. *Qui ti*métis Dóminum, laudáte **e**um: * univérsum semen Iacob, magnificá*te* **e**um.

13. *Annun*tiábitur Dómino generátio ven**tú**ra: * et annuntiábunt cæli iustíti*am* **e**ius.

14. *Pópu*lo qui nas**cé**tur, * quem fe*cit* **Dó**minus.

Or, another simplified version:

II.

D

E- us, * De- us me-

us, réspi-ce in me: qua-re me de-re-li-quí-

sti? ℣. 1. Longe a sa-lú-te me-a verba de-lictó-rum me-ó-

rum. ℣. 2. De- us me-us clamábo per di- em, nec exáudi- es:

in nocte, et non ad insi-pi- énti- am mi- hi. ℣. 3. Tu autem

in sancto há-bi-tas, laus Isra- el. ℣. 4. In te spe-ravé-runt

patres nostri: spe-ravé-runt, et li-be-rásti e- os. ℣. 5. Ad te

cla-mavé-runt, et salvi facti sunt: in te spe-ravé-runt, et non sunt

confú- si. ℣. 6. Ego au- tem sum vermis, et non ho-

mo: oppróbri- um hóminum, et abiécti- o ple- bis.

℣. 7. Omnes qui vi-débant me, aspernabántur me: locú-ti sunt lá-

bi- is et mové-runt ca- put.   ℣. 8. Spe-rá-vit   in Dómi-

no, e-rí-pi- at e-um: salvum fá-ci- at e-um, quóni- am vult e-

um.   ℣. 9. Ipsi ve-ro consi-de-ravé-runt, et conspexé-runt

me: di-vi-sé-runt si-bi vestiménta me- a, et super vestem me-am

mi-sé-runt sortem.   ℣. 10. Lí- be-ra me de o-re le- ónis:

et a córni-bus uni-cornu-ó-rum humi-li-tá-tem me- am.

℣. 11. Qui timé-tis Dóminum, laudá-te e- um: uni-vérsum semen

Iacob, magni-fi-cá-te   e-um. ℣. 12. Annunti- á-bi-tur Dómino

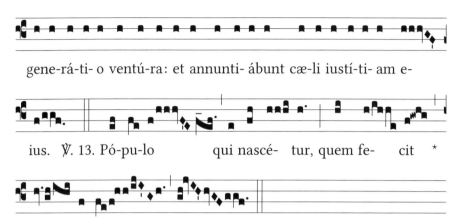

gene-rá-ti- o ventú-ra: et annunti- ábunt cæ-li iustí-ti- am e-

ius. ℣. 13. Pó-pu-lo qui nascé- tur, quem fe- cit ⋆

Dó- mi-nus.

HOLY THURSDAY

Hymn for the Blessing of the Holy Oils

¶ *From the Pontifical Chrism Mass.*

II. *Cantors:* Liber Usualis 665

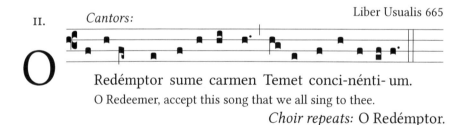

O Redémptor sume carmen Temet conci-nénti- um.
O Redeemer, accept this song that we all sing to thee.
Choir repeats: O Redémptor.

Cantors:

Audi, iudex mortu- ó- rum, Una spes mortá- li- um,
Hear, O Judge of the dead, one hope of humankind,

Audi vo-ces pro-fe-réntum Do-num pa-cis prǽvi- um.
listen to the voices of those who take the gift that precedes the peace.
Choir: O Redémptor.

Cantors:

Arbor fœta alma luce Hoc sacrándum pró-tu-lit, Fert hoc
On the fertile tree, the kindly sunlight formed this offering,

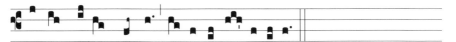

pro-na præsens turba Salva-tó-ri sǽcu-li.   *Choir:* O Redémptor.
which, bowed down, your people bring to the Savior of the world.

Cantors:

Stans ad a-ram imo supplex Infu-lá-tus Pónti-fex, Dé-bi-tum
Standing in front of the altar, deeply pleading, the adorned pontiff

persólvit omne consecrá-to Chrísma-te.   *Choir:* O Redémptor.
repairs all debts with the consecrated oil.

Cantors:

Consecrá- re tu digná- re, Rex per- énnis pá- tri- æ,
Deign to consecrate, sublime King of the earth,

Hoc o-lí-vum, signum vi-vum, Iu-ra contra dǽmonum.
this olive oil, a living sign, to combat the power of evil.

Choir: O Redémptor.

Cantors:

Ut nové-tur sexus omnis Uncti- ó-ne Chrísma-tis: Ut sa-
So may all, both men and women, Who are by the chrism sealed,

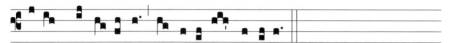

né-tur sau-ci- á-ta   digni-tá-tis gló-ri- a.   *Choir:* O Redémptor.
Be renewed, that human nature's Wounded glory may be healed.

Cantors:

Lo- ta mente sacro fonte Aufugántur crí- mi- na,
Bathing in the sacred fountain Shall the mind from sin redeem;

Uncta fronte sacro-sáncta   Influ-unt cha- rísma-ta.
Where the forehead is anointed Charismatic graces stream.

Choir: O Redémptor.

Cantors:

Corde na- tus ex Pa- réntis Alvum implens Vírgi- nis,
Of the Father's love begotten, Gracing once the Virgin's womb,

Præsta lucem, claude mortem Chrísma-tis con-sórti-bus.
Enlighten all who share this chrism; Close the door that leads to doom.

Choir: O Redémptor.

Cantors:

Sit hæc di- es festa no-bis, Sæcu-ló-rum sǽ-cu- lis Sit sacrá-
Let this be for us a feast day, While the ages pass away,

ta digna laude, Nec senéscat témpo-re. *Choir:* O Redémptor.

Sanctified by worthy praises, And undimmed by time's decay.

Mass IX

(Cum iubilo)

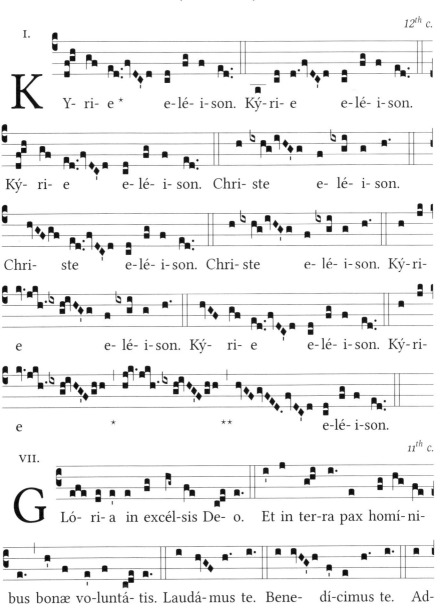

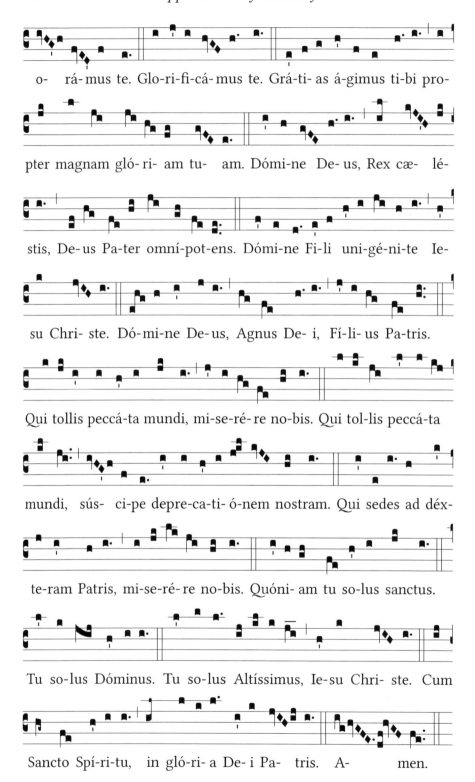

o- rá-mus te. Glo-ri-fi-cá-mus te. Grá-ti- as á-gimus ti-bi pro-

pter magnam gló-ri- am tu- am. Dómi-ne De- us, Rex cæ- lé-

stis, De- us Pa-ter omní-pot-ens. Dómi-ne Fi-li uni-gé-ni-te Ie-

su Chri- ste. Dó-mi-ne De- us, Agnus De- i, Fí-li- us Pa-tris.

Qui tollis peccá-ta mundi, mi-se-ré- re no-bis. Qui tol-lis peccá-ta

mundi, sús- ci-pe depre-ca-ti- ó-nem nostram. Qui sedes ad déx-

te-ram Patris, mi-se-ré- re no-bis. Quóni- am tu so-lus sanctus.

Tu so-lus Dóminus. Tu so-lus Altíssimus, Ie-su Chri- ste. Cum

Sancto Spí-ri-tu, in gló-ri- a De- i Pa- tris. A- men.

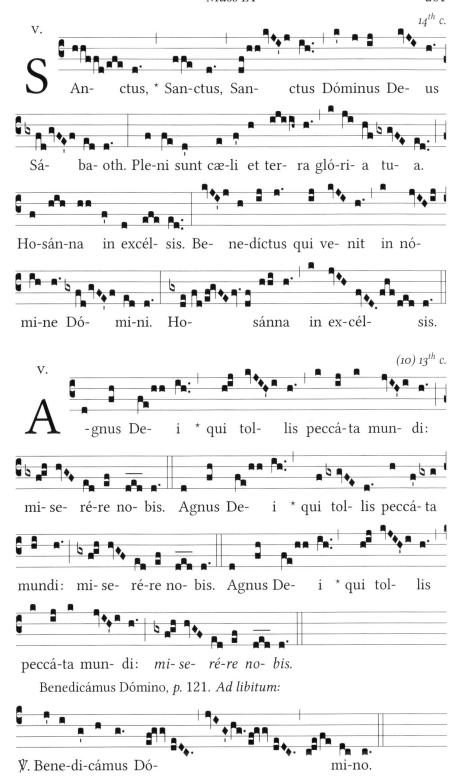

v. 14th c.

S An- ctus, * San-ctus, San- ctus Dóminus De- us

Sá- ba- oth. Ple-ni sunt cæ-li et ter- ra gló-ri- a tu- a.

Ho-sán-na in excél- sis. Be- ne-díctus qui ve- nit in nó-

mi-ne Dó- mi-ni. Ho- sánna in ex-cél- sis.

v. (10) 13th c.

A -gnus De- i * qui tol- lis peccá-ta mun- di:

mi- se- ré-re no- bis. Agnus De- i * qui tol- lis peccá- ta

mundi: mi- se- ré-re no- bis. Agnus De- i * qui tol- lis

peccá-ta mun- di: *mi- se- ré-re no- bis.*

Benedicámus Dómino, *p.* 121. *Ad libitum:*

℣. Bene-di-cámus Dó- mi-no.

℟. De- o grá- ti- as.

Additional Psalms at Communion

cf. Liber Usualis 680-84

Psalm 22

1. Dóminus re-git me, et ni-hil mi-hi **dé**-e-rit: * in loco páscu-æ

i-bi me col*loc*á-vit.

The Lord ruleth me: and I shall want nothing. He hath set me in a place of pasture.

2. Super aquam refectiónis edu**cá**vit me: * ánimam meam *con***vér**tit.

He hath brought me up, on the water of refreshment; he hath converted my soul.

3. Dedúxit me super sémitas ius**tí**tiæ: * propter no*men* **su**um.

He hath led me on the paths of justice, for his own name's sake.

4. Nam, et si ambulávero in médio umbræ mortis, non timébo **mal**a: * quóniam *tu* **me**cum es.

For though I should walk in the midst of the shadow of death, I will fear no evils, for thou art with me.

5. Virga tua, et báculus **tu**-us: * ipsa me con*sol*á**ta** sunt.

Thy rod and thy staff, they have comforted me.

6. Parásti in conspéctu meo **men**sam, * advérsus eos, qui trí*bu***lant** me.

Thou hast prepared a table before me against them that afflict me.

7. Impinguásti in óleo caput **me**-um: * et calix meus inébrians quam *præ***clá**rus est!

Thou hast anointed my head with oil; and my chalice which inebriateth me, how goodly is it!

8. Et misericórdia tua subsequétur me * ómnibus diébus vit*æ* me*æ*.	And thy mercy will follow me all the days of my life.
9. Et ut inhábitem in domo **Dó**mini, * in longitúdinem *di*érum.	And that I may dwell in the house of the Lord unto length of days.

The antiphon Dóminus Iesus *is repeated, p.* 117.

Psalm 71

1. De- us, iudí-ci- um tu-um **re**-gi da: * et iustí-ti- am tu- am fí-

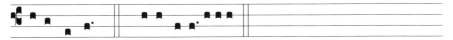

li- *o* **re**-gis. *Flex:* Ará-bi- æ, †

Give to the king thy judgment, O God: and to the king's son thy justice.

2. Iudicáre pópulum tuum in iustítia, * et páuperes tuos in *iu*dício.	To judge thy people with justice, and thy poor with judgment.
3. Suscípiant montes pacem **pó**pulo: * et colles *iu*stítiam.	Let the mountains receive peace for the people: and the hills justice.
4. Iudicábit páuperes pópuli, et salvos fáciet fílios **páu**perum: * et humiliábit calumni*a*tórem.	He shall judge the poor of the people, and he shall save the children of the poor: and he shall humble the oppressor.
5. Et permanébit cum sole, et ante **lu**nam, * in generatióne et genera*ti*ónem.	And he shall continue with the sun, and before the moon, throughout all generations.
6. Descéndet sicut plúvia in **vel**lus: * et sicut stillicídia stillántia su*per* **ter**ram.	He shall come down like rain upon the fleece; and as showers falling gently upon the earth.

7. Oriétur in diébus eius iustítia, et abundántia **pa**cis: * donec auferá*tur* **lu**na.

In his days shall justice spring up, and abundance of peace, till the moon be taken sway.

8. Et dominábitur a mari usque ad **ma**re: * et a flúmine usque ad términos orbis ter**rá**rum.

And he shall rule from sea to sea, and from the river unto the ends of the earth.

9. Coram illo prócident Æthí-opes: * et inimíci eius ter*ram* **lin**gent.

Before him the Ethiopians shall fall down: and his enemies shall lick the ground.

10. Reges Tharsis, et ínsulæ múnera **óf**ferent: * reges Arabum et Saba dona ad**dú**cent.

The kings of Tharsis and the islands shall offer presents: the kings of the Arabians and of Saba shall bring gifts.

11. Et adorábunt eum omnes reges **ter**ræ: * omnes gentes sérvi*ent* **e**i:

And all kings of the earth shall adore him: all nations shall serve him.

12. Quia liberábit páuperem a po**tén**te: * et páuperem, cui non erat ad**iú**tor.

For he shall deliver the poor from the mighty: and the needy that had no helper.

13. Parcet páuperi et **ín**opi: * et ánimas páuperum sal*vas* **fá**ciet.

He shall spare the poor and needy: and he shall save the souls of the poor.

14. Ex usúris et iniquitáte rédimet ánimas e**ó**rum: * et honorábile nomen eórum co*ram* **il**lo.

He shall redeem their souls from usuries and iniquity: and their names shall be honorable in his sight.

15. Et vivet, et dábitur ei de auro Arábiæ, † et adorábunt de ipso **sem**per: * tota die bene**dí***cent* ei.

And he shall live, and to him shall be given of the gold of Arabia, for him they shall always adore: they shall bless him all the day.

16. Et erit firmaméntum in terra in summis móntium, † superextollétur super Líbanum fructus **e**ius: * et florébunt de civitáte sicut fe*num* **ter**ræ.

And there shall be a firmament on the earth on the tops of mountains, above Libanus shall the fruit thereof be exalted: and they of the city shall flourish like the grass of the earth.

17. Sit nomen eius benedíctum in **sǽ**cula: * ante solem pérmanet no*men* **e**ius.

Let his name be blessed for evermore: his name continueth before the sun.

18. Et benedicéntur in ipso omnes tribus **ter**ræ: * omnes gentes magnificá*bunt* **e**um.

And in him shall all the tribes of the earth be blessed: all nations shall magnify him.

19. Benedíctus Dóminus, Deus **Is**raël, * qui facit mirabíli*a* **so**lus.

Blessed be the Lord, the God of Israel, who alone doth wonderful things.

20. Et benedíctum nomen maiestátis eius in ætérnum: † et replébitur maiestáte eius omnis **ter**ra * fi*at*, **fi**at.

And blessed be the name of his majesty for ever: and the whole earth shall be filled with his majesty. So be it. So be it.

The antiphon Dóminus Iesus *is repeated, p.* 117.

Psalm 103

1. Béne-dic ánima me- a, **Dó**mino: * Dómi-ne, De- us me- us, ma-

gni-fi-cá-tus es ve*hemén*ter. *Flex:* Dómi-ne! †

Bless the Lord, O my soul: O Lord my God, thou art exceedingly great.

2. Confessiónem, et decórem induísti: * amíctus lúmine sicut ve*stimén*to.

Thou hast put on praise and beauty: and art clothed with light as with a garment.

3. Exténdens cælum sicut **pel**lem: * qui tegis aquis superió*ra* **e**ius.

Who stretchest out the heaven like a pavilion: who coverest the higher rooms thereof with water.

4. Qui ponis nubem ascénsum **tu**um: * qui ámbulas super pennas ven**tó**rum.

Who makest the clouds thy chariot: who walkest upon the wings of the winds.

5. Qui facis ángelos tuos, **spí**ritus: * et minístros tuos ignem u**rén**tem.

Who makest thy angels spirits: and thy ministers a burning fire.

6. Qui fundásti terram super stabilitátem **su**am: * non inclinábitur in sǽcu*lum* **sǽ**culi.

Who hast founded the earth upon its own bases: it shall not be moved for ever and ever.

7. Abýssus, sicut vestiméntum, amíctus **e**ius: * super montes sta*bunt* **a**quæ.

The deep like a garment is its clothing: above the mountains shall the waters stand.

8. Ab increpatióne tua **fú**-gient: * a voce tonítrui tui for*mi***dá**bunt.

At thy rebuke they shall flee: at the voice of thy thunder they shall fear.

9. Ascéndunt montes: et descéndunt **cam**pi * in locum, quem fundá*sti* **e**is.

The mountains ascend, and the plains descend into the place which thou hast founded for them.

10. Términum posuísti, quem non transgrediéntur: * neque converténtur operíre **ter**ram.

Thou hast set a bound which they shall not pass over; neither shall they return to cover the earth.

11. Qui emíttis fontes in conváll-libus: * inter médium móntium pertransí*bunt* **a**quæ.

Thou sendest forth springs in the vales: between the midst of the hills the waters shall pass.

12. Potábunt omnes béstiæ **a**-gri: * exspectábunt ónagri in s**i***ti* **su**a.

All the beasts of the field shall drink: the wild asses shall expect in their thirst.

13. Super ea vólucres cæli ha-bi**tá**bunt: * de médio petrárum da*bunt* **vo**ces.

Over them the birds of the air shall dwell: from the midst of the rocks they shall give forth their voices.

14. Rigans montes de supe-rióribus **su**is: * de fruc-tu óperum tuórum satiábi*tur* **ter**ra:

Thou waterest the hills from thy upper rooms: the earth shall be filled with the fruit of thy works:

15. Prodúcens fœnum iu**mén**-tis: * et herbam servitú*ti* **hó**minum:

Bringing forth grass for cattle, and herb for the service of men.

16. Ut edúcas panem de **ter**-ra: * et vinum lætíficet *cor* **hó**minis:

That thou mayst bring bread out of the earth: And that wine may cheer the heart of man.

17. Ut exhílaret fáciem in ó-
leo: * et panis cor hóminis
*con*fír*m*et.

That he may make the face cheerful
with oil:　and that bread may
strengthen man's heart.

18. Saturabúntur ligna campi, et
cedri Líbani, quas plan**tá**vit: *
illic pásseres nidi*fi*cá*bu*nt.

The trees of the field shall be filled,
and the cedars of Libanus which he
hath planted: there the sparrows shall
make their nests.

19. Heródii domus dux est eórum: † montes excélsi **cer**vis: *
petra refúgium h*erin*á*c*iis.

The highest of them is the house of
the heron. The high hills are a refuge
for the harts, the rock for the irchins.

20. Fecit lunam in **tém**pora: *
sol cognóvit occá*sum* **su**um.

He hath made the moon for seasons:
the sun knoweth his going down.

21. Posuísti ténebras, et facta
est nox: * in ipsa pertransíbunt
omnes béstiæ **silv**æ.

Thou hast appointed darkness, and it
is night: in it shall all the beasts of
the woods go about:

22. Cátuli leónum rugiéntes, ut
rápiant: * et quærant a Deo
e*scam* **si**bi.

The young lions roaring after their
prey, and seeking their meat from
God.

23. Ortus est sol, et congregá-
ti sunt: * et in cubílibus suis
collo*ca*bún*t*ur.

The sun ariseth, and they are
gathered together: and they shall lie
down in their dens.

24. Exíbit homo ad opus **su**-
um: * et ad operatiónem suam
usque *ad* **vé**sperum.

Man shall go forth to his work, and
to his labor until the evening.

25. Quam magnificáta sunt ópe-
ra tua, Dómine! † óm-
nia in sapiéntia fe**cí**sti: * impléta est terra possessió*ne*
tua.

How great are thy works, O Lord?
thou hast made all things in wisdom:
the earth is filled with thy riches.

26. Hoc mare magnum, et
spatiósum **má**nibus: * illic
reptília, quorum non *est*
númerus.

So is this great sea, which stretcheth
wide its arms: there are creeping
things without number:

27. Animália pusílla cum **ma**-gnis: * illic naves per*transí*-bunt.

Creatures little and great. There the ships shall go.

28. Draco iste, quem formásti ad illudéndum **ei**: * ómnia a te exspéctant ut des illis escam *in* **tém**pore.

This sea dragon which thou hast formed to play therein. All expect of thee that thou give them food in season.

29. Dante te illis, **cól**ligent: * aperiénte te manum tuam, ómnia implebúntur bo*ni***tá**te.

What thou givest to them they shall gather up: when thou openest thy hand, they shall all be filled with good.

30. Averténte autem te fáciem, turbabúntur: † áuferes spíritum eórum, et de**fí**cient, * et in púlverem suum re*ver*téntur.

But if thou turnest away thy face, they shall be troubled: thou shalt take away their breath, and they shall fail, and shall return to their dust.

31. Emíttes spíritum tuum, et crea**bún**tur: * et renovábis fáci*em* **ter**ræ.

Thou shalt send forth thy spirit, and they shall be created: and thou shalt renew the face of the earth.

32. Sit glória Dómini in **sæ**-culum: * lætábitur Dóminus in opéri*bus* **su**is:

May the glory of the Lord endure for ever: the Lord shall rejoice in his works.

33. Qui réspicit terram, et facit eam **tré**mere: * qui tangit montes, *et* **fú**migant.

He looketh upon the earth, and maketh it tremble: he toucheth the mountains, and they smoke.

34. Cantábo Dómino in vita **me**-a: * psallam Deo meo, quám*diu* sum.

I will sing to the Lord as long as I live: I will sing praise to my God while I have my being.

35. Iucúndum sit ei elóquium **me**um: * ego vero delectábor *in* **Dó**mino.

Let my speech be acceptable to him: but I will take delight in the Lord.

36. Defíciant peccatóres a terra, et iníqui ita ut **non** sint: *

Let sinners be consumed out of the earth, and the unjust, so that they be

bénedic, ánima me*a*, **Dó**mino. | no more: O my soul, bless thou the Lord.

The antiphon Dóminus Iesus *is repeated, p.* 117.

Psalm 150

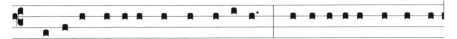

1. Laudá-te Dóminum in sanctis **e**-ius: * laudá-te e-um in firma-

ménto virtú-*tis* **e**-ius. *Flex:* bene-sonánti-bus: †

Praise ye the Lord in his holy places: praise ye him in the firmament of his power.

2. Laudáte eum in virtútibus **e**-ius: * laudáte eum secúndum multitúdinem magnitúdi*nis* **e**ius.

Praise ye him for his mighty acts: praise ye him according to the multitude of his greatness.

3. Laudáte eum in sono **tu**-bæ: * laudáte eum in psaltério, *et* **cí**thara.

Praise him with sound of trumpet: praise him with psaltery and harp.

4. Laudáte eum in týmpano, et **cho**ro: * laudáte eum in chordis, *et* **ór**gano.

Praise him with timbrel and choir: praise him with strings and organs.

5. Laudáte eum in cýmbalis benesonántibus: † laudáte eum in cýmbalis iubilatiónis: * omnis spíritus lau*det* **Dó**minum.

Praise him on high sounding cymbals: praise him on cymbals of joy: let every spirit praise the Lord.

And conclude with the same antiphon Dóminus Iesus *is repeated, p.* 117.

Alternate Dismissal

Ad libitum, when Mass IV is sung:

I.

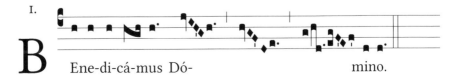

B Ene-di-cá-mus Dó-   mino.

℟. De-o   grá-ti- as.

GOOD FRIDAY

Tract (Responsory) in a Psalm-tone

After the First Lesson

Liber Usualis 723

1. Domi-ne, * audí-vi audí-tum tu-um, et **tí**mu- i: * consi-de-rá-vi

ópe-ra tu-a, et *ex***pá**-vi. *Flex:* inno-tescé-ris: †

The intonation is repeated at each verse.

2. In médio duórum animálium innotescéris: † dum appropinquáverint anni, cogno**scé**ris: * dum advénerit tempus, o*stend***é**ris.

3. In eo, dum conturbáta fúerit ánima **me**a: * in ira, misericórdiæ me*mor* **e**ris.

4. Deus a Líbano **vé**niet, * et Sanctus de monte umbróso et *con***dén**so.

5. Opéruit cælos maiéstas eius: * et laudis eius plena *est* **ter**ra.

Or, another simplified version:

II.

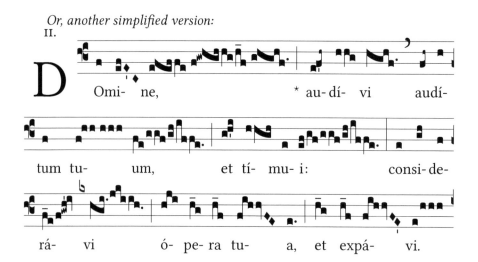

D Omi- ne,   * au- dí- vi   audí-

tum tu-   um,   et tí- mu- i: consi-de-

rá- vi   ó- pe- ra tu-   a, et expá-   vi.

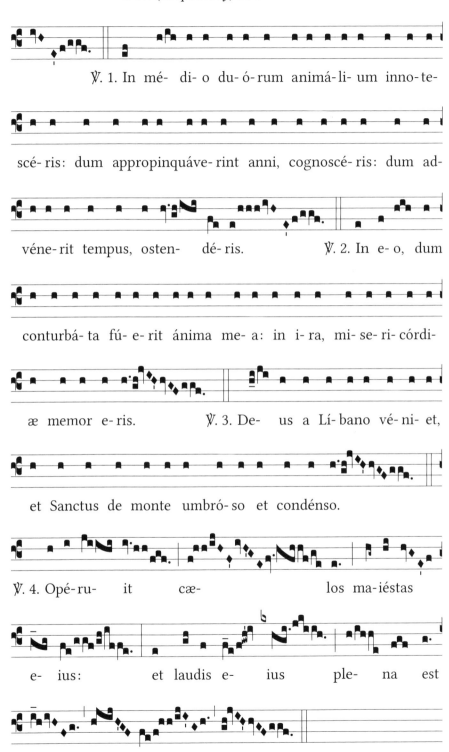

℣. 1. In mé- di- o du- ó- rum animá- li- um inno- te-

scé- ris: dum appropinquáve- rint anni, cognoscé- ris: dum ad-

véne- rit tempus, osten- dé- ris.   ℣. 2. In e- o, dum

conturbá- ta fú- e- rit ánima me- a: in i- ra, mi- se- ri- córdi-

æ memor e- ris.   ℣. 3. De- us a Lí- bano vé- ni- et,

et Sanctus de monte umbró- so et condénso.

℣. 4. Opé- ru- it   cæ-   los ma- iéstas

e- ius: et laudis e-   ius   ple- na   est

* ter-   ra.

Tract (Responsory) in a Psalm-tone

After the Second Lesson

Liber Usualis 727

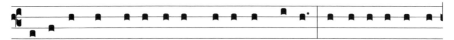

1. E-ri-pe me, Dómi-ne, ab hómi-ne **ma**-lo: * a vi-ro in-íquo

lí-*be*ra me. *Flex:* pecca-tó-ri: †

The intonation is repeated at each verse.

2. Qui cogitavérunt malítias in **cor**de: * tota die constitué*bant* **præ**lia.
3. Acuérunt linguas suas sicut ser**pén**tes: * venénum áspidum sub lábiis *e*órum
4. Custódi me, Dómine, de manu peccat**ó**ris: * et ab homínibus iníquis líbera me.
5. Qui cogitavérunt supplantáre gressus **me**os: * abscondérunt supérbi láque*um* **mi**hi.
6. Et funes extendérunt in láqueum pédibus **me**is: * iuxta iter scándalum posué*runt* **mi**hi.
7. Dixi Dómino: Deus meus **es** tu: * exáudi, Dómine, vocem oratió*nis* **me**æ.
8. Dómine, Dómine virtus salútis **me**æ: * obúmbra caput meum in di*e* **bel**li.
9. Ne tradas me a desidério meo peccatóri: † cogitavérunt ad**vér**sum me: * ne derelínquas me, ne umquam ex*a*l**tén**tur.
10. Caput circúitus *e*órum: * labor labiórum ipsórum opéri*et* **e**os.
11. Verúmtamen iusti confitebúntur nómini **tu**o: * et habitábunt recti cum vul*tu* **tu**o.

Or, another simplified version:
II.

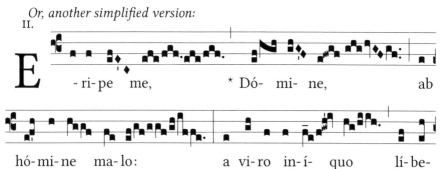

E -ri-pe me, * Dó- mi- ne, ab hó-mi-ne ma-lo: a vi-ro in-í- quo lí-be-

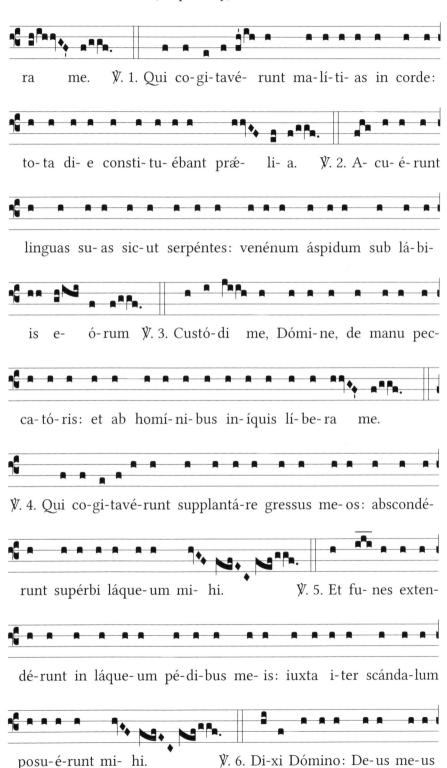

ra me. ℣. 1. Qui co-gi-tavé- runt ma-lí-ti- as in corde:

to- ta di- e consti- tu- ébant præ- li- a. ℣. 2. A- cu- é-runt

linguas su- as sic-ut serpéntes: venénum áspidum sub lá-bi-

is e- ó-rum ℣. 3. Custó-di me, Dómi-ne, de manu pec-

ca-tó-ris: et ab homí-ni-bus in-íquis lí-be-ra me.

℣. 4. Qui co-gi-tavé-runt supplantá-re gressus me- os: abscondé-

runt supérbi láque-um mi- hi. ℣. 5. Et fu- nes exten-

dé-runt in láque-um pé-di-bus me- is: iuxta i-ter scánda-lum

posu-é-runt mi- hi. ℣. 6. Di-xi Dómino: De-us me-us

es tu: exáudi, Dómi-ne, vo-cem o-ra-ti- ónis me-æ.

℣. 7. Dómi-ne, Dómi-ne virtus sa-lú-tis me-æ: obúmbra caput

me-um in di- e bel- li.   ℣. 8. Ne tra-das me a de-si-

dé-ri- o me-o pecca-tó-ri: co-gi-tavé-runt advérsum me: ne de-

re-línquas me, ne umquam exal- téntur.   ℣. 9. Ca- put

circú- i-tus e-ó-rum: labor la-bi- ó-rum ipsó-rum opé-ri- et e-

os.   ℣. 10. Ve-rúmtamen iusti   confi- te-búntur

nómi-ni tu- o: et ha-bi-tábunt re- cti

cum vul- tu * tu- o.

Crux fidelis (Revised)

Instead of the restored hymn Pange, lingua glóriosi prǽlium, *the revised verses, as in the Roman Breviary and Missal, may be sung during the Adoration of the Holy Cross.*

Liber Usualis 742

Crux fi-dé- lis, inter omnes Arbor u-na nó-bi- lis: Nulla

silva ta-lem pro-fert, Fronde, flo-re, gérmi-ne: * Dulce   lignum,

dulces clavos, Dulce pondus sústi-net.

Hymn

PAnge, lingua, glo-ri- ó- si Láure- am certámi-nis, Et

su- per Cru-cis trophǽ-o Dic tri- úmphum nó-bi- lem: Quá-li-

ter Red-émptor orbis   Immo-lá- tus ví-ce-rit.

Repeat Crux fidélis *as far as* * Dulce lignum.

2. De pa-réntis pro-toplá-sti Fraude Factor cóndo-lens, Quando

pomi no-xi- á-lis   In ne-cem morsu ru- it: Ipse   lígnum tunc

no-tá-vit, Damna lign*i* ut sólve-ret. * Dulce lignum.

3. Hoc opus nostræ sa-lú- tis Ordo de-po-pósce-rat: Multi- fór-

mis pro-di-tó-ris Ars ut artem fál-le-ret: Et me- dé-lam ferret

inde, Hostis unde læ-se-rat. Crux fidélis.

4. Quando ve-nit ergo sa-cri Ple-ni-tú-do témpo-ris, Missus est

ab arce Patris Na-tus, orbis Cóndi-tor, Atque ventre virgi-ná-

li Carn*e* amí-ctus pró-di- it. * Dulce lignum.

5. Va-git infans inter arcta Cóndi-tus præ-sé-pi- a: Membra

pannis invo-lú-ta Virgo Ma- ter ál-li-gat: Et De- i ma-nus

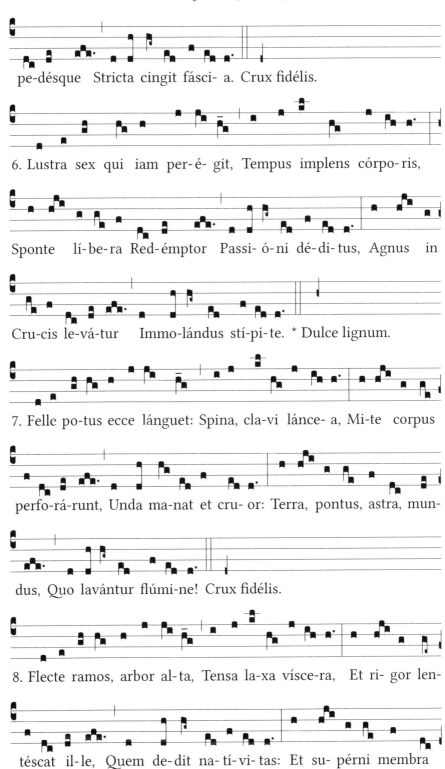

pe-désque Stricta cingit fásci- a. Crux fidélis.

6. Lustra sex qui iam per-é- git, Tempus implens córpo-ris,

Sponte   lí-be-ra Red-émptor Passi- ó-ni dé-di-tus, Agnus   in

Cru-cis le-vá-tur   Immo-lándus stí-pi-te. * Dulce lignum.

7. Felle po-tus ecce lánguet: Spina, cla-vi lánce- a, Mi-te   corpus

perfo-rá-runt, Unda ma-nat et cru- or: Terra, pontus, astra, mun-

dus, Quo lavántur flúmi-ne! Crux fidélis.

8. Flecte ramos, arbor al-ta, Tensa la-xa vísce-ra,   Et ri- gor len-

téscat il-le, Quem de-dit na-tí-vi-tas: Et su- pérni membra

Re-gis Tende mi- ti stí-pi- te. * Dulce lignum.

9. So-la digna tu fu- í- sti Ferre mundi ví-ctimam: Atque portum

præpa-rá-re   Arca mundo náufra-go: Quam sa- cer cru- or per-

únxit, Fusus Agni córpo-re. Crux fidélis.

¶ *The doxology is never omitted:*

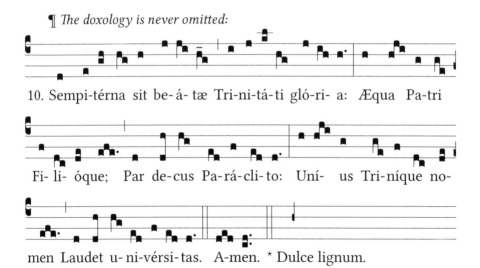

10. Sempi-térna sit be- á- tæ Tri-ni-tá-ti gló-ri- a: Æqua Pa-tri

Fi- li- óque; Par de-cus Pa-rá-cli- to: Uní- us Tri-níque no-

men Laudet u- ni-vérsi- tas. A-men. * Dulce lignum.

Responsories at Communion

From Matins of Good Friday

cf. Job 16: 10, 15 ℣. cf. Ps 68: 22 • Liber Usualis 693

1 Resp.

III.

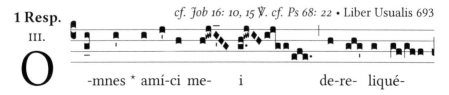

O -mnes * amí-ci me- i   de-re- liqué-

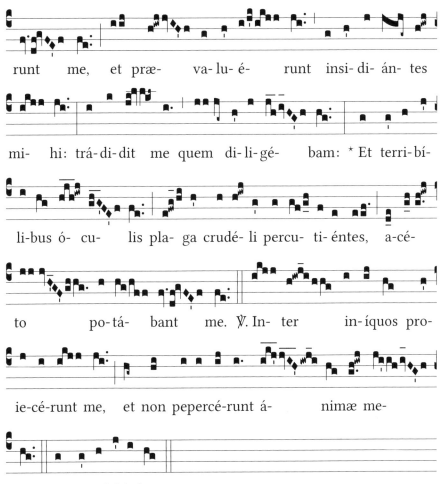

runt me, et præ- va-lu- é- runt insi-di- án- tes

mi- hi: trá-di-dit me quem di-li-gé- bam: * Et terri-bí-

li-bus ó- cu- lis pla- ga crudé- li percu- ti- éntes, a-cé-

to po-tá- bant me. ℣. In- ter in-íquos pro-

ie-cé-runt me, et non pepercé-runt á- nimæ me-

æ. * Et terri-bí-li-bus.

All my friends have forsaken me, and mine enemies have prevailed against me: he whom I loved hath betrayed me: * Mine enemy sharpeneth his eyes upon me, he breaketh me with breach upon breach, and in my thirst they gave me vinegar to drink. ℣. I am numbered with the transgressors, and my life is not spared. * Mine enemy, etc.

2 Resp.

II.

cf. Mt 27: 51, 52; Lk 23: 42 • Liber Usualis 695

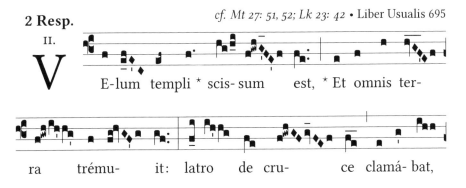

V

E-lum templi * scis- sum est, * Et omnis ter-

ra trému- it: latro de cru- ce clamá- bat,

di- cens: Meménto me- i, Dómi- ne, dum vé- ne-

ris in regnum tu- um. ℣. Pe- træ scissæ sunt,

et monuménta apérta sunt, et multa córpo-ra sanctó-rum,

qui dormí- e-rant, surre- xé- runt. * Et omnis.

The veil of the temple was rent in twain, * And all the earth did quake: the thief on the cross cried, saying: Lord, remember me when thou comest into thy kingdom. ℣. The rocks rent, and the graves were opened, and many bodies of the saints, which slept, arose. * And all the earth, etc.

3 Resp.

VIII.

cf. Jer 2: 21 ℣. Is 5: 2 • Liber Usualis 697

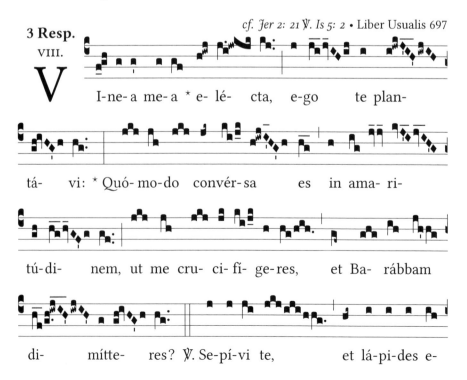

V

I-ne- a me- a * e- lé- cta, e-go te plan-

tá- vi: * Quó- mo-do convér-sa es in ama- ri-

tú-di- nem, ut me cru- ci- fí- ge-res, et Ba- rábbam

di- mítte- res? ℣. Se-pí-vi te, et lá-pi-des e-

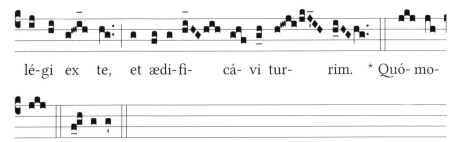

lé-gi ex te, et ædi-fi- cá- vi tur- rim. * Quó- mo-

do. ℟. Ví-ne- a.

O my chosen vineyard: * How then art thou turned to bitterness, that thou should crucify me, and release Barabbas? ℣. I fenced thee, and gathered out the stones from thee, and built a tower in the midst of the land. * How then art thou, etc. ℟. O my chosen, etc.

4 Resp.

VIII.

cf. Mt 26: 55, 27: 26, 31; Mk 14: 46, 48-49 • Liber Usualis 702

T Amquam * ad latrónem e-xístis cum glá-di- is et

fú- sti-bus comprehén- de- re me: * Quo-tí- di-

e apud vos e- ram in templo do- cens, et non

me tenu- í- stis: et ecce flagellá- tum dú- ci- tis

ad cru- ci- fi- gén- dum. ℣. Cumque inie-cís-

sent manus in Ie-sum, et te-nu- íssent e- um, di- xit ad

e-   os.   * Quo-tí- di- e.

Are ye come out, as against a thief, with swords and staves, for to take me: * I was daily with you, teaching in the temple, and ye laid no hold on me: and, now when ye have scourged me, ye lead me away to crucify me. ℣. And when they had laid hands on Jesus, and taken him, he said unto them: * I was daily, etc.

5 Resp.   *cf. Mt 27: 45-46; Jn 19: 20* ℣. *Lk 23: 46* • Liber Usualis 703

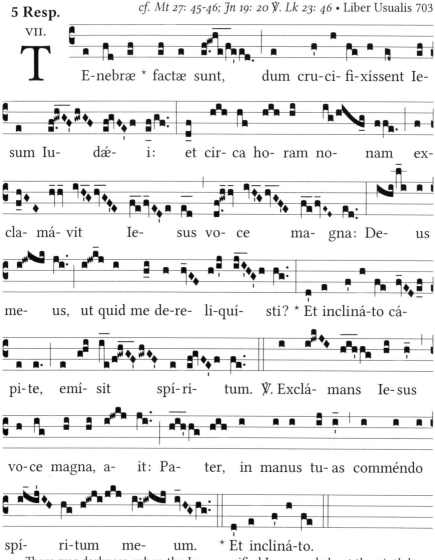

TE-nebræ * factæ sunt,   dum cru-ci- fi-xíssent Ie-

sum Iu-   dǽ-   i: et cir- ca ho- ram no-   nam   ex-

cla- má- vit   Ie-   sus vo- ce   ma- gna: De-   us

me-   us, ut quid me de-re- li-quí-   sti? * Et inclina-to cá-

pi-te, emí- sit   spí-ri-   tum. ℣. Exclá- mans   Ie-sus

vo-ce magna, a-   it: Pa-   ter, in manus tu- as comméndo

spí-   ri-tum   me-   um.   * Et inclina-to.

There was darkness, when the Jews crucified Jesus: and about the ninth hour Jesus cried with a loud voice: My God, why hast thou forsaken me? * And he bowed his head, and gave up the ghost. ℣. When Jesus had cried with a loud voice, he said: Father, into thy hands I commend my spirit. * And he bowed, etc.

cf. Jer 12: 7, 8, 9-11 • Liber Usualis 704

6 Resp.

VIII.

A-nimam me-am * di-lé-ctam trá-di- di in ma-

nus in-iquó- rum, et facta est mi- hi he-ré-di- tas

me- a sic-ut le- o in silva: de-dit contra me

vo-ces adver-sá- ri- us, di-cens: Congregá- mi- ni,

et pro-pe-rá- te ad devo-rán-dum illum: po-su-

é-runt me in de- sérto so-li- túdi- nis, et lu-

xit super me omnis ter- ra: * Qui- a non est invéntus

qui me agnó-sce- ret, et fá- ce- ret be- ne. ℣. Insurre-

xé-runt in me vi-ri absque mi-se-ri-córdi- a, et non

pepercé-runt á- ni-mæ me- æ. * Quia. ℟. Animam.

I have given the dearly-beloved of my soul into the hand of her enemies and mine heritage is become unto me as a lion in the forest: the enemy crieth out against me, saying: Assemble yourselves together, hasten to devour him: they have made my portion a desolate wilderness, and the whole land mourneth unto me: * Because there is none found that will know me, nor do well. ℣. There be risen up against me such as breathe out cruelty, and they have not spared my soul. * Because there is none, etc. ℟. I have given, etc.

7 Resp. *cf. Job 16: 12, 14, 15; Is 53: 12* ℣. *Ps 53: 5* • *Liber Usualis* 710

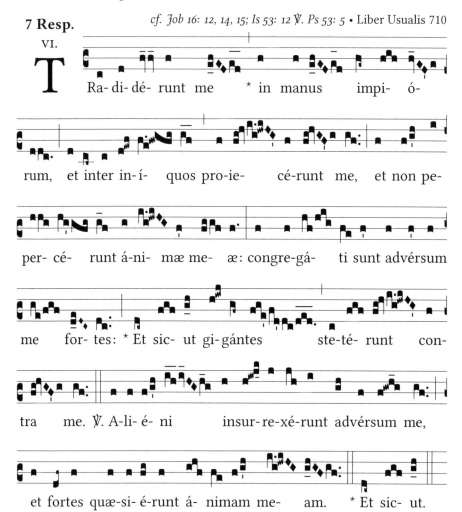

et fortes quæ-si- é-runt á- nimam me- am. * Et sic- ut.

They have turned me over into the hands of the wicked, they also have numbered me with the transgressors, neither have they spared my life: the mighty are gathered together against me: * And stand up against me like giants. ℣. Strangers are risen up against me, and oppressors seek after my soul. * And stand up, etc.

8 Resp.

VIII.

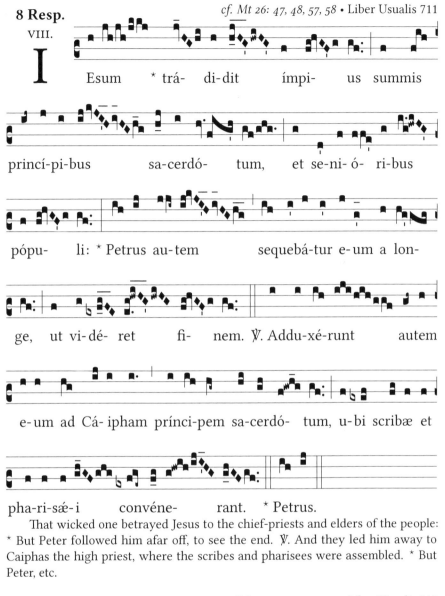

cf. Mt 26: 47, 48, 57, 58 • Liber Usualis 711

Esum * trá- di-dit ímpi- us summis

princí-pi-bus sa-cerdó- tum, et se-ni- ó- ri-bus

pópu- li: * Petrus au-tem sequebá-tur e-um a lon-

ge, ut vi-dé- ret fi- nem. ℣. Addu-xé-runt autem

e-um ad Cá- ipham prínci-pem sa-cerdó- tum, u-bi scribæ et

pha-ri-sǽ- i convéne- rant. * Petrus.

That wicked one betrayed Jesus to the chief-priests and elders of the people: * But Peter followed him afar off, to see the end. ℣. And they led him away to Caiphas the high priest, where the scribes and pharisees were assembled. * But Peter, etc.

9 Resp.

V.

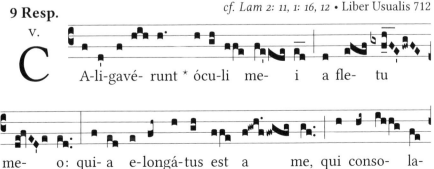

cf. Lam 2: 11, 1: 16, 12 • Liber Usualis 712

A-li-gavé- runt * ócu-li me- i a fle- tu

me- o: qui-a e-longá-tus est a me, qui conso- la-

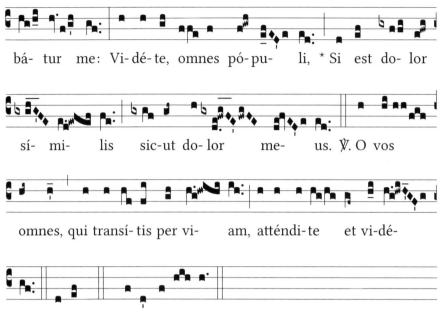

bá- tur me: Vi-dé-te, omnes pó-pu- li, * Si est do- lor

sí- mi- lis sic-ut do- lor me- us. ℣. O vos

omnes, qui transí-tis per vi- am, atténdi-te et vi-dé-

te. * Si est. ℟. Ca-li-gavé- runt.

Mine eyes do fail with tears: because the Comforter that should relieve me is far from me: behold, O all ye nations * If there be any sorrow like unto my sorrow. ℣. O all ye that pass by, behold, and see. * If there be, etc. ℟. Mine eyes do fail, etc.

Vexilla regis

Fortunatus († 609) • Vatican Gradual 191

Hymn

I.

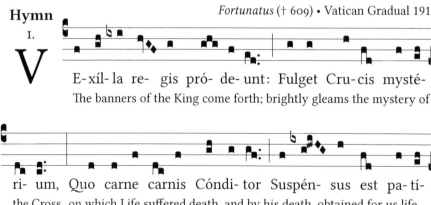

E-xíl-la re- gis pró- de-unt: Fulget Cru-cis mysté-
The banners of the King come forth; brightly gleams the mystery of

ri- um, Quo carne carnis Cóndi-tor Suspén- sus est pa-tí-
the Cross, on which Life suffered death, and by his death, obtained for us life.

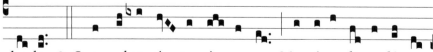

bu-lo. 2. Quo vulne-rá- tus ín-su-per Mucróne di-ro lánce-
He was wounded by the cruel point of a spear,

æ, Ut nos la-vá-ret crími-ne, Ma-ná- vit un-da et sángui-

and to cleanse us from the defilements of sin, there issued forth water

ne. 3. Implé- ta sunt quæ cón-ci-nit Da-vid fi-dé-li cármi-

and blood.   Now is fulfilled what David foretold in faithful song,

ne, Di-cens: In na-ti-óni-bus Regná- vit a ligno De- us.

saying to the nations: "God has reigned from a Tree."

4. Arbor de-córa et fúl-gi-da,   Orná-ta re-gis púrpu-ra,

O beautiful and resplendent Tree   adorned with the purple of the King,

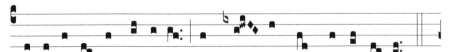

E-lécta digno stí-pi-te Tam san-cta membra tánge-re!

chosen to bear on thy worthy trunk, limbs so holy.

5. Be- á- ta, cu- ius brá-chi- is Sæcli pe-péndit pré-ti- um,

O blessed Tree upon whose branches   hung the ransom of the world;

Sta- té- ra facta córpo- ris, Præ- dámque tu- lit tárta- ri.

it was made the balance of the body, and snatched away hell's expected prey.

6. O Crux, ave, spes ú- ni- ca, Hoc Passi- ó- nis témpo- re,
Hail O Cross our only hope!   In this Pasiontide,

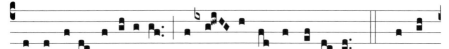

Auge pi- is iustí-ti- am Re- ís-que do-na vé-ni- am. 7. Te sum-
increase grace in the just, and for sinners, blot out their sins. Thee, Most high,

ma, De- us, Trí- ni-tas, Colláudet omnis spí- ri-tus: Quos per
O God, O Trinity!   May every spirit sing thy praise: Whom by

Cru-cis mysté-ri- um Sal-vas, re-ge per sǽ-cu-la.   A-men.
the mystery of the Cross   thou dost save and rule forever.

Stabat Mater

Hymn
VI.   *Fra Jacopone da Todi* († 1306) • Liber Usualis 1874

S Tabat Ma-ter do-lo-ró-sa Iuxta crucem lacrimó-sa,

Dum pendébat Fí-li- us,
Sorrowful, weeping stood the Mother by the cross on which hung her Son.

2. Cuius ánimam geméntem,   Through her heart, His sorrow sharing,
Contristátam et doléntem   all His bitter anguish bearing,
   Pertransívit gládius.   now at length the sword has passed.

3. O quam tristis et afflícta   O how sad and sore distressed
Fuit illa benedícta,   was that Mother, highly blest,
   Mater Unigéniti!   of the sole-begotten One.

4. Quæ mærébat, et dolébat,   Christ above in torment hangs

Pia Mater, dum vidébat
    nati pœnas ínclyti.

she beneath beholds the pangs
of her dying, glorious Son.

5. Quis est homo, qui non fleret,
Matrem Christi si vidéret
    In tanto supplício?

Is there one who would not weep,
whelmed in miseries so deep,
Christ's dear Mother to behold?

6. Quis non posset contristári,
Christi Matrem contemplári
    Doléntem cum Fílio?

Can the human heart refrain
from partaking in her pain,
in that Mother's pain untold?

7. Pro peccátis suæ gentis
Vidit Iesum in torméntis,
    Et flagéllis súbditum.

For the sins of His own nation,
she saw Jesus wracked with torment,
all with scourges rent:

8. Vidit suum dulcem Natum
Moriéndo desolátum,
    Dum emísit spíritum.

She beheld her tender Child,
saw Him hang in desolation,
till His spirit forth He sent.

9. Eia, Mater, fons amóris
Me sentíre vim dolóris
    Fac, ut tecum lúgeam.

O thou Mother! fount of love!
touch my spirit from above,
make my heart with thine accord:

10. Fac, ut árdeat cor meum
In amándo Christum Deum
    Ut sibi compláceam.

Make me feel as thou hast felt;
make my soul to glow and melt
with the love of Christ my Lord.

11. Sancta Mater, istud agas,
Crucifíxi fige plagas
    Cordi meo válide.

Holy Mother! pierce me through,
in my heart each wound renew
of my Savior crucified:

12. Tui Nati vulneráti,
Tam dignáti pro me pati,
    Pœnas mecum dívide.

Let me share with thee His pain,
who for all my sins was slain,
who for me in torments died.

13. Fac me tecum pie flere,
Crucifíxo condolére,
    Donec ego víxero.

Let me mingle tears with thee,
mourning Him who mourned for me,
all the days that I may live:

14. Iuxta Crucem tecum stare,
Et me tibi sociáre
    In planctu desídero.

By the Cross with thee to stay,
there with thee to weep and pray,
is all I ask of thee to give.

15. Virgo vírginum præclára,
Mihi iam non sis amára,
   Fac me tecum plángere.
	Virgin of all virgins blest,
	listen to my fond request:
	   let me share thy grief divine;

16. Fac, ut portem Christi mortem,
Passiónis fac consórtem,
   Et plagas recólere.
	Let me, to my latest breath,
	in my body bear the death
	   of that dying Son of thine.

17. Fac me plagis vulnerári,
Fac me Cruce inebriári,
   Et cruóre Fílii.
	Wounded with His every wound,
	steep my soul till it hath swooned,
	   in His very Blood away;

18. Flammis ne urar succénsus,
Per te, Virgo, sim defénsus
   In die iudícii.
	Be to me, O Virgin, nigh,
	lest in flames I burn and die,
	   in His awful Judgment Day.

19. Christe, cum sit hinc exíre,
Da per Matrem me veníre
   Ad palmam victóriæ.
	Christ, when Thou shalt call me hence,
	be Thy Mother my defense,
	   be Thy Cross my victory;

20. Quando corpus moriétur,
Fac, ut ánimæ donétur
   Paradísi glória. Amen.
	While my body here decays,
	may my soul Thy goodness praise,
	   safe in Paradise with Thee. Amen.

EASTER VIGIL

Inventor rutili

Ancient hymn that preceded the blessing of the fire on Holy Saturday in several medieval rites.

Hymn   *Prudentius († 410) • ed. Sandhofe*

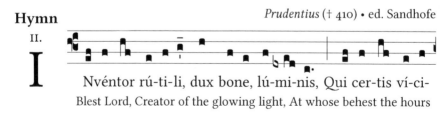

Nvéntor rú-ti-li, dux bone, lú-mi-nis, Qui cer-tis ví-ci-
Blest Lord, Creator of the glowing light, At whose behest the hours

bus témpo-ra dí-vi-dis, Merso so-le cha-os íngru-it hórri-dum,
successive move,   The sun has set: black darkness broods above:

Lucem redde tu- is Chri-ste fi-dé-li-bus. *Repeat:* Invéntor.
Christ! Light thy faithful through the coming night.

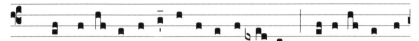

1. Quamvis innúme-ro sí-de-re ré- gi- am, Luna-ríque po-
Thy courts are lit with stars unnumberèd, And in the cloudless vault

lum Lámpade pínxe-ris, Incussu sí-li-cis lúmi-na nos tamen
the pale moon rides; Yet Thou dost bid us seek the fire that hides

monstras, sa-xi-géno sémi-ne quǽre-re. Invéntor.
Till swift we strike it from its flinty bed.

2. Ne nescí-ret homo spem si-bi lú-mi-nis, In Chri-sti só-li-
So man may learn that in Christ's body came The hidden hope of light

do córpo-re cóndi-tam, Qui di-ci stá-bi-lem se vó-lu- it petram
to mortals given: He is the Rock—'tis his own word—that riven

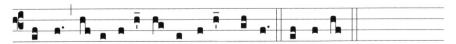

nostris, Igní-cu-lis unde genus ve-nit. Invéntor.
Sends forth to all our race the eternal flame.

The Sacrament of Baptism

If the sacrament of Baptism[1] is to be administered, it is given in the usual way. Nevertheless, especially if several are to be baptized, the ceremonies of the Roman Ritual which precede the actual conferring of Baptism, i.e. for the Baptism of Infants until the words Credis in Deum,[2] *and for the Baptism of Adults until the words* Quis vocaris?[3] *may be anticipated on the morning of Holy Saturday.*

The celebrant, to administer Baptism, changes his violet stole and cope for white ones; these he may keep on for the procession to the font.

Each adult candidate is asked separately:

Quis vocáris?	What is your name?
℞. *N.* (his name)	℞. *N.* (his name)

He asks, by name, each separately (the godfather answers for infants):

N. Credis in Deum Patrem omnipoténtem, Creatórem cæli et terræ?	*N.*, do you believe in God, the Father almighty, creator of heaven and earth?
℞. Credo.	℞. I do believe.
Credis in Iesum Christum, Fílium eius únicum, Dóminum nostrum, natum, et passum?	Do you believe in Jesus Christ, his only Son, our Lord, who was born into this world and who suffered?
℞. Credo.	℞. I do believe.
Credis in Spíritum Sanctum, sanctam Ecclésiam cathólicam, Sanctórum communiónem, remissiónem peccatórum, carnis resurrectiónem, vitam ætérnam?	Do you believe also in the Holy Spirit, the holy Catholic Church, the communion of saints, the forgiveness of sins, the resurrection of the body, and life everlasting?
℞. Credo.	℞. I do believe.
N. Vis baptizári?	*N.* do you wish to be baptized?
℞. Volo.	℞. I do.

---

[1]In the United States, approval was given in 1954 and 1959 for parts of certain rites of the Ritual to be translated and performed in the vernacular, including baptism. The text here is from the 1961 edition of the U.S. *Collectio Rituum*.

[2]tit. II, chap. II, n. 17

[3]tit. II, chap. IV, n. 38

If the candidate is an adult:

N. Quid petis?
 ℟. Baptísmum.
Vis baptizári?
 ℟. Volo.

N. What is it that you are seeking?
 ℟. Baptism.
Do you wish to be baptized?
 ℟. I do.

The form of the sacrament:

N., Ego te baptízo in nómine Pa✝tris, et Fíl✝ii, et Spíritus ✝ Sancti.

Deus omnípotens, Pater Dómini nostri Iesu Christi, qui te regenerávit ex aqua et Spíritu Sancto, quique dedit tibi remissiónem ómnium peccatórum, ipse te líniat ✝ Chrísmate salútis in eódem Christo Iesu Dómino nostro in vitam ætérnam. ℟. Amen.

℣. Pax tibi (*to an adult:* tecum).
℟. Et cum spíritu tuo.

Accipe vestem cándidam, quam pérferas immaculátam ante tribúnal Domini nostri Iesu Christi, ut hábeas vitam ætérnam. ℟. Amen.

Accipe lámpadem ardéntem, et irreprehensíbilis custódi Baptísmum tuum: serva Dei mandáta, ut, cum Dóminus vénerit ad núptias, possis occúrrere ei una cum ómnibus Sanctis in aula cælésti, et vivas in sǽcula sæculórum. ℟. Amen.

N., *I baptize you in the name of the Father, and of the Son, and of the Holy Spirit.*

May the Almighty God, the Father of our Lord Jesus Christ, Who has regenerated you by water and the Holy Ghost, and who has given you the remission of all your sins, may he himself anoint you with the Chrism of Salvation, in the same Christ Jesus our Lord, unto life eternal.

℣. Peace be with (to) you.
℟. And with your spirit.
Receive this white garment. Never let it become stained, so that, when you stand before the judgment seat of our Lord Jesus Christ, you may have life everlasting. ℟. Amen.
Receive this burning light, and keep the grace of your baptism throughout a blameless life. Observe the commandments of God. Then, when the Lord comes to the heavenly wedding feast, you will be able to meet him with all the saints in the halls of heaven, and live forever and ever. ℟. Amen.

The celebrant then says (in the singular or the plural):

N., Vade (Ite) in pace, et Dóminus sit tecum (vobíscum).
℟. Amen.

N., go in peace, and the Lord be with you.
℟. Amen.

The Sacrament of Confirmation

If the sacrament of Confirmation is to be administered to any of the neophytes—by the local ordinary, another bishop, or a priest lawfully delegated—it is given in the usual way.

The neophytes to be confirmed kneel. The celebrant stands and says:

Spíritus Sanctus supervéniat in vos, et virtus Altíssimi custódiat vos a peccátis. ℟. Amen.

May the Holy Spirit come down upon you, and the may the virtue of the Most High guard you from all sin.

℣. Adiu✠tórium nostrum in nómine Dómini.

Our help is in the name of the Lord.

℟. Qui fecit cælum et terram.

Who made heaven and earth.

℣. Dómine exáudi oratiónem meam.

O Lord, hear my prayer.

℟. Et clamor meus ad te véniat.

And let my cry come unto thee.

℣. Dóminus vobíscum.

The Lord be with you.

℟. Et cum spíritu tuo.

And with thy spirit.

Orémus.

Let us pray.

Omnípotens sempitérne Deus, qui regeneráre dignátus es hos fámulos tuos ex aqua et Spíritu Sancto; quique dedísti eis remissiónem ómnium peccatórum; emítte in eos septifórmem Spíritum tuum Sanctum Paráclitum de cælis. ℟. Amen.

Almighty everlasting God, who once gave new life to these servants of thine by water and the Holy Spirit, forgiving them all their sins; send forth on them from heaven thy Holy Spirit, the Advocate, along with his sevenfold gifts.

Spíritum sapiéntiæ, et intelléctus. ℟. Amen.

The Spirit of wisdom and understanding.

Spíritum consílii, et fortitúdinis. ℟. Amen.

The Spirit of counsel and fortitude.

Spíritum sciéntiæ, et pietátis. ℟. Amen.

The Spirit of knowledge and piety.

Adímple eos Spíritu timóris tui, et consígna eos signo Cru✠cis Christi, in vitam propitiátus ætérnam. Per eúndem Dóminum.

Fill them with the Spirit of thy fear, and sign them with the sign of the Cross of Christ unto everlasting life. Through the same Lord.

The celebrant dips his thumb into the Chrism, addresses each candidate by name, and anoints the forehead saying:

N., signo te signo Cru✝cis: et confírmo te chrísmate salútis: In nómine Pa✝tris, et Fí✝lii, et Spíritus ✝ Sancti. ℞. Amen.	*N.*, I sign thee with the sign of the Cross, and I confirm thee with the chrism of salvation; In the name of the Father, and of the Son, and of the Holy Spirit.

He gently strikes the candidate on the cheek, saying:

Pax tecum.	Peace be with thee.

When all have been confirmed, the celebrant washes his hands and the antiphon is sung or said:

Ps 67: 29-30 • Liber Usualis 1844

Ant.
VIII. C

Onfírma hoc De- us, quod ope-rá-tus es in no-bis:

a templo sancto tu- o, quod est in Ie-rú-sa-lem. ℣. Gló-ri- a

Patri, et Fí-li- o, et Spi-rí-tu- i Sancto. ℞. Sic-ut e-rat in princí-

pi- o, et nunc, et semper, et in sǽcu-la sæcu-ló-rum. Amen.

Repeat: Confírma hoc.

Confirm this, O God, which thou hast wrought in us, from thy holy temple, which is in Jerusalem.

℣. Osténde nobis, Dómine, misericórdiam tuam.	Show us, O Lord, thy mercy.
℞. Et salutáre tuum da nobis.	And give us thy salvation.
℣. Dómine exáudi oratiónem meam.	O Lord, hear my prayer.
℞. Et clamor meus ad te véniat.	And let my cry come unto thee.
℣. Dóminus vobíscum.	The Lord be with you.
℞. Et cum spíritu tuo.	And with thy spirit.

The newly confirmed kneel, and the celebrant continues:

Orémus.

Let us pray.

Deus, qui Apóstolis tuis Sanctum dedísti Spíritum et per eos, eorúmque successóres, céteris fidélibus tradéndum esse voluísti; réspice propítius ad humilitátis nostræ famulátum, et præsta; ut eórum corda, quorum frontes sacro chrísmate delinívimus, et signo sanctæ Crucis signávimus, idem Spíritus Sanctus in eis supervéniens, templum glóriæ suæ dignánter inhabitándo perfíciat: Qui cum Patre, et eódem Spíritu Sancto vivis et regnas Deus, in sǽcula sæculórum. ℟. Amen.

O God, thou gave thy Holy Spirit to thy apostles, and will that through them and their successors the same gift should be delivered to all the faithful. Look graciously on the service we humbly render to thee; grant that the same Spirit, coming down upon those whose foreheads we have anointed with the holy chrism and marked with the sign of the holy Cross, may make their hearts a temple of glory. Thou who lives and reigns with the Father and the same Holy Spirit, one God, for ever and ever.

Ecce sic benedicétur omnis homo, qui timet Dóminum.

Behold, thus shall every man be blessed who fears the Lord.

Then the celebrant turns to bless the newly confirmed:

Bene✠dícat vos Dóminus ex Sion, ut videátis bona Ierúsalem ómnibus diébus vitæ vestræ, et habeátis vitam ætérnam. ℟. Amen.

May the Lord bless you from Sion, that you may see the good things of Jerusalem all the days of your life, and may have everlasting life.

Hymn at Communion

Though the Easter Vigil has no appointed antiphon at Communion, the hymn Adóro te *may be sung, as below, or, the antiphon* Ubi cáritas et amor, *with its verses, as at the Washing of Feet on Holy Thursday, p.* 111.

Adoro te devote

St. Thomas Aquinas († 1274) • Liber Usualis 1855

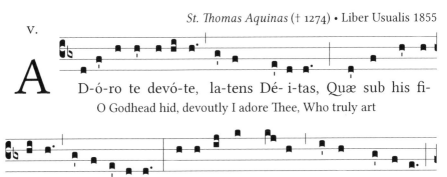

A D-ó-ro te devó-te, la-tens Dé- i-tas, Quæ sub his fi-
O Godhead hid, devoutly I adore Thee, Who truly art

gú-ris ve-re lá-ti-tas: Ti-bi se cor me- um to-tum súb-i-cit,
within the forms before me;   To Thee my heart I bow with bended knee,

Qui- a te contémplans, to-tum dé-fi-cit.
As failing quite in contemplating Thee.

2. Visus, tactus, gustus in te fállitur,	Sight, touch, and taste in Thee are each deceived;
Sed audítu solo tuto créditur;	The ear alone most safely is believed:
Credo quidquid dixit Dei Fílius,	I believe all the Son of God has spoken,
Nil hoc verbo veritátis vérius.	Than Truth's own word there is no truer token.
3. In Cruce latébat sola Déitas.	God only on the Cross lay hid from view;
At hic latet simul et humánitas:	But here lies hid at once the Manhood too:
Ambo tamen credens, atque cónfitens,	And I, in both professing my belief,
Peto quod petívit latro pǽnitens.	Make the same prayer as the repentant thief.

298 Appendix: Easter Vigil

4. Plagas, sicut Thomas, non intúeor,

Deum tamen meum te confíteor:

Fac me tibi semper magis crédere,

In te spem habére, te dilígere.

5. O memoriále mortis Dómini,

Panis vivus vitam præstans hómini:
Præsta meæ menti de te vívere,
Et te illi semper dulce sápere.

6. Pie pellicáne Iesu Dómine,
Me immúndum munda tuo Sángui-
ne:
Cuius una stilla salvum fácere
Totum mundum quit ab omni scéle-
re.

7. Iesu, quem velátum nunc aspício,
Oro, fiat illud, quod tam sítio,
Ut, te reveláta cernens fácie,

Visu sim beátus tuæ glóriæ. Amen.

Thy wounds, as Thomas saw, I do not
see;
Yet Thee confess my Lord and God to
be:
Make me believe Thee ever more and
more;
In Thee my hope, in Thee my love to
store.

O thou Memorial of our Lord's own
dying!
O Bread that living art and vivifying!
Make ever Thou my soul on Thee to live;
Ever a taste of Heavenly sweetness give.

O loving Pelican! O Jesu, Lord!
Unclean I am, but cleanse me in Thy
Blood;
Of which a single drop, for sinners spilt,
Is ransom for a world's entire guilt.

Jesu! Whom for the present veil'd I see,
What I so thirst for, O vouchsafe to me:
That I may see Thy countenance unfold-
ing,
And may be blest Thy glory in behold-
ing.

EASTER SUNDAY

Processional Hymn

In some places, sung in procession before High Mass on Easter Sunday.

Venantius Fortunatus († 609) • OHS (Monastic) 426

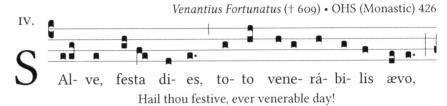

Al- ve, festa di- es, to- to vene- rá- bi- lis ævo,
Hail thou festive, ever venerable day!

Qua De- us inférnum vi- cit et astra tenet. *All repeat:* Salve.
hell is conquered and heaven is won by God.

1. Ecce renascéntis testá- tur grá- ti- a mundi
Lo! the earth bears witness that with the Lord,

Omni- a cum Dómino dona re-dísse su-o. Sal-ve.
she has had all her gifts restored.

2. Namque tri- umphánti post trísti- a tárta-ra Christo
For now the woods with their leaves, and the meadows with their flowers,

Undique fronde nemus, grámina flo-re favent. Sal-ve.
pay homage to Jesus' triumph over the gloomy tomb.

3. Qui cru-ci-fi-xus e-rat De- us, ecce per ómni- a regnat;
The crucified God now reigns over all things;

Dantque Cre-a- tó-ri cuncta cre-á-ta pre-cem. Sal-ve.
and every creature to its Creator tells a prayer.

4. Christe, sa-lus re-rum, bone Cóndi-tor atque Redémptor,
O Jesus! Savior of the world! Loving Creator and Redeemer!

U-ni-ca pro-gé-ni- es ex De- i-tá-te Patris. Sal-ve.
Only-begotten Son of God the Father!

5. Qui genus humá- num cernens mersísse pro- fúndo,
Seeing the human race was sunk in misery deep,

Ut hómi-nem e-rí-pe-res, es quoque factus homo. Sal-ve.
thou were made Man, that thou might rescue man.

6. Fúne- ris exséqui- as pá- te-ris vi- tæ auctor et orbis;
Thou, the author of life and of all creation,

Intras mor-tis i-ter, dando sa-lú-tis opem. Sal-ve.
was buried in the tomb; treading the path of death, to give us salvation.

7. Trísti- a cessé- runt inférnæ víncu- la le- gis,
The gloomful bonds of hell were broken;

Expa-vítque cha- os lúmi-nis o-re premi. Sal-ve.
the abyss shook with fear, as the light shone upon its brink.

8. Pollí-ci-tam sed redde fi-dem, pre-cor, alma pot-és-tas:
But, redeem thy promise, I beseech thee, merciful King!

Tér-ti- a lux réd-i- it, surge, sepúlte me-us. Sal-ve.
This is the third day; arise, my buried Jesus!

9. Non de-cet ut húmi-li túmu-lo tu-a membra te-gántur,
'Tis not meet, that thy Body lie in the lowly tomb,

Non pré-ti- um mundi ví-li- a saxa premant. Sal-ve.
or that a sepulchral stone should keep imprisoned the ransom of the world.

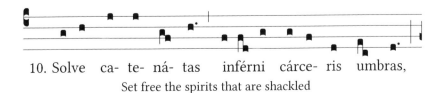

10. Solve ca- te- ná- tas inférni cárce- ris umbras,
Set free the spirits that are shackled

Et révo-ca sursum quidquid ad ima ru- it. Sal-ve.
in limbo's prison. Raise up all fallen things.

11. Redde tu- am fá-ci- em, ví- de- ant ut sǽcu-la lumen;
Show us once more thy face, that all ages may see the light!

Redde di- em qui nos, te mo-ri- énte, fu-git. Sal-ve.
Bring back the day, which fled when thou didst die.

12. Infe- rus insa-tu- ra- bí- li- ter cava gúttu- ra pandens,
The greedy monster, whose huge throat

Qui rápu- it semper, fit tu-a prǽda, De-us. Sal-ve.
had swallowed all mankind, is now thy prey, O God!

13. Rex sa-cer, ecce tu- i rá-di- at pars magna tri- úmphi,
O King divine! Lo! Here a bright ray of thy triumph—

Cum pu-ras ánimas sancta lavácra be- ant. Sal-ve.
the souls made pure by the holy font.

14. Cándidus egré- di- tur ní- ti- dis exérci- tus undis,

The white-robed troop comes from the limpid waters;

Atque ve-tus ví-ti- um purgat in amne novo. Sal-ve.

and the old iniquity is cleansed in the new stream.

15. Fulgéntes ánimas vestis quoque cándi- da signat,

The white garments symbolize unspotted souls;

Et grege de ní-ve- o gáudi- a pastor habet. A-men. Sal-ve.

and the Shepherd rejoices in his snow-like flock:

℣. Gloria Patri at the Introit

℣. Gló-ri- a Patri, et Fí-li- o,   et Spi- rí-tu- i Sancto. *

Sic-ut e-rat in princí-pi- o,   et nunc, et semper, et in sǽcu-la

sǽcu-la sǽcu-ló-rum. Amen.   Re-sur-ré-xi.

PRAYER CONCLUSIONS

Where the prayer is addressed to God the Father:

Per Dóminum nostrum Iesum Christum, Fílium tuum: Qui tecum vivit et regnat in unitáte Spíritus Sancti Deus, per ómnia sǽcula sǽculórum.

Through our Lord Jesus Christ, thy Son: Who lives and reigns with thee in the unity of the Holy Spirit, one God, forever and ever.

Where the prayer is addressed to God the Father, but God the Son is mentioned also:

Per eúndem Dóminum nostrum Iesum Christum, Fílium tuum: Qui tecum vivit et regnat in unitáte Spíritus Sancti Deus, per ómnia sǽcula sǽculórum.

Through the same our Lord Jesus Christ, thy Son: Who lives and reigns with thee in the unity of the Holy Spirit, one God, forever and ever.

Where the prayer is addressed to God the Father, but God the Son is mentioned towards the end:

Qui tecum vivit et regnat in unitáte Spíritus Sancti, Deus, per ómnia sǽcula sǽculórum.

Who lives and reigns with thee in the unity of the Holy Spirit, one God, forever and ever.

Where the prayer is addressed directly to God the Son:

Qui vivis et regnas cum Deo Patre, in unitáte Spíritus Sancti, Deus, per ómnia sǽcula sǽculórum.

Who live and reign with God the Father, in the unity of the Holy Spirit, one God, forever and ever.

INDEX OF CHANTS

ANTIPHONS

HYMNS

RESPONSORIES

INTROIT ANTIPHONS

GRADUALS

ALLELUIA VERSES

TRACTS

OFFERTORY ANTIPHONS

COMMUNION ANTIPHONS

VARIOUS

MASS ORDINARY PARTS

GENERAL INDEX

Made in the USA
Monee, IL
04 February 2022